100 100383

D1800162

PRIVATE OPINIONS PUBLIC POLLS

PRIVATE OPINIONS PUBLIC POLLS

LESLIE WATKINS
ROBERT M. WORCESTER

THAMES AND HUDSON

Where percentages do not add up to 100 or to the total shown this is a result either of computer rounding or of multiple answers.

Printed and bound in Hungary

Contents

Left-handed women are different

Who takes longer to impregnate his wife after marriage – a stockbroker or a deckchair attendant?

What is the *second* thing American women notice when meeting a new man?

Do women with left-wing political views make love more often – or less often – than those who support the right?

Here are the surprising, definitive answers to these questions – and to thousands of others which are equally intriguing. Through the rich seams of information provided by international public opinion polls, this book gives vivid and unexpected insights into other people's lives and minds. The guarantee of anonymity helps them shed their inhibitions. They talk more frankly and truthfully to pollsters – about their fears, fantasies and phobias, for instance – than to their friends and neighbours.

That's why we can reveal that 35 per cent of American executives admit having fiddled their taxes, that only 16 per cent of British couples want their first child to be a girl, that on a typical day in 1981 4 per cent of Swedes admitted having read someone else's letter or private diary without permission. We also strip away the myths to show how in-laws really rate as marriage-wreckers . . . which civilized country cares least about religion . . . and which is keenest on premarital sex.

How much do Europeans trust Americans? Or the French trust the West Germans? How do young people really feel about their jobs in Britain and Japan? And which nation has the most smiling faces?

How does the escalation of crime – and national attitudes to it – differ on the two sides of the Atlantic? In which country is it considered more acceptable to burgle a house than a museum? And where do people regard a car-theft as less excusable than a killing?

Again, here are the answers.

In establishing such an amazing range of international truths – about beliefs, attitudes, experiences and behaviour – pollsters have a first-rate method which rather resembles that of a wine connoisseur. One sip enables him to judge accurately a whole bottle. That principle also applies to pollsters. By carefully questioning a small but scientifically selected sample of people, researchers can amass great quantities of accurate information which applies to huge communities and which can often be used with confidence to predict or even to mould future events.

No subject is outside the scope of these highly skilled professional pollsters whose fascinating findings have created a multi-billion-dollar international industry. Governments, political parties, the media, major companies, professional bodies, pressure groups and other specialist organizations are among those who rely heavily in decision-making on the computerized deluge of statistics and opinions provided each week by the polls.

Polls also have a history. Thanks to the work of pioneering pollster, Seebohm Rowntree, for example, we know that at the turn of the century a British housewife, if she was immensely thrifty, could feed her husband each week for 3s 3d (about 21 cts).

Women were apparently more self-sacrificing, for, by monitoring the weekly budgets of sample households in York, Rowntree also established that a woman could be nourished for 2s 9d (about 18cts) a week. Food for children aged 8–16 could be bought for as little as 2s 7d a week and for younger children it need cost only 2s 1d.

Passionately aware of the need for social reform, Rowntree used the power of survey research to spotlight the harshness of life on the poverty line, and in 1906 he proved through another survey that 52.5 per cent of working-class children under the age of one in York were living below that line. His published work attracted immense attention and became a major spur towards social changes, such as the introduction of the Old Age Pensions Act in 1908.

Polls have been used to anticipate election results for more than 150 years. In 1824, an American newspaper, the *Harrisburg Pennsylvanian*, conducted one of the early 'straw' polls – questioning people in the street about voting intentions – in anticipation of the imminent Presidential election.

Such polls had become commonplace by the turn of the century and some publications, in order to increase the size of the sample, began sending printed questionnaires through the post. It was then believed that the accuracy of a poll would automatically be increased if more people were questioned. That is a fundamental fallacy. One of the secrets of being a successful pollster is getting a correctly balanced cross-section of people.

The technique of postal polling was discredited in 1936 after the *Literary Digest* posted questionnaires about the US Presidential election to more than ten million people – their names taken from such sources as telephone directories and lists of registered car owners.

Only the comparatively wealthy then had such luxuries as telephones and cars and so there was no chance of the sample mirroring the mood of the across-the-board electorate.

More than two million replies were returned to the *Digest* and the editors then confidently predicted a landslide victory for Republican Alf Landon. The election was won by Franklin D. Roosevelt of the Democratic Party, with 61 per cent of the votes.

However, Roosevelt's victory was accurately anticipated by an enterprising young pollster named George Gallup, the late father of modern polling, who used a properly balanced sample of only 2,000.

Gallup's success confirmed that a properly selected sample of thousands or even hundreds can produce results far more reliable than one of millions. That remains true for all types of mass surveys – whether they are about attitudes to politicians or weather forecasting, artificial fertilizers or nude cycling in the Alps. Nevertheless, unrepresentative polls, phone-in polls, coupon-clipping polls and biased polls still continue to be taken.

Although professional pollsters are sometimes wrong, mostly they are accurate to within plus-or-minus 2 or 3 per cent. On the day of the 1983 British General Election MORI forecast Tories 44 per cent, Labour 28 per cent and Alliance 26 per cent – and they were exactly right. In the 1984 US Presidential election Gallup correctly forecast Reagan's victory over Mondale by 59 per cent to 41 per cent.

In this book we occasionally dip into the past, but concentrate mainly on today's world. Here is a splendid opportunity to peep into other people's minds – to discover what they really think. And at the same time, here are serious insights into the attitudes and patterns of behaviour that are helping to shape our modern world.

Did you know, for instance, that 14 per cent of American bosses admit having dodged work by feigning illness? Or that Britain's upper- and upper-middle classes shrank from being 8 per cent of the total population in 1949 to 2 per cent in 1984?

Or that in so many ways – such as being more than twice as likely as right-handers to vote for right-wing politicians and having had their first period, on average, seven months earlier – left-handed women are different?

SECTION I

SEX, LOVE AND MARRIAGE

1 Cupid under the microscope

American women are far less interested in men's faces – when they meet for the first time – than men are in women's faces. For women, the way men are dressed makes more of an initial impact. So does the expression in their eyes.[1]

Short men may also be gratified to know that a man's height is not so important in creating first impressions. Nor is the state of his teeth. And balding men can be reassured that having a splendid head of hair is less important than having a pleasantly warm smile.

It's different when women are first appraising other women. Hair (condition and styling) is then instantly significant and takes priority over face, figure and smile – although still not nearly as interesting, of course, as what the other ladies are wearing.

What usually strikes a man first about a woman is her figure, but he is more likely to notice her face than the way she is dressed. When he first meets another man, however, he tends to be more impressed by the clothing than by the face.

In 1983, Americans of both sexes were shown a card listing aspects of appearance and were then asked by the Roper Organization: 'When you first meet a person of the opposite sex, which one or two of these things about physical appearance do you tend to notice first?'

Here are the results:

	Women meeting Men	Percentage
1	How dressed	35
2	Eyes	30
3	Figure, build	29
4	Face	27
4	Smile	27
6	Hair	16
7	Teeth	11
8	Height	8
9	Hands	2
10	Legs	–

	Men meeting Women	Percentage
1	Figure, build	45
2	Face	34
3	How dressed	29
4	Smile	24
5	Eyes	22
6	Hair	16
7	Legs	6
8	Teeth	5
9	Height	3
10	Hands	1

The same questions were then asked in respect of first meetings with people of the same sex. Here are the results:

	Women meeting Women	Percentage
1	How dressed	41
2	Hair	27
3	Face	26
4	Figure, build	20
4	Smile	20
6	Eyes	16
7	Teeth	5
8	Height	2
8	Hands	2
10	Legs	–

	Men meeting Men	Percentage
1	How dressed	39
2	Face	28
3	Figure, build	16
3	Smile	16
5	Height	15
6	Hair	13
7	Eyes	9
8	Hands	4
9	Teeth	3
10	Legs	–

Apparently most women pay no attention, or hardly any, to other women's legs – and female legs are well down the list of attractions for men. So has the come-on importance of shapely legs been traditionally overstated – maybe as a lingering legacy of Betty Grable? That certainly appeared to be the case in 1982 when Americans were asked how they felt about the miniskirt coming back in style.[2]

The 19 per cent who really wanted it back were heavily outnumbered by the 33 per cent who really did not. Three per cent gave no opinion and the bulk of Americans, 45 per cent, obviously considered the miniskirt a great yawn – saying they didn't care one way or the other.

The survey also established that exactly a quarter of Americans, 25 per cent, felt that men are more attracted to blondes. Nineteen per cent did not feel qualified to give an opinion. And a whacking great 56 per cent dismissed the idea as a load of nonsense.

In Britain a quarter of husbands fell in love with their wives at first sight. Only 21 per cent of wives were so impetuous – and a further 21 per cent initially didn't even like their menfolk.[3]

In America, according to an Audits & Surveys poll for the Merit Report in 1983, two-thirds of men (66 per cent) and 57 per cent of women believe in love at first sight.[4] Over a quarter (27 per cent) of Americans think themselves 'very romantic' and an overwhelming 94 per cent think that the traditional courtesies between a man and a woman should be preserved.

However, most single men in America (74 per cent) admit they are confused about how to treat women and nearly as many single women (71 per cent) agree, according to a Black Corp. poll for *USA Today*.[5] But most single men (52 per cent) also agree that 'a liberated woman is a better marriage partner'. Only a third (31 per cent) of married and newly divorced men agree.

And in America similar interests are thought to be ten times as important as income or physical attractiveness in looking for a mate or lasting relationship.[6]

In the early tentative steps towards a British romance, on the other hand, appearances are considered more important than personality by 40 men in 100, but by only 23 per cent of women.[7] Which could explain, perhaps, why a Gallup poll discovered that only 12 women in 100 consider their husbands or boyfriends are worth photographing.

(Incidentally, men are twice as keen to have their wives as photographic models. They might care to note that (only) 71 per cent of women aged 16–44 would refuse to be photographed topless on foreign holidays, although 84 per cent would refuse while holidaying in Britain.)

When choosing their ideal mates, only 3 per cent of women consider that a passionate nature adds to a man's attractiveness and 37 women in 100 actually feel that men have too much sex drive. Seven per cent, on the other hand, say that men have too little sex drive.

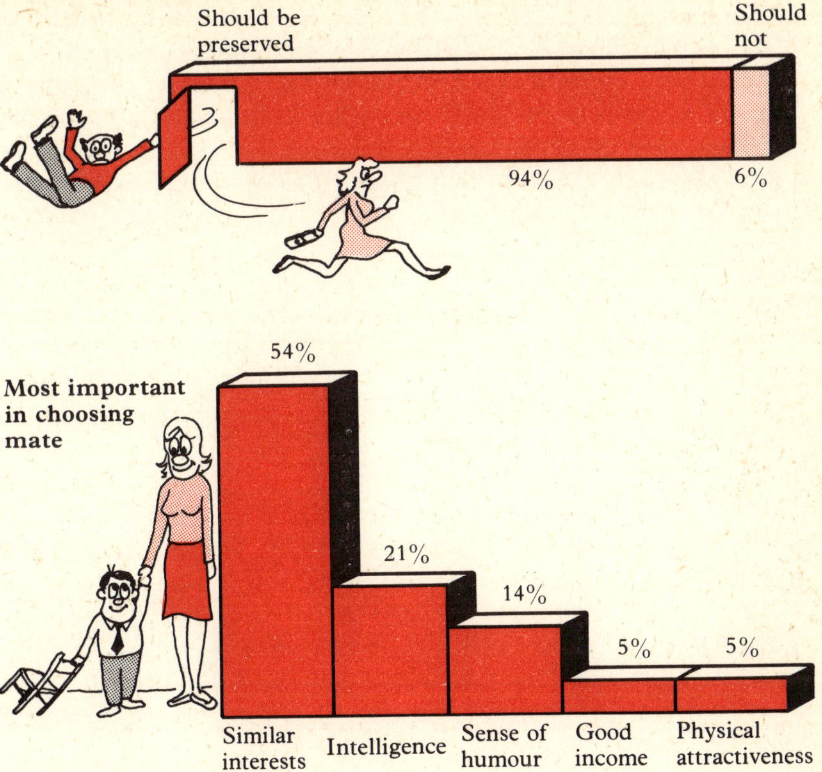

On one issue there is almost universal feminine agreement: the belief that women are attracted by power, that it is a form of aphrodisiac, is a hoary fallacy. Less than 1 per cent regard power or status as a turn-on and most women – by a vote of three to two – would prefer to receive a box of chocolates than a bottle of perfume.

How well do you appreciate the nuances of modern romance and courtship? Judge for yourself by answering these questions:

1 **Tenderness and intelligence are among the five qualities women consider most important in men with whom they intend spending the rest of their lives.** TRUE OR FALSE?

2 **Physical attractiveness is among the four qualities men consider most important in women with whom they intend spending the rest of their lives.** TRUE OR FALSE?

3 **Most young women, if given the opportunity, would sooner marry the boy next door than a prince or a pop star.** TRUE OR FALSE?

4 **The most romantic gesture a man could make on St Valentine's Day, in the opinion of the majority of women, would be to take his wife or girlfriend out for a candle-lit dinner.** TRUE OR FALSE?

5 **When assessing a man's physical attractiveness, women are keener for him to have long legs than a large penis.** TRUE OR FALSE?

6 **After a broken love affair, women are more likely than men to dream about their former partners.** TRUE OR FALSE?

Take two marks for each correct answer – given and amplified below – to check your affinity with Cupid in the 1980s.

QUESTION ONE **Tenderness and intelligence are among the five qualities women consider most important in men with whom they intend spending the rest of their lives.** FALSE Women are realists. They prefer potential husbands to be reliable and hard-working rather than intelligent or tender – and neither intelligence nor tenderness are included among the five top priority qualities. What women do insist on most is a sense of humour – with 56 per cent saying so – and consideration takes second place with a vote of 49 per cent. The rest of their top ten desired qualities, in order of importance, are faithfulness (47 per cent), reliability (43), hard-working character (32), loving nature (30), intelligence (20), practicality (11), tenderness and physical attractiveness (8 each).[10]

QUESTION TWO **Physical attractiveness is among the four qualities men consider most important in women with whom they intend spending the rest of their lives.** FALSE Physical attractiveness certainly is important, with men rating it sixth on the list, but it is more important for a woman to be loving and intelligent.

Like women, men regard a sense of humour as the most essential characteristic, with 49 per cent saying so, and faithfulness (47 per cent) comes second – one place higher than with women.

Men are less concerned than women that their partners should be hard-working, putting that quality ninth rather than fifth, but are keener on them being loving – rating that third rather than sixth.

Unexpectedly, one man in ten also wants his wife to be strong-willed – possibly a legacy from having been accustomed as a boy to domination by his mother.

Here, in order of preference, are the ten qualities desired most by men: sense of humour (with a 49 per cent vote), faithfulness (47), loving nature (37), consideration (34), intelligence and physical attractiveness (both 28), reliability (26), practicality (24), hard-working character (17) and a strong will (10).

QUESTION THREE **Most young women, if given the opportunity, would sooner marry the boy next door than a prince or a pop star.** TRUE In 1982, more than 1,000 women were asked which of the following types they would most want to marry, if they had the choice, and which they would least like to marry: 'Sportsman, politician, doctor, film star, lawyer, prince, pop star, millionaire, boy next door.'[11]

Millionaires won, with a vote of 15 per cent, but were only marginally ahead of the boy next door – regardless of whether or not he had money.

Doctors and sportsmen were in fourth and fifth places. Only 2 women in 100 fancy marrying a prince – 'all those functions and dressing up every night – no thanks!' said one woman – and pop stars are the men they would least like to marry. Explained one woman, 'I couldn't bear to marry a man who was more glamorous than me.' Another added, 'You'd never trust him, would you – not with all those young girls around.'

QUESTION FOUR **The most romantic gesture a man could make on St Valentine's Day, in the opinion of the majority of women, would be to take his wife or girlfriend out for a candle-lit dinner.** FALSE That is what most men believe, but most women – particularly those aged 15–34 – would much prefer to be given a dozen red roses.[12]

For every woman who would appreciate a Valentine's Day gift of perfume, there are four who would prefer breakfast in bed.

QUESTION FIVE **When assessing a man's physical attractiveness, women are keener for him to have long legs than a large penis.** TRUE Women consider long legs to be three times as admirable as a large penis – which comes below good hair texture in their priorities – although most men believe that a large penis is six times more of an asset than long legs.

Other male misconceptions about female preferences were toppled when the New York newspaper *Village Voice* asked 100 men to list masculine physical characteristics most regarded as a 'turn on' by women. A hundred women were asked to provide a similar list and they proved that most men, when hoping to attract the opposite sex, are ignorant of their own most valuable attributes.

Men concentrated most heavily on the more obvious signs of strength and virility – 21 plumping for muscular chest and shoulders, 18 for muscular arms and 15 for a large penis. Fourth in the male list, with a vote of 13, was tallness.

Not one of those four characteristics was at the top of the list provided by women. In fact, muscular chest and shoulders got only 1 vote and muscular arms scored a zero. Small buttocks were the most important feature – rated number one by 39 of the 100 women – followed by slimness (15), a flat stomach (13) and expressive eyes (11).

Fifth in the men's list was slimness with 7 votes – less than half the number given to it by women – and hair texture was sixth equal with 4. Buttocks and eyes also scored 4 each and the list was completed by long legs (3) and a good neck (2).

Fifth in the women's list were long legs (6), followed by tallness and hair (5 each) and neck (3).

The large penis prized so highly by the men attracted only 2 votes from the women – hardly a twentieth of those awarded to buttocks – and the only other features considered to be worth even a single combined vote were muscular chest and shoulders.

The survey boosted the self-esteem of men who, in the words of the advertisement, tend to have sand kicked in their eyes.

QUESTION SIX **After a broken love affair, women are more likely than men to dream about their former partners.** FALSE In this situation, men are more likely than women to be the backward-glancing dreamers – whether asleep or awake – although, on average, they recover more quickly from the trauma of a shattered romance. That was established in one of the most interesting studies into the aftermath of broken affairs, published by American sociologists Clifford Kirkpatrick and Theodore Caplow in 1945, and based on interviews with several hundred students.[13]

Although breaks which followed one of the partners becoming involved with someone else were more than twice as likely to have been instigated by the women, there was a tendency among more women than men to preserve keepsakes (11 per cent compared with 7) and to re-read old love letters (9 compared with 7).

However, the men were more prone to dreaming about former partners, with 16 per cent doing so compared with 11 per cent of women, and to fantasizing about them – 14 per cent compared with 9. Women are twice as likely as men to remember only unpleasant things about a broken affair. Four per cent admitted doing so, compared with 2 per cent of men. Far more of both sexes – 16 per cent in each case – claimed to remember only things that were pleasant. Which, of course, could explain many of those masculine dreams.

How accurate was your judgment? Scores of 0–4 suggest that you are hardly on nodding terms with Cupid, 6–8 show that you are well tuned-in to modern romance, 10–12 reflect an exceptional understanding.

2 Modern marriage – the uncensored facts

Bridal virginity is now considered completely unnecessary by most women – as well as by most men – and the popularity of trial marriages has soared in Britain.

In 1982, more than one bride in five aged 16–34 and married between 1979 and 1981 had lived with her future husband – compared with only one in ten during the early 1970s.[1]

In 1982, more than half the women in the country were in favour of couples living together before marriage.[2] And in 1984 there was evidence of an even more relaxed attitude to female chastity – with only 28 per cent of women considering that brides should be virgins when taking their vows.[3] That contrasted starkly with a survey in 1970 when less than a quarter of the nation's women, under 45, approved of premarital sex for women.[4]

Attitudes to premarital sex for men also changed dramatically among women between 1970 and 1984. In 1970, nearly half the women frowned on it.[5] In 1984, only 18 per cent felt that bridegrooms should be virgins.[6]

In 1983, about 380,000 couples were wed in Britain – with drinks worth £68 million being downed, incidentally, to help wish them all luck – at an average cost of £2,000 per wedding reception.

What tempted all those brides into marriage?

This question was asked in a 1982 MORI poll in which a range of possible reasons for marriage was shown to more than 1,000 women who were then asked: 'When you got married, which two or three of these reasons do you think were the most important?'[7]

Here, in descending order, are the replies:

Marrying because

		Percentage
1	I loved him	90
2	To have children	33
3	For financial security	10
4	To get away from home	8
5	It was expected of me	7
6	I was pregnant	6
7	I was lonely	4
7	Passion/lust	4
9	All my friends did	3
10	Rebelling against parents	2
10	Other reason	2
12	Don't know	1

Most of 1983's brides, who paid an average of £202 for their wedding dresses, could hardly be accused of rushing into matrimony. The average engagement in Britain lasts 19 months[8] – a far longer time than in Russia where more than a third of marriages are between couples who have known each other for less than 6 months.[9] A 1984 Russian survey established that many newly-weds there are 'sexually illiterate' (sic) and it was recommended, as a result, that sex education be improved.

Seven British brides in every 100 would sooner keep their maiden surnames after marriage. Fifty-six per cent would prefer to adopt their husbands'. Thirty-three per cent feel it makes no difference and the others do not know.[10]

And should they conceal their new marital status – as feminists insist they ought to – by using the title 'Ms' rather than 'Mrs'?

Not in the view of the majority.

Questioned about the word 'Ms' by NOP in November 1980, only 3 Britons in every 100 'liked it a lot'. A further 9 per cent admitted to 'liking it a little'.[11]

Forty-seven per cent 'didn't like it much' or 'didn't like it at all' and 9 per cent hated it. How many always used it? Only 1 in 100.

How accurate are your opinions on the true state of modern marriage? Find out by answering these questions:

1 **Understanding and tolerance between partners are as important – as ingredients of a successful marriage – as fidelity or a happy sexual relationship.** TRUE OR FALSE?
2 **Middle-class fathers spend more time mothering young children – bathing them, dressing them, changing diapers – than fathers in the working class.** TRUE OR FALSE?
3 **Wives tend to be more relaxed than husbands about their partners having close friends of the opposite sex.** TRUE OR FALSE?
4 **Problems with in-laws are more likely to break up marriages than violence or excessive drinking.** TRUE OR FALSE?
5 **The proportion of divorcees whose marriages end within four years is higher among women who were teenage brides – rather than among those who were 40 or older at the time of their wedding.** TRUE OR FALSE?
6 **Husbands are twice as likely as wives to wish they had married someone else.** TRUE OR FALSE?
7 **Most American wives who have had affairs regret them.** TRUE OR FALSE?

Answers start on the next page.

QUESTION ONE **Understanding and tolerance between partners are as important – as ingredients of a successful marriage – as fidelity or a happy sexual relationship.** TRUE Although faithfulness and sexual harmony are considered extremely important – more so than good housing or an adequate income – most couples give as much priority to understanding and tolerance.

In 1982, Gallup invited 1,000 Britons to rate 'good marriage' ingredients in order of importance.[12]

Highest scores were given to 'mutual respect and appreciation' and 'understanding and tolerance' – with 97 per cent describing them as 'very important' or 'rather important'. Only 1 in 100 felt that mutual respect was 'not very important'.

Faithfulness had a 96 per cent vote, but 3 per cent considered it to be not very important.

Happy sexual relationships got a vote of 93 per cent – with 4 per cent considering it not very important and 2 per cent saying they didn't know.

Money and housing were placed fourth and fifth, with 85 per cent and 83 per cent respectively, although each had 4 per cent saying they were not very important.

Music-hall jokes about mothers-in-law, and possibly fathers-in-law as well, seem to be justified by the 80 per cent agreement that it was important to live away from them. This was considered more significant than the sharing of household chores, which had a 75 per cent rating.

Having children was considered as important in a happy marriage as a willingness to do dishes (and other household chores) together – and 23 per cent considered that children were not very important, with a further 3 per cent not knowing.

Nearly half the couples (47 per cent) felt it was important to have the same social background, but 51 per cent disagreed.

Shared religious beliefs (37 per cent) were considered more important than agreement on politics (18 per cent) – with a massive 80 per cent dismissing politics as 'not very important'. This reply was endorsed, incidentally, by a 1982 MORI poll which showed that fewer than half the wives in Britain believe their political views are taken seriously by their husbands.[13]

In the MORI survey, women were also asked: 'How important do you consider sexual love is in marriage?' Here are the replies:

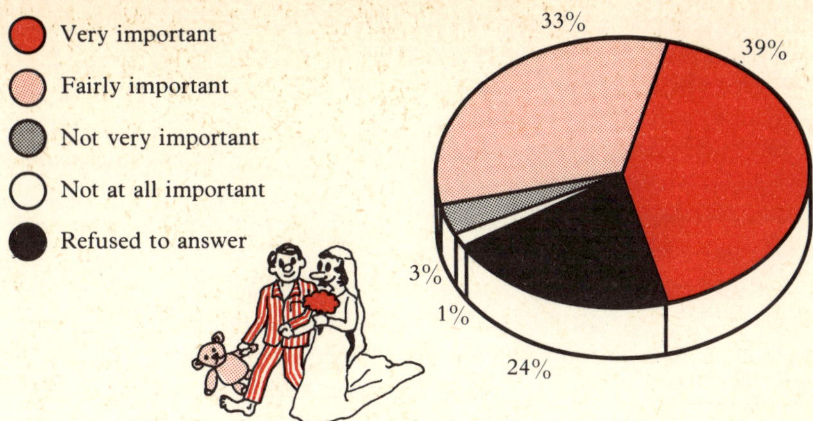

The women were then asked: 'How satisfying would you say sexual intercourse is for you?' Here are the replies:

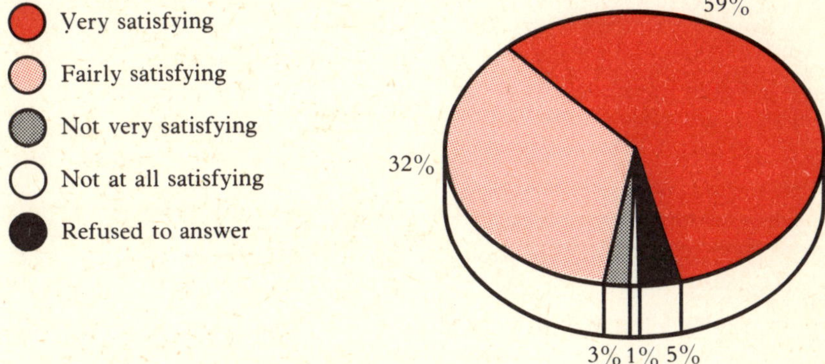

On the basis of the answers to that last question, it would seem that 11,400 of the 1983 brides will probably regard marital intercourse as not very satisfying and 3,800 will consider it not at all satisfying – with the true figures being even higher if one considers the 5 per cent who refused to answer.

QUESTION TWO **Middle-class fathers spend more time mothering young children – bathing them, dressing them, changing diapers – than fathers in the working class.** TRUE Generally, men do not do enough to look after their children – in the view of 53 per cent of men and women, with only 26 per cent disagreeing – but fathers in the ABCl social groups (middle-class) do more than (working-class) DE fathers.[14]

Change diapers? Never or rarely, admit 43 per cent of the ABCls compared with 46 per cent of the C2DEs.

Prepare meals? Never or rarely, admit 46 per cent of the ABCls – compared with 54 per cent of the C2DEs.

Bath babies? Never or rarely, admit 33 per cent of the ABCls – compared with 46 per cent of the C2DEs.

Dress children? Never or rarely, admit 22 per cent of the ABCls – compared with 33 per cent of the C2DEs.

Tuck them into bed? Never or rarely, admit 15 per cent of the ABCls – compared with 25 per cent of the C2DEs.

Middle-class fathers are just as likely as working-class fathers to play with their children, with only 3 in 100 never or rarely doing so – compared with 4 in 100 among the C2DEs.

Sixteen per cent of fathers claim to bath children every day or most days and 15 per cent claim to change diapers just as regularly – a claim backed up by wives, 14 per cent of whom say father does the diaper-changing.

Two fathers in every 100 prepare children's meals every day and 46 in 100 say they play with children every day. Two per cent admit they rarely play with their children, 1 per cent say they never do and 7 per cent claim not to know whether they do or not.

If a mother is working, the father should spend as much time as she does in looking after the children. That is agreed by 87 per cent of both men and women.

When a child is ill in the night, it is better if the mother tends to it rather than the father. Fifty-five per cent of men agree. So do 61 per cent of women.

Who should punish a naughty child? Mother or father? More than half (52 per cent) disagreed with the old notion that punishment is best left to the father, while less than a quarter (23 per cent) agreed that it should be his job.

QUESTION THREE **Wives tend to be more relaxed than husbands about their partners having close friends of the opposite sex.**
FALSE Fifty-one per cent of wives would not be comfortable with the idea of their partners having such friends, compared with 43 per cent of husbands. That was established through a 1982 American survey by the magazine *Better Homes and Gardens*.[15] Five per cent of the husbands surveyed felt that, when they were talking, their spouses were not usually listening. So did 13 per cent of the wives.

The survey also showed that 38 per cent of wives considered men should be doing more of the household chores – while 8 per cent of husbands felt women were not doing enough. So it is hardly surprising that a 1982 MORI poll in Britain should show that domestic quarrels are just as likely to be sparked off by housework (6 per cent) as by sex (4 per cent) or even more likely than by drink (2 per cent).[16]

Squabbles flare most frequently over money – 19 per cent do – and 16 per cent are over children. Other significant causes are His Family (5 per cent), Her Family and Car-Driving (both 3 per cent).

A quarter of British married couples never quarrel, according to their wives.

QUESTION FOUR **Problems with in-laws are more likely to break up marriages than violence or excessive drinking.** TRUE In Britain, 21 per cent of women regard in-law troubles as the biggest single cause of broken marriages – with 11 per cent blaming violence and only 9 per cent blaming drink. That was established by MORI in 1982.[17]

Adultery is the principal cause of marriages foundering – 35 per cent of women say so – and 12 per cent put the blame on a poor sex life. Working-class wives get more hurt over unfaithfulness than those in the upper-middle class. Women with higher education consider it far less important than those who left school at 16.

Other factors seen as marriage-wreckers are lack of respect between partners (14 per cent), boredom (6 per cent) and children (2 per cent).

Attitudes to infidelity vary dramatically between countries. Surveys of young Americans at college (18–24 years old) showed that in the early 1980s 85 per cent of them considered that adultery was either 'always wrong' or 'almost always wrong'. Incidentally, in the early 1970s the figure was 68 per cent.[18] A survey in Switzerland[19] in 1977, among people aged 18–24, produced a very different picture. Only 16 per cent felt strongly that fidelity is essential in marriage.

QUESTION FIVE **The proportion of divorcees whose marriages end within four years is higher among women who were teenage brides – rather than among those who were 40 or older at the time of wedding.** FALSE Twenty-nine per cent of divorces involving women who wed between 40 and 44 happen within the first four years. The percentage increases to 35 among women who were 45 or older when they were married. Among teenage brides it is 26.[20]

Statistics confirm the reality of the 'seven-year-itch' by showing that the most hazardous period for marriages is between the 5th and 9th years. That period produces 30 per cent of all divorces. Nineteen per cent of divorces come between the 10th and 14th years, nine per cent between the 20th and 24th years, and one per cent happen within the first 24 months.

Although a third of British marriages are ending in divorce, people are showing an increasing determination to try again. A third of the 388,000 marriages in 1981 were actually remarriages. And 18 per cent of the 159,000 divorces in 1982 ended marriages in which one or both partners had already experienced an earlier divorce.

In 1982, MORI also discovered that 19 per cent of women still living with their husbands had seriously considered leaving them. What stopped them? The most common answer – given by 47 per cent – was the welfare of the children. Only 6 per cent stayed because of money.[21]

QUESTION SIX **Husbands are twice as likely as wives to wish they had married someone else.** FALSE Twelve American wives in every 100 – compared with 6 American husbands in every 100 – wish they had married someone else.[22] Fifteen German wives in every 100 – compared with 7 German husbands in every 100 – wish they had married someone else.[23]

If they had their time over again, 6 per cent of the American wives would not have got married at all – a view echoed by only 5 per cent of their husbands.[24]

In 1978, 9 per cent of German wives aged 20–30 admitted having found consolation in the beds of other men – three times as many as in 1963 – and 24 per cent of husbands made comparable admissions.[25]

More than half the married women in Germany (51 per cent) have considered prostitution to be a 'necessary evil' and a further 37 per cent have regarded it as a 'useful institution'.[26]

On both sides of the Atlantic, wives are equally as enthralled as husbands by the delights of marriage. In America, 78 per cent of women – compared with 82 per cent of men – consider their expectations of happiness in marriage are being realized.[27] In Britain, 16 women out of every 100 told MORI in 1982 that marriage was worse than they had expected, while 28 per cent had found it better; and for 45 per cent it was as they had expected. However, 42 per cent of British women felt that men got the best deal out of marriage – 35 per cent more than those who felt women got the best deal.[28] In Germany, 63 per cent of women said that, if they were born again, they would choose to be a woman. Only 6 per cent of men would prefer to be a woman.[29]

QUESTION SEVEN **Most American wives who have had affairs regret them.** FALSE Half of married women in America aged 20–60 say they have unsatisfactory marriages and have extramarital affairs mainly because they want deeper emotional intimacy, according to a Seton Hall

University sociologist who surveyed 150 USA wives. She found only 2 per cent were 'swept away' in a moment of madness; most knew their partner as a friend first. Only one in four said she felt guilty and none regretted her affair, not even the one woman in the sample who said her affair ended her marriage. On average, the affairs lasted one year with weekly meetings of a couple of hours.

How accurate were your opinions? Take two marks for each correct answer. Scores of 0–4 show you have a great deal to learn about modern marriage; 6–8 indicate a good average awareness; 10–14 reflect an exceptional degree of insight.

3 International sex – the amazing numbers game

Among every 100 young men in Sweden there are 18 who have made love, between them, to not less than 360 and possibly to as many as 900 women. Each has had between 20 and 50 partners.[1]

That sample fact comes from the intriguing pattern of sexual attitudes and behaviour which has been discovered by pollsters. Here, taken at random, are more:

- Nearly 60 per cent of British women are prepared to initiate intercourse – if their partners are too slow or shy – and 16 out of every 100 wish they were men.[2]
- American women are more in favour of extramarital sex than American men. Eighteen out of every 100 consider it is 'not wrong at all' or only 'sometimes wrong' – a view shared by only 13 per cent of men.[3]
- A quarter of the girls in France have lost their virginity by the age of 15. So have more than half the boys.[4]

More generalizations and false assumptions are made about sex than almost any other subject. Such questions as the following of double standards or increasing promiscuity – among the middle-aged as well as the young – are debated across the world. Many of the arguments are fuelled by gut feeling or by suspect stories in the more lurid newspapers. But scientific research has now established that the truths are often more surprising than the surmises. Extensive and meticulously conducted polls have provided a penetrating insight into international sexuality.

How do your instincts – or prejudices – rate against such research? Find out by answering the following questions:

1 **Being less inhibited than their contemporaries in Britain, France and West Germany, American youngsters are more likely to endorse premarital sex.** TRUE OR FALSE?

2 **Slim girls keep their virginity longer than plump girls.** TRUE OR FALSE?

3 **At least 1 out of every 12 American women now (1985) aged 26–28 had intercourse with 6 partners or more before her 19th birthday.** TRUE OR FALSE?

4 **Two out of every 100 Canadian men now (1985) aged 30–32 had intercourse for the first time before their 12th birthday.** TRUE OR FALSE?
5 **British wives had intercourse far more often in 1984 than in 1970.** TRUE OR FALSE?
6 **Australian wives are more than 10 times as likely to commit adultery – or to admit doing so – as wives in Britain.** TRUE OR FALSE?
7 **Working-class women are more likely to make the first moves in lovemaking than middle-class women.** TRUE OR FALSE?
8 **In Britain, the pleasures of sex are rated more highly by women who vote Conservative than by those who support Labour or the Liberal-Social Democratic Alliance.** TRUE OR FALSE?

Take two marks for each correct answer – given and amplified below – to measure the accuracy of your judgment.

QUESTION ONE **Being less inhibited than their contemporaries in Britain, France and West Germany, American youngsters are more likely to endorse premarital sex.** FALSE Although the American entertainment industry is often blamed for subverting teenage morals – its critics claiming that it unjustifiably exploits sex – American youngsters are more disapproving of premarital sex than those in Britain, France and West Germany. That fact has remained unchanged for at least a decade – as evidence from polls in 1973 and 1983 shows.[5]

In the 1973 poll, Gallup International established that 78 per cent of Americans aged 14 to 18 saw nothing wrong in premarital sex. That figure may have provoked raised eyebrows among puritans in America – particularly as 19 per cent of the youngsters considered it was 'all right even if the parties concerned are not in love' – but the percentage also revealed that young Americans were less in favour of premarital sex than their contemporaries in Britain (83 per cent), France (87) and West Germany (88).

In Sweden, land of long nights and liberated love, youngsters were far keener on high jinks. Ninety-four out of every 100 voted for premarital sex – with 38 per cent dismissing love as irrelevant – and that put the country top of the international league. Switzerland took second place, with 91 per cent approving sex before marriage.

Three-quarters of the youngsters in Yugoslavia, a higher percentage than elsewhere, believed that such lovemaking was acceptable only if the couples were in love. With that proviso, 82 per cent were in favour and so Yugoslavia became sixth in the 'will do' league – after Sweden, Switzerland, West Germany, France and Britain.

America was seventh, followed by Japan (72 per cent), the Philippines (62) and Brazil (60).

Chastity was most highly valued among youngsters in India, where 73 per cent said that premarital sex 'should be avoided under any circumstances'.

By 1983, however, France had taken over first place, increasing its percentage from 87 to 95. Sweden slipped to second place on 94, while Switzerland, Great Britain and Yugoslavia all shared third place on 91.

West Germany was sixth, just ahead of America which stayed at seventh. Japan had moved down to ninth place, below predominantly Catholic Brazil.

QUESTION TWO **Slim girls keep their virginity longer than plump girls.** FALSE The more weight a woman carries, the less enthusiastic she is about sex. Thirty-four per cent of those who are overweight believe that females do not care about sex – a view held by only 17 per cent of slim women.[6] Average age for a slim woman in Britain to have her first experience of lovemaking is 19 years, 2 months. Average for plump women: 20 years, 6 months.

QUESTION THREE **At least 1 out of every 12 American women now (1985) aged 26–28 had intercourse with 6 partners or more before her 19th birthday.** TRUE Between 1971 and 1976 there was a sharp increase in the number of American girls aged 15–19 who could justifiably be described as having 'slept around'.[7] In 1971, more than a quarter of them had had intercourse with two or three men and 6 per cent had had six or more partners. By 1975, 31 per cent had had two or three partners and 10 per cent had had six or more.

In Britain, a direct link has been established between a woman's politics and her number of sex partners.[8]

In a 1984 survey of women, MORI posed this question: 'Have you ever had sex with anybody besides your present partner?'

Twenty-six per cent of Labour women said 'yes'. Thirty-three per cent of Conservative women and those in the Liberal-Social Democratic Alliance said 'yes'. The fact that older women have a stronger affiliation to the Conservative Party than younger women may have something to do with this, however; they've simply had more time to expand their horizons. One per cent of Conservative women also answered, puzzlingly, that they did not know – indicating, perhaps, that they were not particularly observant or that they had poor memories. (The pollsters – and the University of London sexologist advising them – believe the 1 per cent represented a lesbian encounter.)

Not surprisingly, some of the most dramatic statistics come from Sweden. A 1967 survey[9] showed that more than 9 women out of 100 then aged 18–30 admitted having had between 6 and 12 partners and 2 per cent admitted having been bedded by between 20 and 50 men.

In the same age group, more than 18 per cent of men confessed to having had between 6 and 12 partners and almost the same number, exactly 18 in every 100, said that they had had intercourse with between 20 and 50 women.

Such statistics conjure a bizarre picture of life in any Swedish town or city which, like Stockholm, has at least 15,000 men between the ages of 18 and 30. Among those men would be an enterprising 2,700 who, in total, would have made love to between 54,000 and 135,000 women.

QUESTION FOUR **Two out of every 100 Canadian men now (1985) aged 30–32 had intercourse for the first time before their 12th birthday.** TRUE Male Canadians now aged 30–32 showed their share of enterprise as small boys, with 2 per cent of them having had sexual intercourse before the age of 12.[10] More than 38 per cent of them, compared with 29 per cent of women, first had it when they were 16 or 17.

Through the late 1970s and early 1980s, probably partly because of faster maturity, girls were losing their virginity at an earlier age. Most of the women surveyed by MORI in 1984, for instance, had had their first period before their 14th birthday and 5 per cent had had it at 10. Physically, if not emotionally, they had become grown-ups at a younger age than their mothers and the presumed consequences, accelerated by changing moral attitudes, were reflected graphically in the results of the polls.

In 1970, only 2 per cent of French girls had had intercourse by the age of 15,[11] although through the 1970s, as we have seen, French youngsters were among the principal advocates of premarital sex.

In 1976, 17 per cent of British girls then aged 18 to 26 reported having had intercourse by the age of 15.[12] The trend towards earlier experience was evidenced by an analysis of the findings of this survey. The younger the women were at the time of the survey, the more likely they were to have had sex before their 16th birthday – with each passing year, apparently, intercourse at a younger age was becoming more fashionable. Only 3 per cent in the oldest bracket – 24–26 – had had it before their 16th birthday. Among those aged 21–22, the percentage jumped to 22. Among those aged 18–20, it climbed to 26.

In 1977, another survey among 15-year-olds in France, published in September that year by *L'Express*, confirmed that early-teen promiscuity had increased greatly there since 1970.[13] Twenty-eight per cent of the girls had had intercourse and 11 per cent of those who had lost their virginity had had sex 'several times'. Fifty-four per cent of the boys had had sex, nearly half of those having had it 'several times'.

Most of the girls had had their first experience with boys their own age, but most of the boys had been initiated by older women.

QUESTION FIVE **British wives had intercourse far more often in 1984 than in 1970.** TRUE In 1970 three times a week was considered a 'high rate of intercourse' for women under 45,[14] but in 1984 two or three times a week was no more than average. The average rates of having intercourse increased by about 20 per cent in the 14-year period – probably because of more liberal attitudes towards sex and because of improved methods of contraception – and by 1984, 4 per cent of British women were having sex at least once a day.[15]

Nine per cent were having it at least five times a week and more than a quarter of all women were having it at least three times a week.

QUESTION SIX **Australian wives are more than 10 times as likely to commit adultery – or to admit doing so – as wives in Britain.** TRUE Australian wives are far more likely to admit they cheat on their husbands than British wives. Extramarital sex has been admitted by only 3 per cent of wives in Britain[16] – which makes them 1 per cent more adulterous than wives in the Netherlands.[17] Among Australian wives, the number who have admitted extramarital pranks is 34 in every 100.[18]

Between the ages of 41 and 50, Aussie wives were particularly likely to have been flighty, with admissions of unfaithfulness having been made by 46 out of 100.

Maybe this reflects dissatisfaction with the lovemaking of their husbands, for another survey[19] has shown that only 45 Australian women in every 100 rate their sex lives as 'very enjoyable' – compared with 70 per cent of men.

Fourteen per cent of Australian women gave their love-life the lukewarm rating of 'occasionally pleasant' – more than three times as many as men – and 2 in every 100 dismissed it as 'very unpleasant'.[20]

American women also feel more strongly than their menfolk that there may well be benefits in extramarital sex. Only 60 per cent of them, compared with 72 per cent of men, consider it is 'always wrong.'[21] In America, the possibility of justification because of extenuating circumstances was apparently recognized by the 13 per cent of both sexes who considered it 'almost always wrong'. It may not be wrong, in other words, if there's a good reason.

Eighteen per cent of women and only 13 per cent of men felt it was 'not wrong at all' or only 'sometimes wrong'.

In Britain, adulterous husbands are apparently more than twice as common as adulterous wives – with 7 out of 100 having admitted infidelity[22] – but the double-standard gap is far higher in the Netherlands. Eleven husbands in every 100 there, compared with only 2 wives in every 100, have bedded other partners since their marriage.[23]

And Australian husbands? No figures are available.

QUESTION SEVEN **Working-class women are more likely to make the first moves in lovemaking than middle-class women.** FALSE Middle-class women (15 per cent of them) are more likely to initiate lovemaking than working-class women (11 per cent).[24] Most modern women are certainly not reluctant to make their needs known in bed and nearly 60 per cent are prepared to make the first moves towards sexual intercourse – particularly if they feel their partners are being too slow – but the number of times they actually do take the initiative depends to a great extent on the length of the relationship and on their social class.

A quarter do so often or always in the first 4 years of a relationship, but only one in ten does so after 15 years. Those over 45 who are still taking the initiative have sex twice as often as those who take it 'sometimes or rarely'.

QUESTION EIGHT **In Britain, the pleasures of sex are rated more highly by women who vote Conservative than by those who support Labour or the Liberal-Social Democratic Alliance.** TRUE Although Conservative wives lag behind their sisters in frequency of sex, they are more universally enthusiastic about its pleasures. Seventy-six per cent believe that women enjoy sex at least as much as men, compared with 75 per cent of Alliance women and 69 per cent of Labour women. Which may suggest that true-blue men make the best lovers.[25]

How accurate were your answers? Scores of 0–6 indicate that, on this subject, you are out-of-touch; 8–12 indicate average awareness of modern trends in sexuality; 14–18 indicate an exceptional awareness.

4 Homosexuality and morality

Twenty per cent or more of American men are homosexuals and the same proportion of American women are lesbians – in the opinion of more than a quarter of the population.

A massive 66 per cent also believe that homosexuality is more prevalent in the country than during the 1950s – with women being at least as likely to hold that view as men.

These findings emerged from a 1977 poll in the USA by Gallup.[1]

A large cross-section was asked this question: 'Just your best guess, what percentage of men in the United States do you think are homosexuals?' Twenty per cent felt the total was less than 10 per cent, and nearly as many, 19 per cent, felt that between 10 and 19 per cent of men were homosexuals. The biggest positive vote, 27 per cent, supported the view that at least one man in every five was a homosexual. (The other 34 per cent gave no answer.)

Women were more likely to give the higher estimate, with 35 per cent plumping for it, compared with 19 per cent of men.

The next question – 'What percentage of women in the United States do you think are homosexuals?' – brought this response:

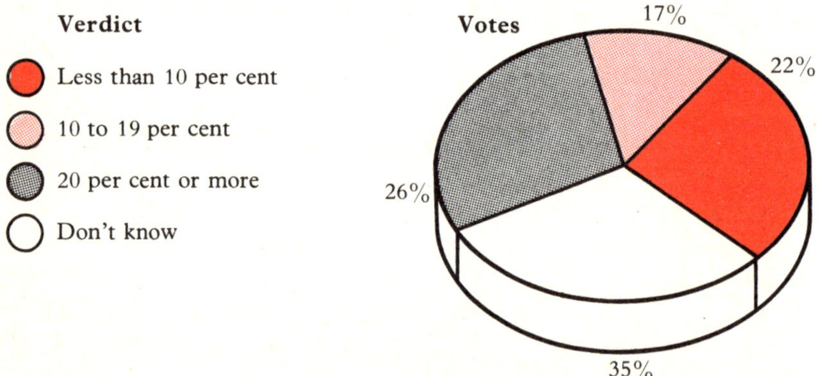

Once again, women favoured the higher estimate, with 31 per cent choosing it, compared with 19 per cent of men.

A 1981 British poll[2] also established that there were believed to be more homosexuals in Britain than there had been 25 years earlier. Forty-six per cent of Britons said so, outnumbering those who disagreed (22 per cent) by more than two to one – but 32 per cent offered no opinion.

Sixteen British men in every 100 said they had been the target for a homosexual approach – and a further 9 per cent reported such an approach having been made to them as children.

Many of the opinions in this poll mirrored those highlighted by a 1975 British survey conducted by NOP for the newspaper *Gay News*.[3] Forty per cent of Britons then felt that homosexual couples should be able to live openly together – with 31 per cent disagreeing and 28 per cent giving no opinion – and a 16 per cent minority considered that such couples should be allowed to marry. Fifty-three per cent disagreed with the marriage idea and 31 per cent said they 'didn't know'.

Gay News reported: 'The homosexual was seen typically as being male, middle or upper class in upbringing, and well educated. Opinions differed widely on why some people were gay and others weren't. Some spoke of hormones and hereditary factors, others of environmental conditioning. One man had a simpler explanation – 'A result of inbreeding amongst the upper classes'.

Lesbianism was seen as rarer than male homosexuality.

NOP were also offered this explanation by one male: 'Women are notoriously less driven sexually than men. Sex to many women soon becomes a marital duty, sex to them is definitely a part of marriage, of love for the husband . . . and an urge for children. This means that there will be fewer lesbians because they can obtain no motherly gratification from it.'

The *Gay News* report continued: 'When asked to discuss other forms of sexual expression, such as bisexuality, transvestism and fetishism, two interesting types of result were obtained.

'Firstly, while respondents in general seemed familiar with the idea of homosexuality, there was some amount of ignorance with regard to other forms of sexual expression. Certain respondents, for example, had no idea that bisexual behaviour existed.

'A second result concerned the relative "status" of homosexuality. It seems that homosexuality is regarded basically as an *alternative* to heterosexuality.

'The phenomena of bisexuality, transvestism and even promiscuity were seen as perversions of an individual's sexuality, whether this was heterosexual or homosexual in nature. As such, they were more blameworthy than homosexuality in most respondents' eyes. Homosexuality was a complete sexual code in itself and was respected – although not necessarily approved – as such.'

A typical comment supporting this view was made to the pollsters by a woman: 'They [homosexuals] can't help being like that, can they? There is a difference between being a homosexual and somebody who is oversexed and prepared to go out and pick *anyone* up.'

An opposing view came from a man: 'They are worse than the others because they can't find normal satisfaction at all. The others are at least *partly* normal.'

Six per cent of men aged 20–30 in West Germany, and 5 per cent of women, revealed in 1949 that they had gained their first sexual experiences with partners of their own sex. By 1978, the proportion of men and women saying so was only 2 per cent – which suggests either a difference in patterns of sexual behaviour or a changed attitude to the truth. Seven per cent of men could not remember their first sexual experience. Nor could 7 per cent of women.[4]

Finding satisfaction through masturbation was then three times as common among single men (aged 20–30) as among single women – with 12 per cent saying they masturbated, compared with 4 per cent of women – but women were more likely to get their satisfaction through same-sex relationships. Six per cent described enjoying lesbian acts, but not even 1 per cent of men admitted finding satisfaction in homosexuality.

The sexes in West Germany were fairly equally divided about that time, incidentally, on the subject of prostitution. In 1976, 56 per cent of men saw it as a 'necessary evil'. So did 51 per cent of women. Thirty-eight per cent of men saw it as a 'useful institution'. So did 37 per cent of women. However, women were twice as likely to regard it as a 'danger' – with 12 per cent saying so, compared with 6 per cent of men.[5]

Homosexual drinking bars are considered more acceptable in America than the use of marijuana or the employment of topless waitresses in nightclubs. They are *considerably* more acceptable than nudity in films or beaches for nudists.

That was established in a 1977 survey for *Time* by Yankelovich, Skelly and White.[6]

Although the majority of Americans, 52 per cent, considered homosexual drinking bars were unacceptable, 48 per cent felt they were acceptable – and 47 per cent felt that way about marijuana and topless waitresses.

Attitudes to nakedness in films depended on the sex of the performers. Nude actresses were considered unacceptable by 56 per cent of Americans, but 61 per cent felt that way about nude actors. Sixty-three per cent of Americans considered nude-bathing beaches unacceptable and almost the same proportion, 64 per cent, held that view about massage parlours.

Antagonism towards blatant sexual acts in adults-only movies was expressed by 68 per cent – about the same as the proportion who felt films should not be made about mass murderers.

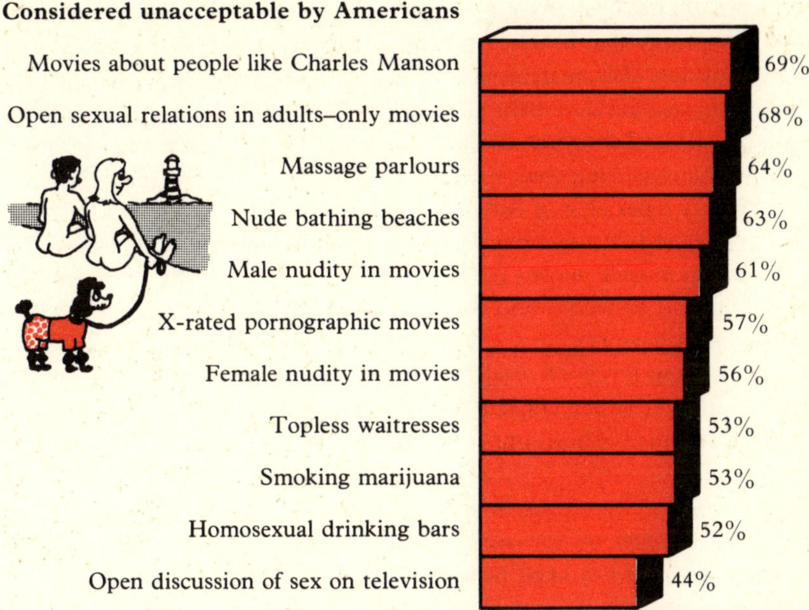

A similar survey by MORI in Great Britain in 1982 showed that Britons consider homosexual relationships between consenting adults as being less morally wrong than prostitution, abortion on demand or pornography in the cinema – with condemnation of them more likely to come from men than women.[7]

Such homosexual relationships were considered morally wrong by 29 per cent of Britons – 34 per cent of the men and 24 per cent of the women.

Prostitution was regarded in this way by 31 per cent – 23 per cent of the men and 37 per cent of the women.

Abortion on demand won similar disapproval from 38 per cent – 31 per cent of the men and 43 per cent of the women. Women were also more opposed than men to pornography in the cinema – with 45 per cent of them, compared with 36 per cent of men, regarding it as morally wrong.

The most emphatic disapproval was aimed at married people who sleep with someone other than their spouses. Such behaviour was rated immoral by 69 per cent of Britons (72 per cent of women and 66 per cent of men) – which showed it is considered more than twice as morally reprehensible as active homosexual behaviour.

It is intriguing to note, incidentally, that the proportion of women who frown on homosexual relationships, 24 per cent, is similar to the proportion of women who consider it morally wrong for newspapers to print pin-up pictures of bare-breasted girls (21 per cent). Their attitude to these girls is shared by 12 per cent of men.

In America, also, marital infidelity is considered to be morally worse than homosexual relationships between consenting adults – with the old double-standard showing, in that women who commit adultery get more of a public censuring than men.[8]

Eighty-two per cent of Americans say it is morally wrong for wives to have affairs and 79 per cent say it is wrong for husbands. Sixty-eight per cent say it is morally wrong for unmarried couples to have babies – if they do not intend to wed – and 66 per cent say it is wrong for unmarried teenagers to have sex.

Below these levels of disapproval, at 58 per cent, come homosexual relationships between consenting adults – considered as less acceptable than having an abortion simply because no more children are wanted (57 per cent).

What is the cause of homosexuality?

That question has been posed in many surveys.

In 1976 nearly half the men in West Germany, 49 per cent, regarded it as a disease. Twenty-five per cent considered it a vice and 13 per cent felt it was 'something very natural'. West German women were also inclined to regard it as a disease, with 46 per cent saying so. Twenty per cent saw it as a vice, but there was also a 20 per cent view that it was 'something very natural'.[9]

The majority of Americans, 56 per cent, believed homosexuality is due to factors such as upbringing and environment – Gallup discovered in 1977 – and 12 per cent believed people are born with it in them.[10]

Another poll in the same year[11] showed that 33 per cent of Canadians believed it stemmed from upbringing and other environmental factors, while 14 per cent regarded it as a mental illness.

A 1968 poll in Holland[12] established that 51 per cent of men and 46 per cent of women there considered it was either 'an innate affliction' or a 'sickness'. Five per cent of Dutch men considered it was 'dirty'. So did 6 per cent of Dutch women.

In 1981, Britons were asked by Gallup's pollsters: 'Is homosexuality something a person is born with or is it due to other factors, such as upbringing or environment?'[13]

Opinions were amplified by respondents to the NOP survey in Britain: 'There's nothing worse than an all-boys school. It's a nest for that sort of thing.' (Female)

'A person can be homosexual because of the fault of his upbringing as a child. Smothering by one parent, it's supposed to be dominated by the mother.' (Female)

'It is like a person being born a villain and dying a villain. It's just as they are and it will never change . . . it's in their brain and their system. It might be hereditary. I think it possibly is.' (Male)

'It must be something to do with hormones or something . . . something they are born with and it comes out later. I would think it can be trained away if you spot it.' (Female)

Can homosexuals be good Christians or good Jews?

That question was asked by Gallup in America in 1977[14] and in Britain in 1981.[15]

In America a little over half, 53 per cent, felt they could be – with 33 per cent disagreeing and 14 per cent giving no opinion. In Britain, more than three-quarters, 77 per cent, felt they could be – with 12 per cent disagreeing and 11 per cent giving no opinion.

In both countries, the majority felt that homosexuals should not be allowed to adopt children. Seventy-seven per cent said so in America. Sixty-three per cent said so in Britain. This slightly more relaxed British attitude was also seen in respect of homosexuals and employment. Homosexuals seeking jobs could expect a better deal in Britain than in America.

Attitudes about employment in the two countries were probed by Gallup with this question: 'In general, do you think homosexuals should or should not have equal opportunities in terms of job opportunities?'

Fifty-six per cent of Americans felt they should,[16] compared with 67 per cent of Britons.[17]

But were there some occupations from which homosexuals should be barred? The replies to this question underlined the difference between the nationalities – particularly when certain occupations were specified.

In America, opinion was split equally on the issue of whether or not homosexuals should be employed as doctors – with 44 per cent in favour, 44 per cent against, and 12 per cent offering no opinion. In Britain, the vote was more decisive – 50 per cent against such employment, 42 per cent favouring it, and 9 per cent offering no opinion.

Should they be hired as junior or elementary school teachers? Sixty-five per cent said 'no' in America and 66 per cent said 'no' in Britain.

The British were more prepared to accept homosexuals as clergymen – with 42 per cent saying so, compared with 36 per cent in America.

Should homosexuals be allowed in the armed forces? Here the two countries were in agreement – with 'yes' votes coming from 51 per cent of Americans and 49 per cent of Britons.

Concern at the prospect of homosexuals being involved with the forces of law and order – the police as well as the armed services – was expressed by many respondents to the NOP survey in Britain.[18]

'If an enemy found out about a soldier, he could blackmail him into being a spy,' said one man. 'And a criminal could force a policeman not to catch him.'

'I can't imagine a homosexual being a policeman,' added a woman. 'They wouldn't like the uniform for a start.'

In Britain, there have been no laws prohibiting lesbianism – as there have been in relation to male homosexuality – for one very simple reason: Queen Victoria refused to believe that lesbianism was possible because women, she insisted, could never behave in such an extraordinary manner.

On another aspect of sexuality, MORI conducted a survey in 1984 to establish the scale of sexual molestation in Britain. The survey was the first ever into this subject and revealed that one in ten of adults in Britain had been sexually abused under the age of 16. It also showed that the problem is not confined to families with problems of other kinds.[19]

A similar survey in America showed that nearly one in five women and one in ten of men reported experiencing sexual abuse that had long-term effects.[20]

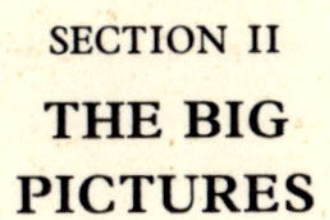

SECTION II

THE BIG PICTURES

5 Prospects of revolution

Disillusionment with the way democracy functions is growing on both sides of the Atlantic – with dissatisfaction increasing in various European countries and suspicions about the government climbing high in America.

That has been demonstrated clearly by surveys in nine European countries – Belgium, Britain, Denmark, France, Holland, Ireland, Italy, Luxembourg and West Germany – between 1973 and 1980,[1] and in America between 1958 and 1980.[2]

A comparison of attitudes between September 1973 and October 1980 shows that, at the later date, a higher proportion of people registered

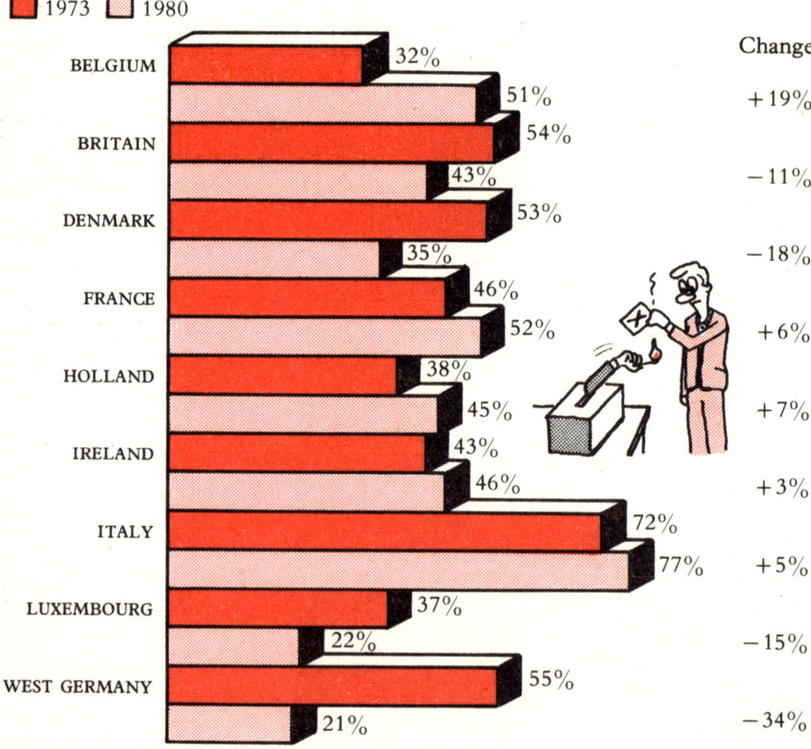

discontent with the operation of democracy in five of the nine European countries – with the exceptions being Britain, Denmark, Luxembourg and West Germany. In each of those four the proportions dropped through the years – from 54 per cent to 43 per cent in Britain, 53 per cent to 35 per cent in Denmark, 37 per cent to 22 per cent in Luxembourg, and 55 per cent to 21 per cent in West Germany.

The most dramatic increase in such dissatisfaction was found in Belgium. In 1973, it was expressed by only 32 per cent, but by 1980 the proportion had grown to 51 per cent, a startling leap of 19 per cent.

Among the European nations surveyed, the Italians were the most vehemently unhappy with their own brand of democracy, with 77 per cent saying so in 1980.

In 1980, Italy had the smallest proportion, 21 per cent, of people voicing satisfaction with the functioning of democracy. Other countries at the bottom were France (36 per cent) and Belgium (34 per cent).

The American surveys evidenced a drastic erosion of confidence in government. Here are typical findings:

1 *There are quite a few crooks in government.* In 1958, 24 per cent of Americans held that view. In 1968, it was being expressed by 25 per cent. By 1978, 40 per cent were in agreement, and by 1980 the proportion was 47 per cent.

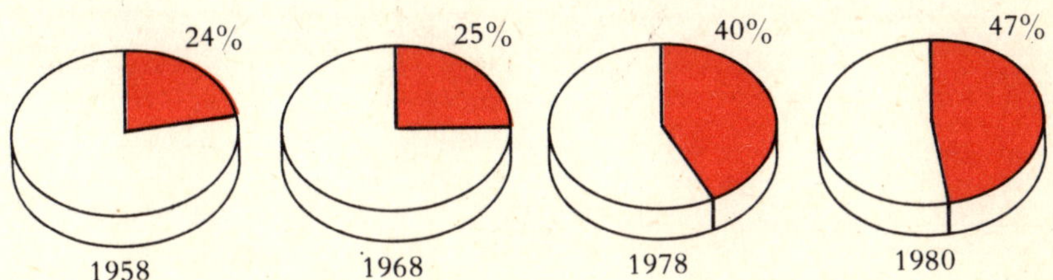

2 *The government wastes a lot of money.* Forty-three per cent of Americans said so in 1958. In 1968, the proportion was 59 per cent. By 1978, it had grown to 77 per cent, and by 1980 it had increased another point to 78.

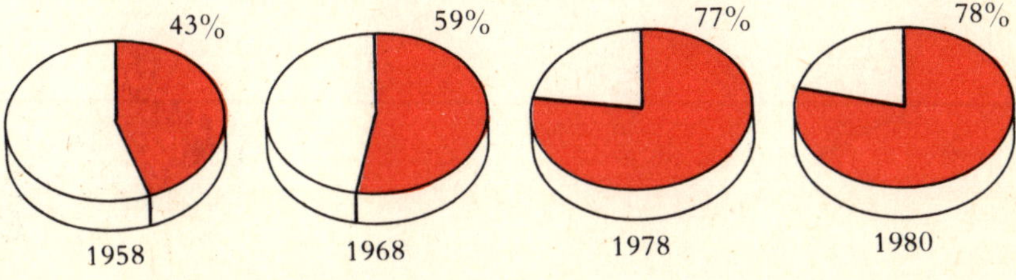

3 *You cannot trust the government to do right most of the time.* In 1958, that statement was endorsed by 23 per cent of Americans. In 1968, the proportion was 36 per cent. By 1978, it was the view of the majority, 68 per cent, and by 1980 nearly three-quarters of Americans, 73 per cent, were in agreement.

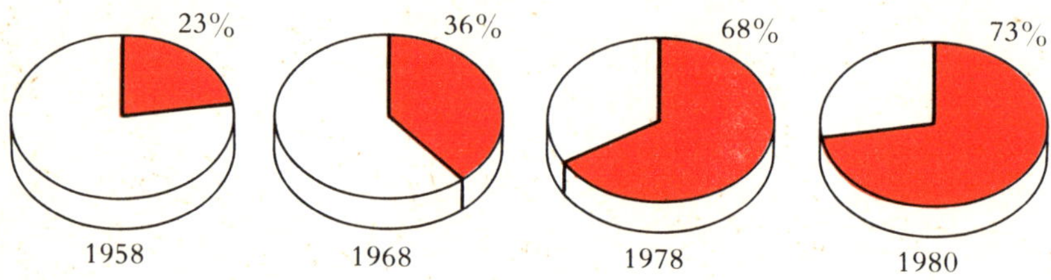

4 *Government is run for the benefit of a few big interests.* Between 1964 and 1968, the proportion of Americans holding that cynical view increased from 29 per cent to 40 per cent – and the rate of increase was accelerating. By 1978, it was being expressed by 67 per cent, and in 1980 it was the avowed belief of 70 per cent.

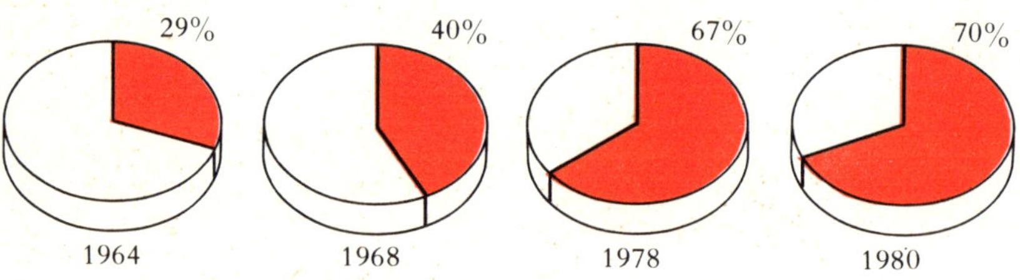

Here is how Americans responded to a related set of questions:

1 *'How much attention do you feel the government pays to what the people think when it decides what to do – a good deal, some, or not much?'* In 1964, 32 per cent felt the government paid 'a good deal' of attention. That tumbled to 11 per cent in 1976, and by 1980 it was only 8 per cent.

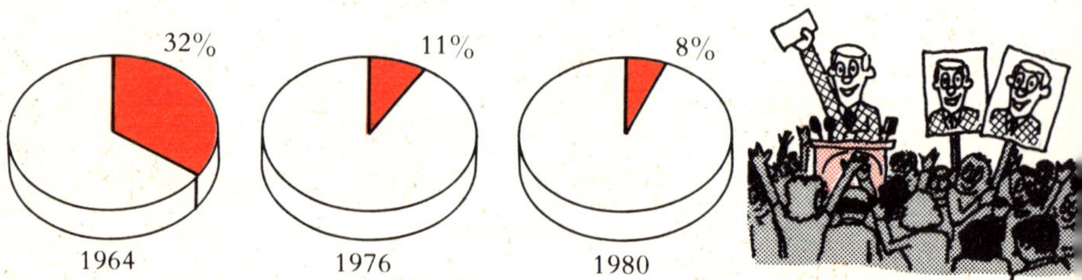

2 *'How much do you feel that political parties help to make the government pay attention to what the people think?'* Forty-two per cent said 'a good deal' in 1964. In 1976, and again in 1980, that was the view of only 16 per cent.

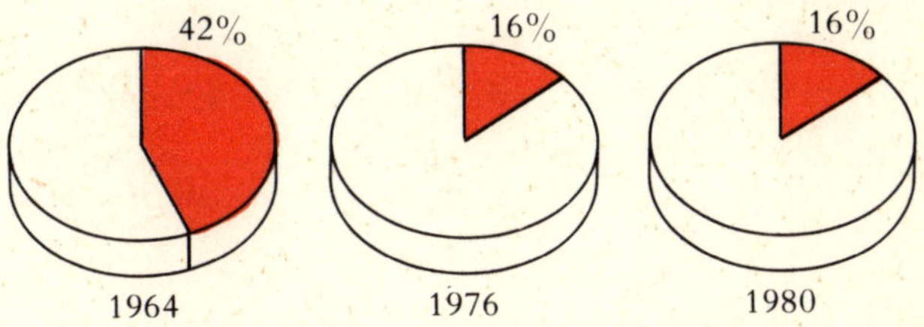

3 *'How much do you feel that having elections makes the government pay attention to what the people think?'* In 1964, 65 per cent felt the answer was 'a good deal'. That portion fell by 1976 to a bare majority, 52 per cent, and again in 1980 – to 51 per cent.

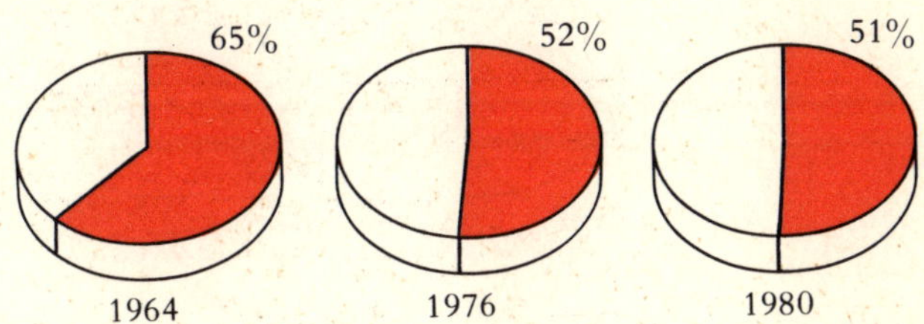

4 *'How much attention do you think most Congressmen pay to the people who elect them when they decide what to do in Congress?'* This won 'a good deal' vote of 42 per cent in 1964, which dropped to 17 per cent in 1976, and to 16 per cent in 1980.

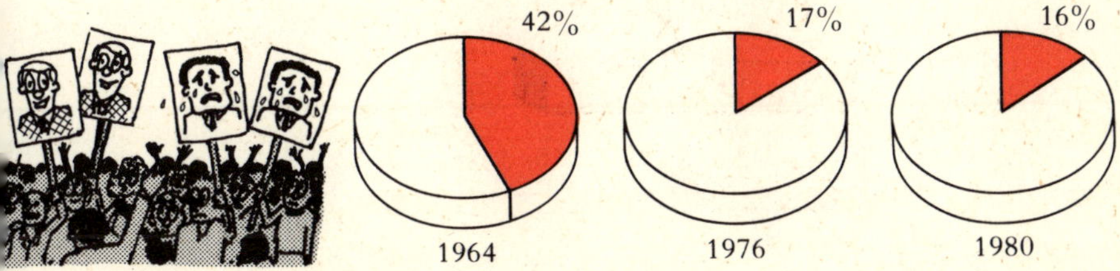

Similar disenchantment with giant corporations has also been charted over the years among Americans.[3]

In 1959, 53 per cent of Americans were prepared to say, 'There is too much power concentrated in the hands of a few large companies for the good of the nation.' By 1969, that view was endorsed by 61 per cent, and in 1981 by 76 per cent. The same statement has been used in Britain, although there has not been such a shift in opinion as in the USA. Sixty-one per cent supported the view in 1969 and virtually the same proportion, 65 per cent, in 1981.[4]

In 1959, 38 per cent of Americans were prepared to say, 'For the good of the country, many of our largest companies ought to be broken up into smaller companies.' By 1969, that view was being endorsed by 45 per cent, and in 1981 by 53 per cent.

In 1959, 55 per cent of Americans were prepared to say, 'As they grow bigger, companies usually get cold and impersonal in their relations with people.' By 1969, this statement was being endorsed by 64 per cent, and

Americans with 'a great deal of confidence' in the top people in

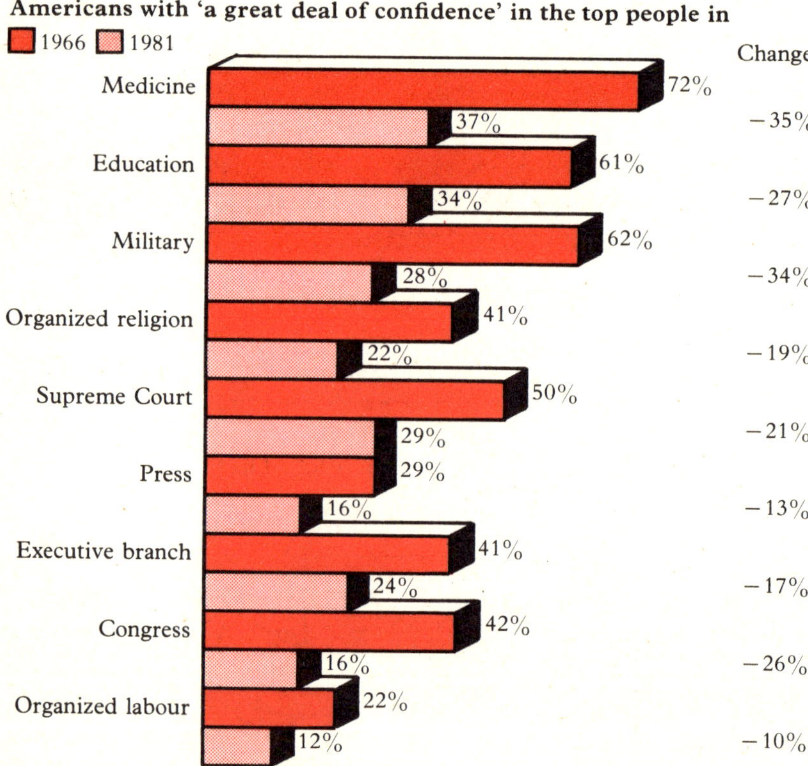

in 1981 by 79 per cent. Britons are even more inclined to take this view than Americans. Seventy-five per cent did so in 1969 and, by 1981, the percentage was 81.[5]

In 1959, 60 per cent of Americans felt able to say, 'The profits of large companies help make things better for everyone.' That expression of confidence was coming from 55 per cent in 1969, and only 39 per cent in 1981.

Overall, between February 1966 and September 1981, the proportion of Americans who had 'a great deal of confidence' in leaders of major companies fell by more than two-thirds – from 55 per cent to 16 per cent.[6]

Over that period, there were also significant drops in the proportions testifying to having 'a great deal of confidence' in the leaders responsible for other aspects of life in America, as is shown in the previous table, with percentages relating to attitudes in February 1966 and in September 1981.

Although Britain had a comparatively small proportion of people expressing dissatisfaction with democracy in 1980, it had a higher proportion of potential revolutionaries – people believing that society 'must be radically changed by revolutionary action' – than deeply disaffected Italy. And it had seven times as high a percentage as Denmark.[7]

Potential revolutionary strengths in

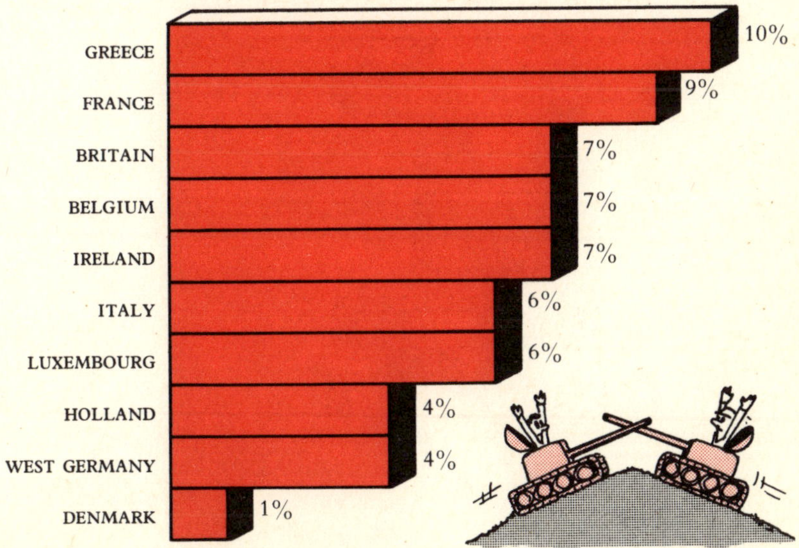

In October 1980, during a Gallup survey which also included Greece, 7 per cent of Britons indicated such feelings, compared with 6 per cent of Italians, 4 per cent of West Germans and only 1 per cent of Danes.

The French were far more revolution-minded, with 9 per cent favouring such action, but the keenest of all were the Greeks, with 10 per cent.

And how vigorous would resistance be in those countries to any revolution? Gallup investigated by measuring the amount of support which would be given to the following statement: 'Our present society must be valiantly defended against all subversive forces.'

The most emphatic endorsement came from the West Germans (46 per cent) and the Danes (45 per cent), which indicates – particularly in view of their low placings in the revolutionary-strength table – that both countries would prove particularly tough targets for would-be revolutionaries.

Holland, with a vote of 35 per cent, would not be much easier, particularly as it also has comparatively few potential revolutionaries.

The proportion supporting the statement in Greece was 30 per cent – the same as in Britain and Italy. In Luxembourg it was 26 per cent, in Belgium 24 per cent, and in France and Italy 22 per cent.

These findings suggest that, out of the ten countries, France offers the most promising scope for any successful revolution.

6 War and peace

Americans are more prepared to risk war, as an alternative to accepting Russian domination, than people in Britain, France, Italy or West Germany.[1] A higher percentage of them would also be prepared to fight for their country.[2]

These facts were established by international surveys in 1982.

And what are the chances of a third world war involving nuclear weapons? Too high – according to the majority of Americans. Sixty-three per cent believe that such a war is 'very likely' or 'somewhat likely' within the next 20 years.[3]

Nearly half the British, 46 per cent, believe there will be a third world war – with only 35 per cent disagreeing and the rest offering no opinion.[4] Ten per cent of those who regard such a war as inevitable say it will come within 20 years. Forty-three per cent say it will start within 10 years and twenty-seven per cent expect it in the next 30 years.

People in five countries – America, Britain, France, Italy and West Germany – were asked by Gallup which of two opinions was closer to their own:

- War is so horrible that it is better to accept Russian domination than to risk war.
- It is better to fight in defence of your country than to accept Russian domination.

In America, 83 per cent opted to fight, 6 per cent opted to accept domination, 11 per cent did not know.

In Britain, 75 per cent opted to fight, 12 per cent opted to accept domination, 12 per cent did not know.

In France, 57 per cent opted to fight, 13 per cent opted to accept domination, 30 per cent did not know.

In Italy, 48 per cent opted to fight, 17 per cent opted to accept domination, 35 per cent did not know.

In West Germany, 74 per cent opted to fight, 19 per cent opted to accept domination, 7 per cent did not know.

If it were to come to war, would you be willing to fight for your country? That question was asked by Gallup International Research Institutes/International Research Associates in America, Europe and Japan.[5]

In America, 71 per cent said they would be willing to fight – with only 22 per cent saying so in Japan and the average in the European countries being 43 per cent.

The British were the most resolute among the Europeans – with 62 per cent saying they would be willing to fight, compared with 42 per cent in France, 35 per cent in West Germany, and only 28 per cent in Italy, where an overwhelming 57 per cent stated that they would not be willing to fight.

Apart from in Italy, those responses matched ones to questions which assessed people's pride in their own country. Eighty per cent of Americans said they were very proud of their nationality. So did 55 per cent of the British and 33 per cent of the French. In Japan, 30 per cent were very proud of their nationality and West Germany's pride level, at only 21 per cent, was about the lowest in Europe. The Italians were the odd ones out for, although they would not fight for their country, they had a higher proportion (41 per cent) of people very proud of their nationality than France or West Germany.

Levels of national dedication in America, Britain, France, Italy and West Germany were also measured in 1983 with this question: 'Would you be willing to volunteer a few days a year, without pay, to defend your country?'[6]

Least enthusiastic were the West Germans. Only 27 per cent said they would be willing to volunteer – and 68 per cent said they would not. The other 5 per cent were undecided. Italians were split right down the middle, with 44 per cent saying 'yes' and 44 per cent saying 'no'. Twelve per cent were undecided.

A little more than half the population of France, 54 per cent, would be prepared to volunteer. Thirty-four per cent would not and 12 per cent were undecided. In Britain, 57 per cent said 'yes' and 23 per cent said 'no' – with 20 per cent being undecided.

Only in America was the idea greeted with immense enthusiasm. Nearly four people in five (79 per cent) said they would be willing to volunteer, with only 13 per cent unwilling and 8 per cent undecided.

Would Western Europe be safer if it moved towards neutrality in the East–West situation? Or would such a move be more dangerous?

The views collected by Gallup in 1983 in five countries are shown opposite.[7]

Some lack of confidence in the Americans is reflected in those European percentages, for more than a quarter of Britons, for instance, believe that America is more likely than Russia to initiate a nuclear attack in Europe.

		Percentage in favour of neutralization	Percentage opposed to neutralization	Percentage of don't knows
1	WEST GERMANY	57	43	—
2	HOLLAND	53	32	15
3	BRITAIN	45	42	13
4	FRANCE	43	41	16
5	AMERICA	41	45	14

So do a fifth of the people in Holland and West Germany. However, in those three countries, there is a more general belief that such an attack is more likely to come from the Soviet Union.

People in five countries were asked whether the Americans or the Russians were the more likely to launch an opening nuclear attack in Europe. Here are the results:

		Percentage saying the Americans	Percentage saying the Russians	Percentage of don't knows
1	BRITAIN	28	48	24
2	HOLLAND	20	31	49
3	WEST GERMANY	20	45	35
4	AMERICA	12	65	23
5	FRANCE	11	49	40

When considering the possibility of a nuclear attack being made initially by America, rather than by Russia, Canadians have been less optimistic about their neighbours than many Europeans. In March 1983, 22 per cent of them told CIPO that such an attack, in their opinion, would come from America. Fifty-two per cent felt it would come from Russia and 26 per cent offered no opinion.[8]

Attitudes on the advisability of providing the Americans with bases – for nuclear missiles or for troops – vary dramatically between European countries. In West Germany, for instance, the American military presence is far more welcome than in Britain. This was established by answers to two questions asked by Gallup during an international survey in 1982:[9]

1 Do you think that having American nuclear missiles stationed in [your country] increases the chances of an attack on this country, provides greater protection against such an attack, or has no effect?

2 Do you think that having American troops stationed in [your country] increases the chances of an attack on this country, provides greater protection against such an attack, or has no effect?

Here are the percentage replies in respect of missiles and troops:

Percentage replies:		Increases chances of attack	Provides greater protection	No effect	Don't know
AMERICA	*Missiles*	14	55	19	12
	Troops	10	61	19	10
BRITAIN	*Missiles*	42	29	24	5
	Troops	25	24	46	5
WEST GERMANY	*Missiles*	27	41	28	4
	Troops	15	48	33	4
BELGIUM	*Missiles*	24	25	21	30
	Troops	22	25	27	26
DENMARK	*Missiles*	21	29	24	26
	Troops	16	33	26	25

In November 1983, a Harris Survey for the *Chicago Tribune*[10] showed that more than half the adults in America – 59 per cent, compared with only 47 per cent in March 1983 – shared a dread with Europeans that 'the deployment of American nuclear missiles in Western Europe will result in a nuclear confrontation, leading to nuclear war, between America and Russia'.

How do people in Britain, for instance, rate their chances of surviving a nuclear attack against the country?

Eighty-seven per cent of the population regards them as 'poor' and 8 per cent as 'fair'.[11] However, the majority feel that unilateral nuclear disarmament would be a bad move – with 65 per cent saying so, compared with 28 per cent who disagree and the rest offering no opinion. As for nuclear weapons, and their effectiveness in maintaining peace, Britons are divided. Forty-one per cent think nuclear weapons help keep the peace while virtually the same proportion, 39 per cent, think they threaten the peace.[12]

And which side would win a nuclear battle between East and West? Twenty-five per cent of Britons say the West but slightly more, 26 per cent, say the East. A bigger proportion, 33 per cent, say, perhaps more realistically, that nobody would win. In addition, a majority of Britons in 1984 – 63 per cent – said they had not very much confidence or none at all in the United States to deal with world problems. Indeed, there was a great deal of scepticism about the United States' approach to arms negotiations talks. Thirty-nine per cent say the USA is making genuine efforts and slightly more, 44 per cent, that it is not making a genuine effort.[13]

Universal anxiety about nuclear warfare certainly continues to mount. In March 1982, 61 per cent of Americans favoured the destruction of all nuclear weapons in the world, with 37 per cent opposing such an idea. By May 1982, there were 74 per cent in favour and 22 per cent against. By March 1983, 80 per cent were in favour and only 17 per cent were against. And nearly nine Americans in every ten wanted an effective East–West agreement for substantial cuts in nuclear weapons.[14]

7 Can foreigners be trusted?

Americans inspire more trust among Europeans than the British, the French or the West Germans. But they are considered more likely to tell lies than the Swiss.

More than 70 per cent of people in ten European countries, questioned by Gallup in 1980, regard the Swiss as the most highly trustworthy race – with the Americans in second place with a vote of 68 per cent.[1]

The Dutch are also highly rated – being acclaimed as trustworthy by 63 per cent – and are ahead of the Belgians and the West Germans (both with 61 per cent).

The British are sixth in the league with a vote of 60 per cent.

Nationalities regarded with more universal suspicion are the French (53 per cent say they can be trusted), the Japanese (49 per cent), the Italians (47 per cent) and the Spanish (41).

Bottom of the list are the Portuguese (33 per cent) and the Russians (20 per cent).

Italians, clearly, do not trust Italians – being the Europeans with the lowest opinion of their own national trustworthiness. They rate it at only 60 per cent – having more confidence in the Americans (68 per cent), the Swiss (63 per cent) and the West Germans. In their view, the British (55 per cent) are less trustworthy than the French (57 per cent).

The Italians are more ready to believe the Russians – 30 per cent say so – than people questioned in any other country.[2] The Greeks are not quite so certain of the Russians but, even so, still regard them as more trustworthy than the Americans.

Attitudes to the Americans vary intriguingly across Europe. The ratings given to them by the various nations are shown opposite.

Which foreigners do the Americans trust most? Nearly half say the Canadians and 18 per cent say the British. The Japanese are rated third with a vote of 7 per cent and the West Germans are in fifth place with 5 per cent. Only 2 per cent have such confidence in the French.

No one has such a high opinion of the British as the British. They awarded themselves a trustworthiness vote of 85 per cent – higher than those they gave to other countries – but how are they rated by other Europeans? The answers are shown opposite.

Attitudes to American trustworthiness

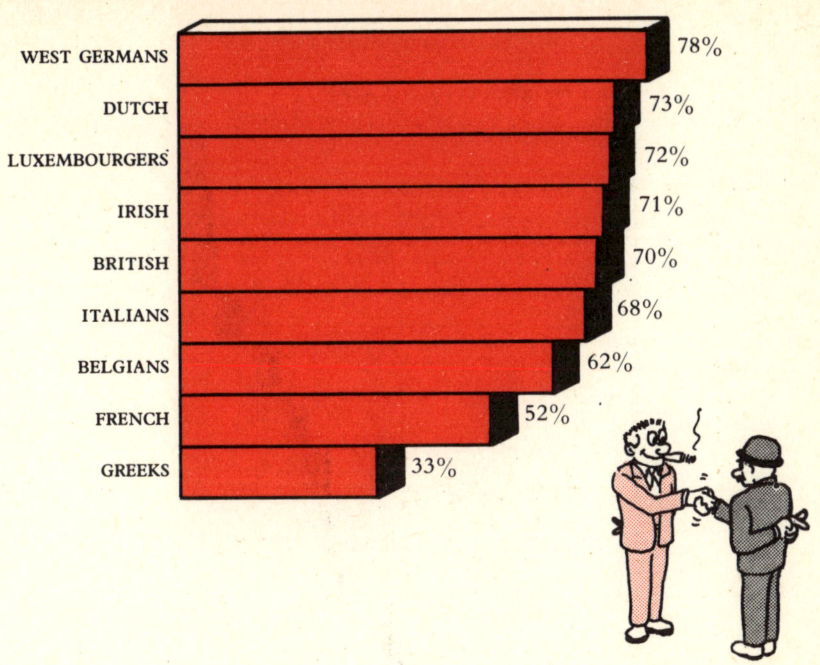

Attitudes to British trustworthiness

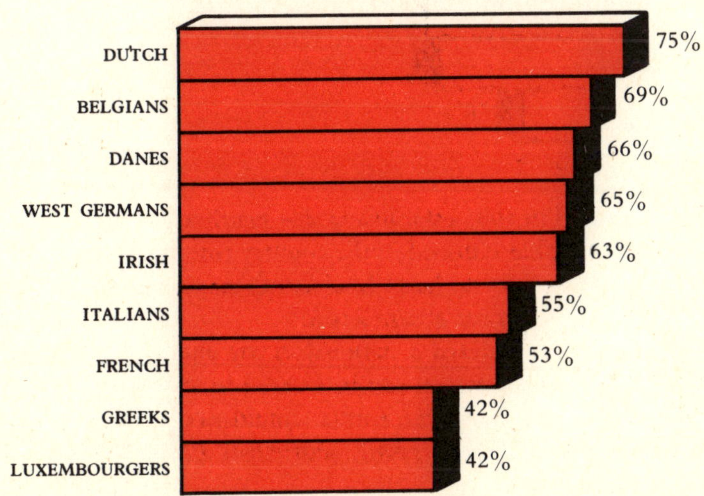

And what level of trustworthiness do the British perceive in foreigners? Here are the British ratings:

British ratings for foreign trustworthiness

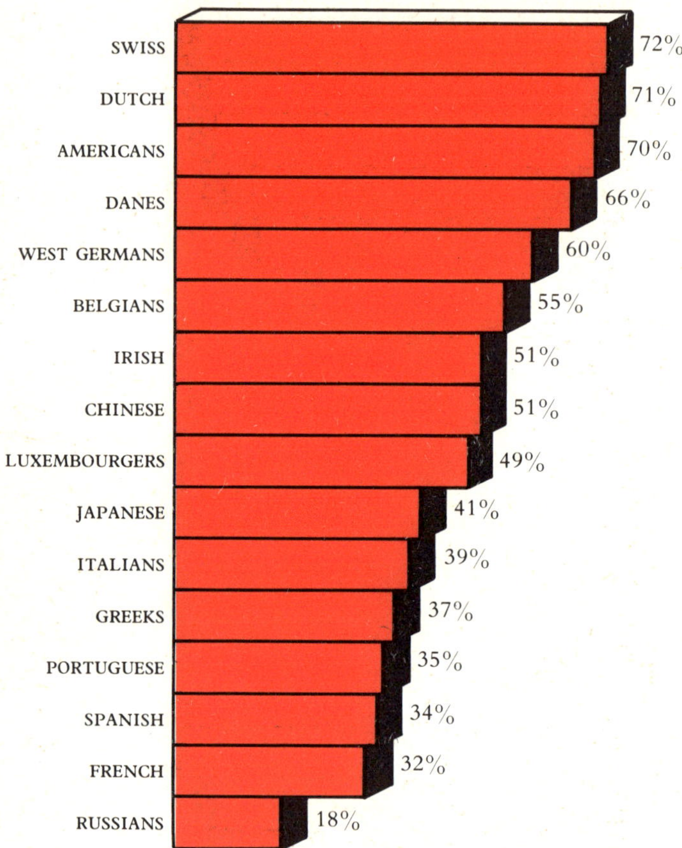

A MORI poll published in 1984 established that nearly three-quarters of Britons feel dishonesty has climbed in the country since the early 1970s and one person in three sees no harm in cheating employers by using a phoney illness as an excuse for absenteeism.[3]

Yet honesty is still considered a national virtue and 57 per cent of Britons believe the average person can be trusted to tell the truth.

Less than half that percentage has similar confidence in businessmen and civil servants (25 per cent each), journalists (23 per cent), or politicians (18 per cent).

Three-quarters of the population told MORI that politicians in general do not tell the truth and 63 per cent hold the same view of civil servants.

The most truthful group are clergymen, according to 85 people in every 100, and doctors come second with a vote of 82 per cent.

Respect for teachers is reflected in the fact that 79 per cent trust them, while judges, whose integrity should be unimpeachable, trail with an endorsement of only 77 per cent. Eighteen people in every 100 believe, disconcertingly, that judges do not tell the truth. Five per cent cannot make up their minds whether they do or not.

British police are the best in the world – 82 per cent of Britons say so – but only 61 per cent feel they tell the truth and the others do not know. In fact, Mr Average would be marginally less ready to accept the word of a British bobby than that of a television newsreader – although one person in four feels that newsreaders tell lies. It is intriguing that newsreaders should inspire more than twice as much trust as journalists – who supply the news they read.

However, journalists can take comfort from the knowledge that they are considered slightly more reliable than politicians and trades union leaders – groups trusted by only 18 people in every 100.

Government ministers come last. Only 16 per cent believe them! Clergymen and doctors also head the list for honesty and high ethics in America – a Gallup survey has established – and are followed by engineers and college teachers.[4]

Bankers are the fourth most-trusted group – a little way ahead of policemen and journalists.

Undertakers and lawyers tie in eighth place – being more trusted than Senators, insurance salesmen, labour union leaders and advertising practitioners.

Bottom of the list in America are car salesmen.

Confidence in national integrity appears to be growing in West Germany. In 1953, 83 per cent of the population felt most people could not be trusted. In 1978, only 51 per cent felt that way.[5]

However, foreigners might justifiably feel that Germans should not be trusted to tell the time. In 1978, 28 per cent of them had watches which were fast, 16 per cent had watches which were slow, and 21 per cent never wore watches.

8 People at the top

Ronald Reagan was the third most-respected head of state in the world in 1984 – being pipped by the late Mrs Indira Gandhi and West Germany's Helmut Kohl – according to major surveys in Britain[1] and France[2].

Kohl won first place in Britain, where Mrs Gandhi was second. In France, their positions were reversed.

In neither country could people vote for their own national leaders in these polls, but that made no difference in France, as far as Reagan's position was concerned, for a separate poll there, conducted in March 1984 by BVA, established that he was more popular with the French than their own François Mitterand.[3]

President Reagan's popularity was also high among voters at home, when compared with that of other leaders such as Margaret Thatcher and President Mitterand. Fifty-four per cent of Americans approved of the way he was handling his job in April 1984 and 36 per cent disapproved – so giving him a total rating of plus 18 per cent.[4] Mrs Thatcher had a rating of minus 9 per cent[5] and François Mitterand one of minus 10 per cent.[6]

That was a dramatic reversal of the positions in March 1983 when Reagan was minus 8 per cent,[7] Thatcher was plus 2 per cent,[8] and Mitterand was plus 13 per cent.[9]

How have Americans rated Reagan, in comparison with their earlier Presidents? Gallup surveys have revealed their feelings about eight Presidents – measuring the percentage of people who approved of how they were handling the job after each had been in office three months.[10]

Approval after 3 months in office

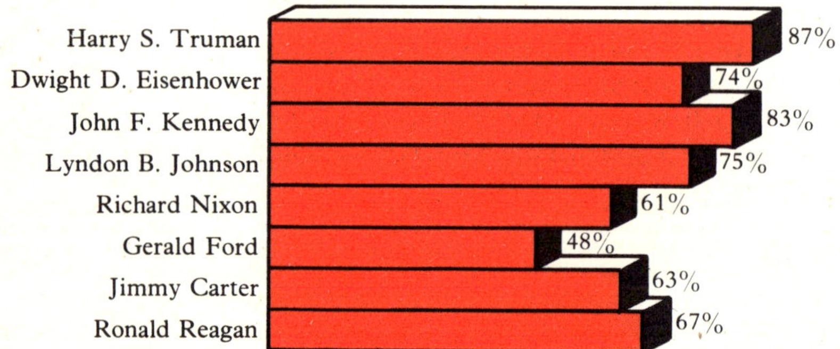

Kennedy was the President who had the most appealing personality and who did most to inspire confidence in the White House. According to Americans, he was also the best in domestic affairs and cared most about the elderly and the poor.

Apart from setting the lowest moral standards, Nixon was best in foreign affairs, and the President apparently least able to get things done was Carter.

Those opinions emerged from a Harris survey for the *Chicago Tribune* in August 1983.[11]

Which President . . .

	inspired confidence	was most appealing personality	was best in domestic affairs	was best in foreign affairs
	Percentage	Percentage	Percentage	Percentage
1	Kennedy 40	Kennedy 60	Kennedy 27	Nixon 25
2	Roosevelt 23	Roosevelt 11	Roosevelt 22	Kennedy 21
3	Truman 8 Eisenhower 8	Reagan 8	Truman 8	Roosevelt 14
4	—	Eisenhower 6	Eisenhower 7	Eisenhower 9 Truman 9
5	Reagan 5	Carter 4	Reagan 6 Johnson 6	—
6	Carter 3	Truman 3	—	Carter 6
7	Ford 2 Nixon 2	Ford 2	Carter 5	Reagan 4
8	—	Nixon 1 Johnson 1	Nixon 4	Ford 2
9	Johnson 1	—	Ford 3	Johnson 1
10	Don't know 7	Don't know 4	Don't know 12	Don't know 9

continued . . .

Which President . . .

	cared most	**cared least**	**set lowest moral standards**	**was least able to get things done**
	Percentage	Percentage	Percentage	Percentage
1	Kennedy 27	Reagan 29	Nixon 46	Carter 35
2	Roosevelt 26	Nixon 18	Kennedy 10	Ford 15
3	Carter 12	Johnson 8	Johnson 7	Nixon 11
4	Johnson 7 Truman 7	Carter 5 Eisenhower 5	Reagan 5	Johnson 9
5	—	—	Carter 4	Reagan 7
6	Reagan 5	Ford 4	Roosevelt 3	Eisenhower 5
7	Eisenhower 3	Kennedy 2 Truman 2 Roosevelt 2	Ford 2 Eisenhower 2 Truman 2	Kennedy 4
8	Ford 2	—	—	Truman 2
9	Nixon 1	—	—	Roosevelt 1
10	Don't know 10	Don't know 25	Don't know 19	Don't know 11

Whatever their views on Reagan's policies, there is certainly no doubt that Americans like him as a man. In November 1981, 74 per cent told Gallup they approved of him as a person.[12] Sixteen per cent disapproved and 10 per cent had no opinion. In April 1981, a survey by CBS News and the *New York Times* revealed that 71 per cent considered he had good judgment under pressure.[13] And in September that year a survey by the Roper Organization showed that 68 per cent approved of his frankness and openness in dealing with the American public, with 19 per cent disapproving and 13 per cent having mixed feelings.[14]

Reagan's standing with the British is an intriguing one for, although he had a higher 'favourable' vote than any other foreign leader in MORI's 1984 poll, he was eventually pushed into third place by also having one of

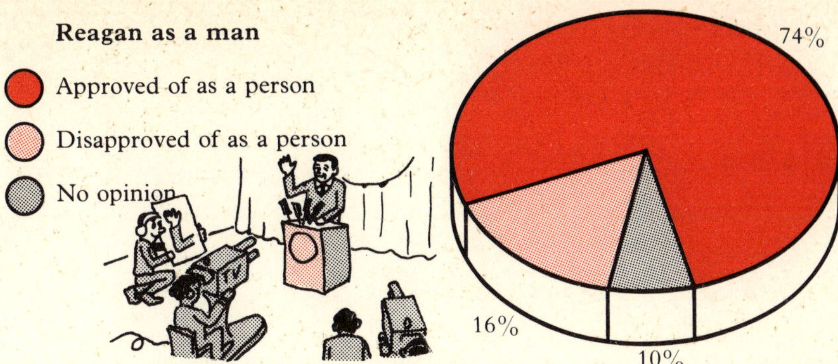

the highest 'unfavourable' votes – with more 'unfavourable' votes being gained only by Konstantin Chernenko of Russia, Fidel Castro, the Ayatollah Khomeini and Colonel Gadaffi.

Here is how Britons voted on their feelings towards foreign leaders:[15]

	Percentage replies:	Favourably	Unfavourably	Neither	Don't know	Rating
1	Helmut Kohl (WEST GERMANY)	42	13	13	32	+29
2	Indira Gandhi (INDIA)	45	27	19	9	+18
3	Ronald Reagan (USA)	47	34	14	5	+13
4	François Mitterand (FRANCE)	40	29	18	13	+11
5	Den Xiaoping (CHINA)	21	11	12	56	+10
6	Olaf Palme (SWEDEN)	17	8	9	66	+9
7	Mario Soares (PORTUGAL)	12	12	12	64	0
7	Andreas Papandreou (GREECE)	20	20	16	44	0
9	Felipe Gonzalez (SPAIN)	12	14	10	64	−2
10	Bettino Craxi (ITALY)	5	13	9	73	−8
11	Konstantin Chernenko (RUSSIA)	8	40	15	37	−32
12	Fidel Castro (CUBA)	8	62	9	21	−54
13	Ayatollah Khomeini (IRAN)	3	82	3	12	−79
13	Colonel Gadaffi (LIBYA)	3	84	4	9	−81

The French were far less generous to Margaret Thatcher than the British were to Mitterand. In fact, she ranks high among their most unpopular people – as can be seen in the French 'favourability' list:[16]

French 'favourability'

		Percentage			Percentage
1	Gandhi	+45	8	Craxi	+ 3
2	Kohl	+42	8	Xiaoping	+ 3
3	Reagan	+27	10	Thatcher	−27
3	Soares	+27	11	Castro	−40
3	Gonzales	+27	12	Chernenko	−42
6	Palme	+21	13	Gadaffi	−70
7	Papandreou	+18	14	Khomeini	−83

Although most people in Britain (60 per cent) say they have some interest in politics, only just over half (54 per cent) could remember their MP's name in 1983.[17] Putting names to faces would not appear to be a British strong point either. Although 99 per cent of those questioned by MORI during the 1983 election campaign correctly identified the Prime Minister's photograph, less than one in five (18 per cent) could correctly identify Cabinet Minister and Conservative Party Chairman Cecil Parkinson, who had featured heavily in party election broadcasts. Only 59 per cent recognized the PM's neighbour, at No 11 Downing Street, the Chancellor of the Exchequer. Fewer than half (40 per cent) could identify another senior Cabinet Minister, the Secretary of State for Employment. Seventy per cent said that unemployment was the most important issue facing the country, but a third of those interviewed either did not know that the minister concerned was a Conservative or thought he belonged to another party.

The British are not alone in experiencing difficulty in recognizing top politicians, however, as a 1982 poll conducted for the German weekly *Der Spiegel* showed.[18] Attempting to gauge the favourability rating of Cabinet Ministers in the Federal Republic of Germany, the pollsters included the name of a nonexistent official on the list. He proved quite popular, coming in sixth, ahead of ten other candidates.

While three-quarters of those Britons questioned in a December 1983 MORI survey for *The Sunday Times* felt they could not trust politicians generally to tell the truth,[19] 16 per cent of Germans questioned in 1982 said that if they had their way a German politician would be permitted to lie on television.[20] When 'to foreign politicians' was substituted for 'on television', the figure assenting rose dramatically, to 39 per cent. Protestants and Catholics were more likely (42 per cent and 39 per cent respectively) to agree than those of other faiths, or no religion at all (24 per cent).

It should perhaps be added that over half (55 per cent) of those questioned thought German politicians should tell the truth to their foreign counterparts, and this may have something to do with the international popularity of the Germans, as witnessed in 1984 surveys in France[21] and Britain.[22] British rated West Germany third in popularity behind Switzerland and Sweden, the French placing her fourth behind Poland.

Since opinion polls are frequently used to measure politicians' popularity, the sad news for Jimmy Carter is that the memory lingers on. More than two years after he was voted out of the White House, the peanut farmer from Georgia came top of a poll among Taiwanese students asked which politician in the world they disliked most; 15 per cent of respondents named the former United States President, making him nearly four times as unpopular as Adolf Hitler or the Ayatollah Khomeini (both 4 per cent), and three times as unpopular as Joseph Stalin (5 per cent) in Taiwan.[23]

If it's any consolation for Mr Carter, his successor as President, Ronald Reagan, also failed to impress the students. Asked which politician in the world they respected most, only 2 per cent chose the current US President. Top of the popularity league was the first President of China, Sun Yat-sen, the choice of 22 per cent. Abraham Lincoln (6 per cent), Winston Churchill and Margaret Thatcher (3 per cent each) also featured, as did India's Indira Gandhi, who was the choice of one person in 50.

Confidence in the institutions of government varies between countries, and an eight-nation study in 1981–82[24] showed that in only Ireland (51 per cent), West Germany (53 per cent) and the United States (53 per cent) did a majority of the population have a great deal, or quite a lot, of confidence in parliament or Congress. At the other end of the scale less than a third of respondents in Japan (30 per cent) and Italy (31 per cent) expressed this level of confidence. The lack of confidence apparently felt by Italians in their system of government also appears in a survey testing satisfaction or dissatisfaction with the way democracy works. Only one Italian in a hundred feels 'very satisfied' with the way democracy works in the country, while nearly four in five (77 per cent) are either 'not very satisfied' or 'not at all satisfied'. Democracy's greatest fans are to be found in Denmark, where only 3 per cent are 'not at all satisfied'. More than seven Danes in ten are either 'very satisfied' or 'fairly satisfied' with the way democracy works in their country.

The extent to which people are willing to express dissatisfaction with a system of government through political participation also varies. When the question of translating political views into action arises, the citizens of Thailand leave the rest trailing.[25] Almost half (46 per cent) of the population claims to be 'often' politically active, according to a 1981 survey. Only one Thai in four never participates in political activity, a disinclination shared by nine out of ten Britons. While only 6 per cent of Americans profess frequent political activity, this figure is three times that for the Japanese or the British.

Despite their relative inactivity, politically speaking, the British are the top petition-signers in Europe, six out of ten having signed one.[26] At the other end of the scale only one Spaniard in five and less than a quarter of Belgians (22 per cent) have done so.

Petitions aside, France harbours the most politically active men and women in Europe, its public being three times as likely as the neighbouring Belgians to join in a boycott. The French are also more likely to have attended 'lawful demonstrations', a quarter (25 per cent) claiming to have done so. This activity does not find favour with the undemonstrative British, a clear majority (57 per cent) saying they would never attend such a form of political protest. In Ulster nearly one in five (18 per cent) has attended such a demonstration, but again over half (53 per cent) would never do so. The average citizen of France is also more likely to have joined an unofficial strike or occupied a building or factory, although two-thirds of their countrymen say they would never engage in such political activities. While the Italians would be twice as likely to have occupied a building or factory as to have joined an unofficial strike, the pattern in other countries is reversed. The Danes and the British are four times as likely to have taken part in an unofficial strike as to have occupied a building or factory, although fewer than one in ten (8 per cent) have done so.

Whenever Danes are gathered together, they'll be four times as likely to be talking politics as the Belgians, and almost eight times as likely as the Japanese, only 3 per cent of whom frequently discuss political matters with their friends. With six out of ten Italians considering themselves close to a particular political party, it is perhaps surprising that only one in eight (12 per cent) frequently engage in political discussions with their friends. In Ireland only one in five of those south of the border and a similar percentage in the north (18 per cent) consider themselves close to a particular party, with fewer than one Irishman or woman in ten frequently discussing politics amongst friends. While almost half the West Germans (49 per cent) feel close to a particular party, less than a quarter (22 per cent) frequently enjoy political conversations with their associates.

Opinion polling also monitors views on the output of government. In 1978 more than a third of a sample of the residents of Cincinnati, Ohio, expressed an opinion on the issue of whether 'the 1975 Public Affairs Act' should be repealed or not. Sixteen per cent of the original sample were in favour of repeal, 18 per cent opposing such a move. The only snag concerned the Act itself; it was totally fictitious, having been dreamed up by George Bishop and his colleagues at the University of Cincinnati as an experiment in opinion-poll question design.

9 How did we get into this mess?

Irresponsible behaviour by trade unions is indicated as a far greater source of concern among people in America and Britain than in countries such as France, Spain or West Germany.

Thirty-seven per cent of Americans identify trade unions as a major cause of their nation's economic problems. So do 41 per cent of Britons who, in fact, regard it as their biggest single handicap.

A nine-nation survey by Harris in 1983 showed Holland as the country most in harmony with its unions. Only 10 per cent of the population believe national prosperity is being damaged by unjustifiable union activities – compared with 14 per cent in Japan, 15 per cent in Norway, 17 per cent in France, 18 per cent in Spain, 20 per cent in West Germany and 32 per cent in Italy.[1]

Pollsters named twelve possible causes of economic difficulties, six internal and six international, and asked people in each country to select those most significant.

'Our society is living beyond its means' was voted as the principal internal culprit in five countries – America, Holland, Norway, Spain and West Germany – and the people least willing to accept that as true were the British.

Spain is the country taking the hardest swipe at its employers – with 31 per cent of the population criticizing them for not being sufficiently dynamic. That view is expressed by about a quarter of the people in France, Norway and West Germany, by 21 per cent in Britain, 16 per cent in America and 12 per cent in Japan.

'Inadequate government economic policies' are seen as the chief internal source in Italy (60 per cent say so) and Japan (53 per cent) – with the same opinion being held by 34 per cent of Americans, 33 per cent of West Germans, 31 per cent of the French and 28 per cent of Britons.

France puts more blame than any other country on 'inadequately modernized industry' – with 30 per cent seeing that as a major problem – while the Norwegians (4 per cent) are, perhaps surprisingly, even more content on this issue than the Japanese (6 per cent) or the West Germans (7 per cent).

Here is how these six internal causes are rated by people in the nine nations:

Employers not dynamic enough

		Percentage
1	SPAIN	31
2	NORWAY	25
3	FRANCE	24
3	WEST GERMANY	24
5	BRITAIN	21
6	AMERICA	16
7	JAPAN	12
8	ITALY	9
9	HOLLAND	8

Inadequate government economic policies

		Percentage
1	ITALY	60
2	JAPAN	53
3	AMERICA	34
4	WEST GERMANY	33
5	FRANCE	31
6	HOLLAND	30
7	BRITAIN	28
7	SPAIN	28
9	NORWAY	26

Restrictions of constrained social legislation and labour costs

		Percentage
1	FRANCE	47
2	HOLLAND	30
3	NORWAY	23
4	AMERICA	20
5	ITALY	19
6	WEST GERMANY	17
6	SPAIN	17
8	JAPAN	13
9	BRITAIN	10

Irresponsible behaviour of labour unions

		Percentage
1	BRITAIN	41
2	AMERICA	37
3	ITALY	32
4	WEST GERMANY	20
5	SPAIN	18
6	FRANCE	17
7	NORWAY	15
8	JAPAN	14
9	HOLLAND	10

Our society is living beyond its means

		Percentage
1	NORWAY	52
2	WEST GERMANY	44
3	FRANCE	39
4	AMERICA	38
5	SPAIN	35
5	HOLLAND	35
7	ITALY	29
8	JAPAN	25
9	BRITAIN	23

Inadequately modernized industry

		Percentage
1	FRANCE	30
2	SPAIN	27
3	BRITAIN	25
4	AMERICA	24
5	ITALY	13
6	HOLLAND	8
7	WEST GERMANY	7
8	JAPAN	6
9	NORWAY	4

There is also a strong tradition of countries putting the blame for their economic problems on foreigners. A quarter of Americans regard Japan's export policies as a key source of their country's troubles and a higher proportion of Japanese, 32 per cent, claim that their difficulties stem largely from the economic policies of America.

Forty per cent of Britons point accusingly at countries with low-cost exports – such as Taiwan and Korea – which are considered to be almost as much of a threat as the British unions. And large proportions of the population in France and West Germany blame America, Japan, Taiwan and Korea – apart from claiming that there is too little economic co-operation among the countries of Europe.

Oil prices are regarded as the most damaging international factor in six countries – America, Japan, Italy, Spain, Holland and Norway – but take second place in Britain and fourth in France and West Germany. The French are far more ready than the others to blame the 'instability of the international monetary system', while the Germans are the most jaundiced about high exports from Japan.

Here is how the international causes are rated in the nine nations:

Major changes in oil prices

		Percentage
1	SPAIN	54
2	ITALY	41
3	JAPAN	35
3	NORWAY	35
5	AMERICA	34
6	FRANCE	28
7	WEST GERMANY	27
7	HOLLAND	27
9	BRITAIN	26

Japan's export policy

		Percentage
1	WEST GERMANY	36
2	JAPAN	27
2	FRANCE	27
4	AMERICA	25
5	HOLLAND	21
6	BRITAIN	18
7	SPAIN	8
8	NORWAY	7
9	ITALY	6

America's economic policy

		Percentage
1	JAPAN	32
2	SPAIN	30
3	FRANCE	27
4	AMERICA	26
4	WEST GERMANY	26
6	HOLLAND	17
7	NORWAY	16
8	ITALY	13
9	BRITAIN	9

Insufficient economic co-operation among European countries

		Percentage
1	FRANCE	38
2	NORWAY	30
3	WEST GERMANY	29
3	SPAIN	29
5	ITALY	27
6	BRITAIN	24
7	HOLLAND	23
8	AMERICA	18
9	JAPAN	13

Low-cost exports from Third World countries such as Taiwan and Korea

		Percentage
1	BRITAIN	40
2	FRANCE	35
3	WEST GERMANY	34
4	AMERICA	33
5	NORWAY	23
6	HOLLAND	21
7	ITALY	12
8	JAPAN	11
9	SPAIN	7

Instability of the monetary system

		Percentage
1	FRANCE	49
2	ITALY	38
3	SPAIN	34
4	AMERICA	25
5	NORWAY	24
6	JAPAN	23
7	BRITAIN	19
8	WEST GERMANY	18
9	HOLLAND	11

One curious fact spotlighted by the survey is that Japan's export policy is considered more as a source of economic problems in Japan than in most other countries, including America and Britain. More than a quarter of Japanese, 27 per cent, consider that many of their economic difficulties stem from that policy. This would suggest that a surprisingly high proportion of the Japanese do not realize how their nation's goods are beginning to dominate world markets – or that they are dissatisfied because the domination is not universal.

Japanese manufacturers deserve to be the international top dogs. They produce high-quality goods – superior to those of America, Britain, France and West Germany – and their sales techniques are considerably more effective.

Their executives are by far the best and their employees, apart from having the most pride in their work, are the hardest-working.

That assessment is from America. It came through a 1982 survey, conducted by Trendex for General Electric, which mirrored one of 1980 and so showed how opinions varied over the two-year period.[2]

Views about attitudes and industrial efficiency in five countries – America, Britain, France, Japan and West Germany – were probed through twelve questions:

1 *Each of these countries makes products such as cars, clothing, appliances, cameras, airplanes and so on. Which makes the highest-quality goods?* When that question was initially asked in 1980, three countries were neck-and-neck as clear front-runners – Japan with a 33 per cent vote, America with 32 per cent, and West Germany with 29 per cent. Britain and France trailed sadly, with 3 per cent and 2 per cent, respectively. By 1982, Japan

had surged ahead triumphantly (41 per cent), while America (30 per cent) and West Germany (22 per cent) had fallen away. Britain had also slipped slightly, to join France with 2 per cent.

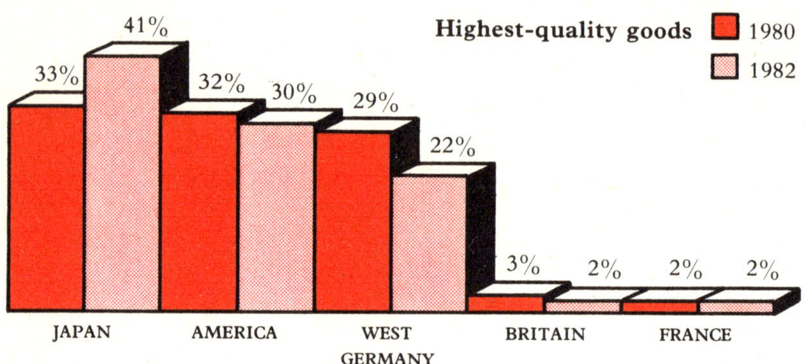

2 *Which makes the best-looking products?* America beat Japan to this accolade in both years, with the margin narrowing over the two years, and West Germany was again in third place. In both years, Britain was regarded as being at the bottom of the heap.

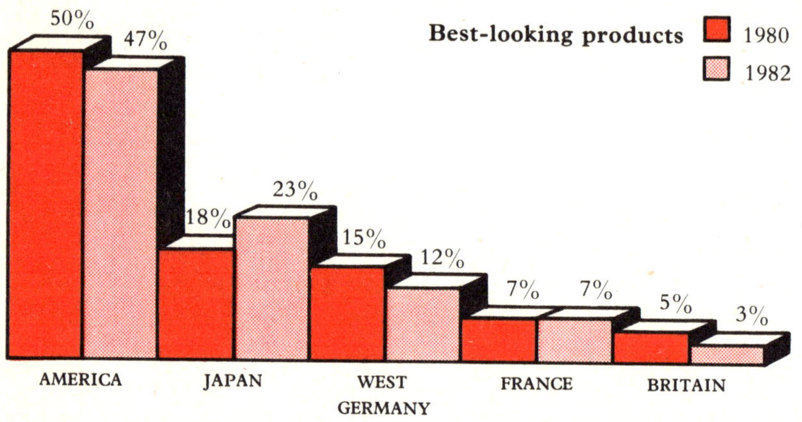

3 *Which has the most advanced technology?* Britain and France were again at the bottom in both years, with West Germany third. In 1980, America was leading decisively from Japan, but was only just ahead by 1982.

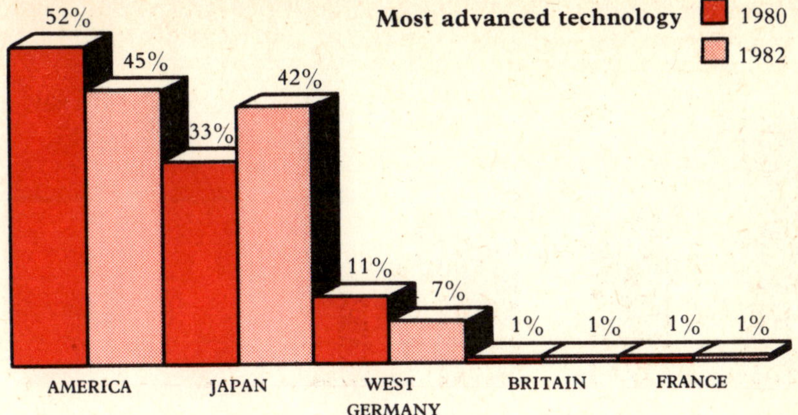

4 *Which does best exporting job?* There was so little respect for British salesmanship in 1980 that the country did not even rate a vote of 1 per cent – the level registered by France. An overwhelming majority, 78 per cent, put Japan in the lead in 1980 – with America second and West Germany third – and that lead was increased still further by 1982.

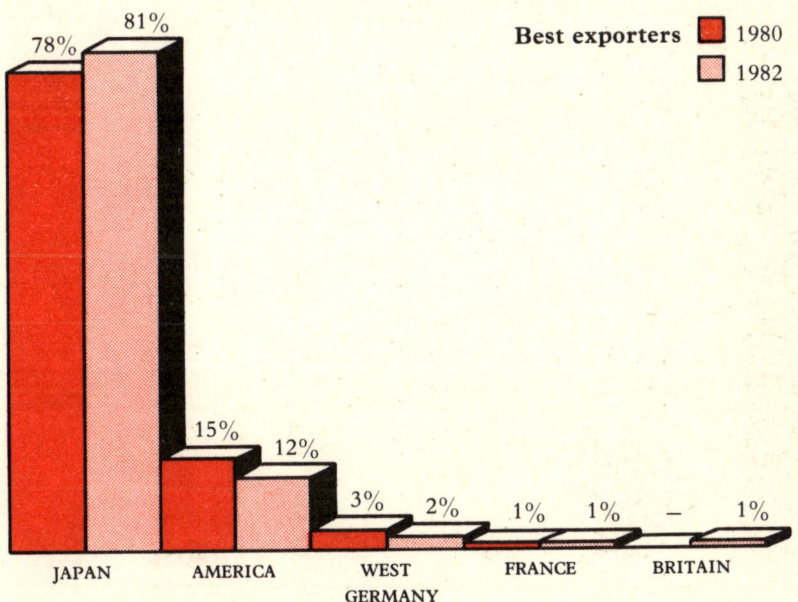

5 *Which has the most highly skilled workers?* Americans are confident that their workers have the highest skills, but also feel that Japanese competition is intensifying. West Germany is again third, with less than

half the votes cast for America, while Britain and France both get a derisory 1 per cent.

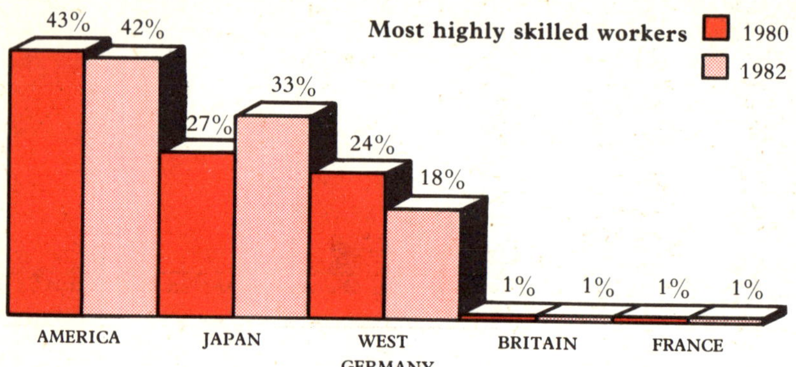

6 *Which pays employees most?* The confidence of Americans that they most certainly have the highest wages was reflected by a vote of 79 per cent in 1980 and an even higher one in 1982. Here, for the first time, the West Germans pushed the Japanese into third place and right at the bottom, yet again, were Britain and France.

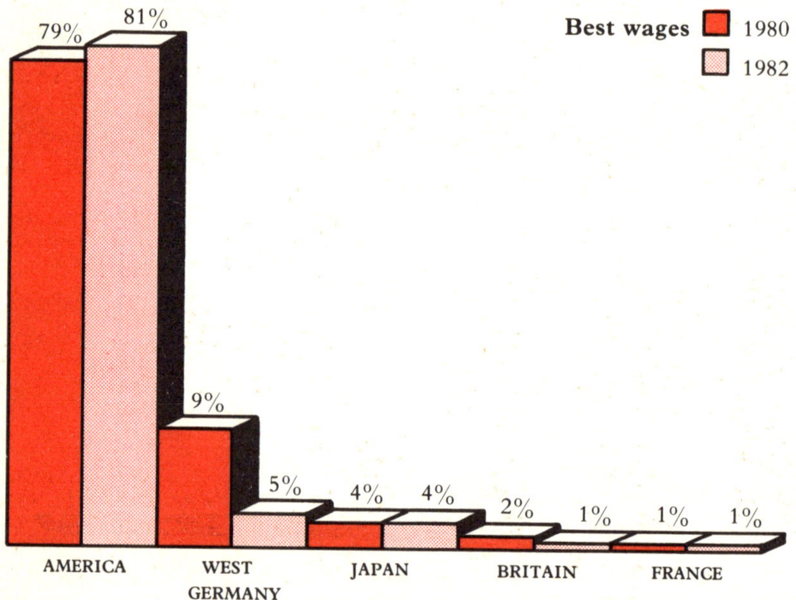

7 *In which do employees have best protection plans for retirement, sickness or unemployment?* All countries were seen as having slipped back on such welfare matters – with the exception of Japan which moved ahead – and

the lead was retained by America. In 1982, Britain was regarded as pegging level with West Germany – and both were put ahead of France.

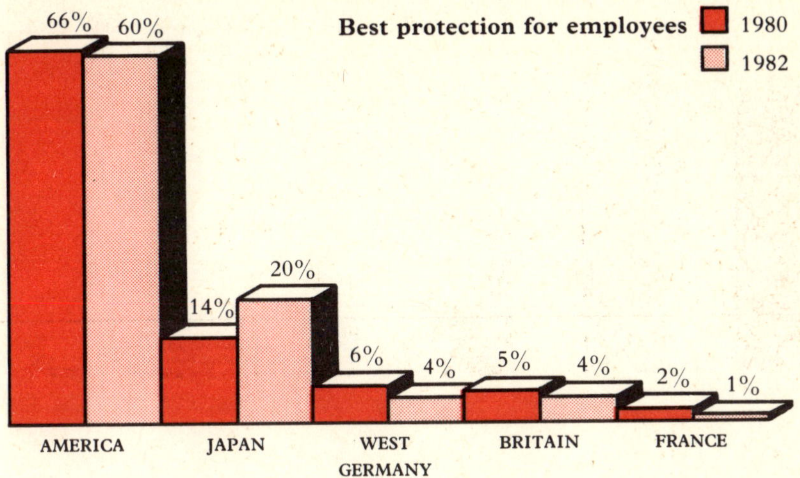

8 *Which has the most up-to-date and best-equipped factories?* In both years, Japan won more votes than all the other countries put together, and was even more dramatically ahead in 1982 than in 1980. America and West Germany remained in second and third places, respectively, while Britain and France, yet again, each scored only 1 per cent of the votes.

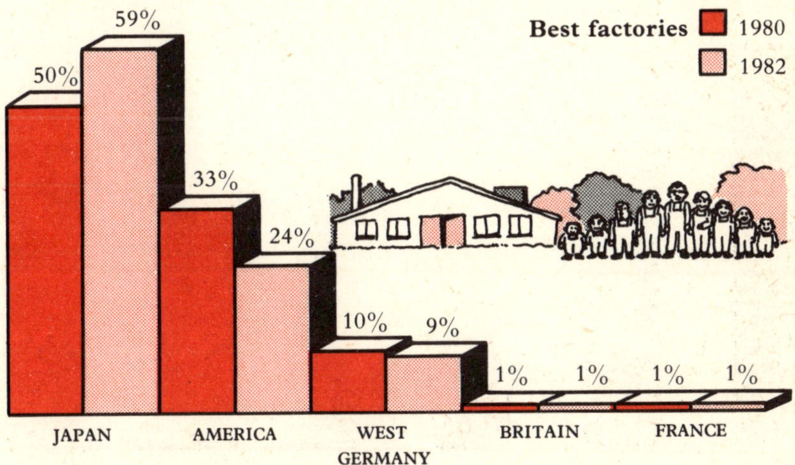

9 *Which has the best-managed companies?* Here is another resounding victory for the Japanese. Fifty-four per cent of Americans say Japan has the best-managed companies, compared with 23 per cent who vote for

America. And, over the two-year period, the gap between the countries widened.

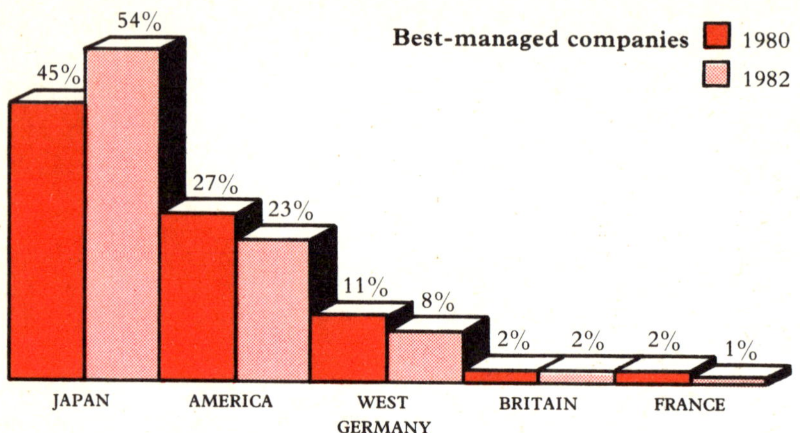

10 *Which has the hardest-working employees?* Americans consider themselves to be hard-working when compared with the Europeans, particularly the British and the French, but feel thoroughly laggardly when assessed against the Japanese. In both years, the Japanese were seen as undisputed champions – with the gap widening between them and the runner-up Americans.

11 *Which has workers with most pride in their work?* Pride in work was seen to have slipped in every country except Japan, which increased its lead over America from 25 per cent to 35 per cent. The French were regarded as those with the least pride.

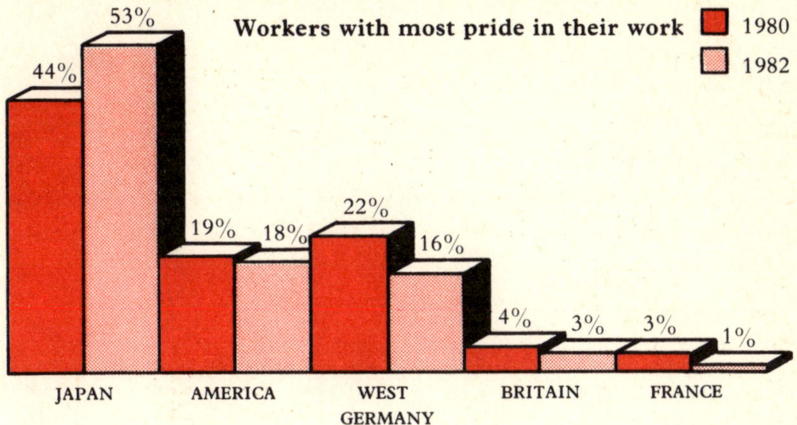

12 *In which does business get most help and support from national government?* America and Japan were considered equal in this respect in 1980, but the position of the Japanese businessman was believed to have improved considerably by 1982. Apart from Japan, France was the only country where such help was felt to have been strengthened but, even so, France eventually shared the lowest place with Britain.

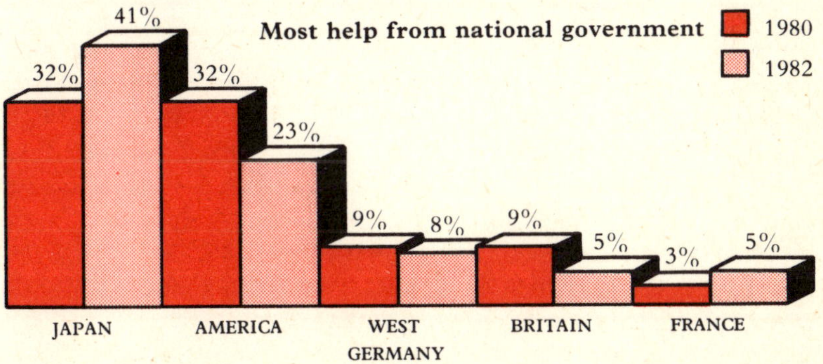

If these opinions are justified, the country facing the bleakest industrial future is France. In common with Britain, it is seen as having workers who are the least skilful and the least hard-working, the worst exporters, the most out-of-date factories, the most retarded technology and the poorest-quality goods. It is also seen as having two other significant handicaps – managers who are less efficient than those in Britain and workers with less pride than the British. And all that, if true, would suggest eventual economic disaster.

10 The rape of the environment

Few issues have provoked more international concern or controversy than man's rape of the environment. In most countries, as surveys have confirmed, at least half the population is alarmed by the increasingly high levels of pollution which are a by-product of so-called progress. And fears for the future continue to mount.

In 1982, 50 per cent of Americans declared that the government was doing too little to improve and protect the environment, and, on an allied issue, 56 per cent said it was doing too little to improve and protect the nation's health.[1]

In the same year, 63 per cent of Japanese decided that, as a priority, protecting the national environment had become more important to them than development work, such as building new factories, homes and roads.[2]

In 1982, also, the people of Taiwan decided that improvements to the environment were as important as the maintenance of law and order – with those two issues both being given a priority vote of 48 per cent, compared with one of 21 per cent urging an improvement in social conditions and one of only 10 per cent in favour of improving housing facilities.[3]

The extent to which hopes for the future are being pervaded by fears about pollution was also graphically demonstrated through a 1982 survey, conducted for the Commission of the European Communities, in ten countries: Belgium, Britain, Denmark, France, Greece, Holland, Ireland, Italy, Luxembourg and West Germany.[4]

When asked to identify their major fears for the next ten to fifteen years, at least half the people in seven of those countries cited the 'despoiling of natural life'.

The West Germans were the most acutely concerned, with 77 per cent saying so, and they rated pollution as the future's biggest single problem – more worrying than the prospect of higher unemployment, anticipated rises in crime and terrorism, or the possibility of a prolonged breakdown in supplies of oil and natural gas.

Next most apprehensive about future pollution were the Greeks, for whom, as a worry, it rated second only to the prospect of rises in crime and terrorism.

The country least concerned was Britain. Only 39 per cent of Britons anticipated pollution becoming a major problem – with bigger proportions being more concerned about matters such as unemployment (61 per cent), rise in social tensions within the country (46 per cent), and increases in crime and terrorism (77 per cent).

Here, with percentages, is how the ten nations expressed anxiety for the future because of pollution:

Anxiety for the future because of pollution

		Percentage			Percentage
1	WEST GERMANY	77	6	ITALY	55
2	GREECE	69	7	BELGIUM	50
3	DENMARK	65	8	IRELAND	48
3	HOLLAND	65	8	FRANCE	48
3	LUXEMBOURG	65	10	BRITAIN	39

However, despite their low placing in that 'future' table, the British do recognize pollution as an immediate problem – and are prepared to pay for remedies. In 1983, for instance, 58 per cent of them told MORI in a study for the 'Earth's Survival' project that they would support any government proposal to increase income tax by one penny in the pound, if such extra money were to be spent on measures ensuring less wastage of natural resources.[5]

During the previous year, MORI had found Britons even more environmental-and-health conscious on the issue of lead in petrol exhaust-fumes. Ninety-one per cent said they believed lead was a potential health hazard and only 4 per cent said it was not. A detailed breakdown showed that 46 per cent rated it a 'very serious hazard', 33 per cent a 'fairly serious hazard' and only 12 per cent a 'slight hazard'.

Ninety per cent said lead should be banned from petrol, with 6 per cent adding that this was 'urgent'.

Three-quarters of those questioned said they would be prepared to pay more for lead-free petrol. This was after they were asked: 'Do you think the government should introduce a law to ensure that all petrol sold in Britain is lead-free, even if this would put up petrol prices by a few pence a gallon?' Seventy-seven per cent said 'yes', 15 per cent said 'no', and 8 per cent gave no opinion.

So, while concern about pollution is universal, its level varies considerably from country to country – depending, largely, on local experiences and on national characteristics. Similarly, the degrees of determination to counter it also vary.

See how accurately you would assess the relative strengths of national concern about this subject by trying the following questions:

1 **Partly because of the high density of traffic in their cities, Americans are more worried about air pollution than the Danes or the French.** TRUE OR FALSE?

2 **Acid rain has become emotively known as the invisible killer from the sky, and concern about the damage it inflicts on the environment is more intense in Canada than in most countries of Europe.** TRUE OR FALSE?

3 **With levels of concern about the future well-being of this planet varying from country to country – often reflecting purely national fears or self-interests – the Dutch and the British, in order to protect the environment, would be more prepared to sacrifice economic growth than the Italians or the French.** TRUE OR FALSE?

4 **Despite priding themselves on being a nation of animal-lovers, the British are six times as likely as the West Germans to be totally unconcerned by the fact that certain animals – and, indeed, plants – are threatened with extinction because of environmental changes.** TRUE OR FALSE?

5 **With the world becoming more reliant on nuclear power, there is increasing concern about the disposal of nuclear waste – and the level of such concern is higher in countries such as Belgium and Denmark than in France or Italy.** TRUE OR FALSE?

6 **With public money often being in short supply, volunteers can play a major role in protecting or preserving the environment – through tasks such as clearing choked streams or helping to transform derelict land into gardens – and youngsters in America are more likely than those in France or Switzerland to join in free-time activities which contribute to improving society.** TRUE OR FALSE?

Answers begin on the next page.

QUESTION ONE **Partly because of the high density of traffic in their cities, Americans are more worried about air pollution than the Danes or the French.** FALSE In most parts of Europe, including France and Denmark, anxieties about air pollution are far higher than in America. Sixty-five per cent of the French worry 'a great deal' or 'a fair amount' about the problem, and so do 60 per cent of the Danes. Such concern is felt by only 40 per cent of Americans.

That was established by surveys on either side of the Atlantic – one in America by Harris in 1981[6] and the other conducted in 1982 for the Commission of the European Communities in ten European countries: Belgium, Britain, Denmark, France, Greece, Holland, Ireland, Italy, Luxembourg and West Germany.[7]

The question asked in America was: 'Do you think that federal air pollution standards are overly protective of people's health, not protective enough, or just about right?'

The dissatisfied 40 per cent felt it was 'not protective enough'. Eighteen per cent considered the standards were 'overly protective of people's health'. The others thought they were 'just about right'.

Anxieties were found to be at their highest in Italy, where they were expressed by 78 per cent of the population, with the Dutch and the West Germans, both with 77 per cent having such fears, being just as worried.

The Europeans most content with their air, with only 54 per cent voicing concern, were the British.

Concern about air pollution

		Percentage			Percentage
1	ITALY	78	7	BELGIUM	60
2	HOLLAND	77	7	DENMARK	60
2	WEST GERMANY	77	9	IRELAND	58
4	GREECE	74	10	BRITAIN	54
5	LUXEMBOURG	70	11	AMERICA	40
6	FRANCE	65			

In fact, another 1981 poll[8] indicated that there was an even lower level of worry among Americans. It showed that 53 per cent of them considered the air around their homes was either 'excellent' or 'good' and 33 per cent considered it was 'fair'. Only 14 per cent described it as 'poor'.

This survey also reflected strong determination among Americans to keep their air that way. Sixty-eight per cent said they would favour air-pollution laws being retained at their tough level, even if that meant the closure of some factories – more than double the 32 per cent who disagreed.

QUESTION TWO **Acid rain has become emotively known as the invisible killer from the sky, and concern about the damage it inflicts on the environment is more intense in Canada than in most countries of Europe.** TRUE In 1980, shortly after Canada and America signed a memorandum of intent to curb acid rain, 79 per cent of Canadians[9] said they considered the problem was 'very urgent' or 'quite urgent'. That was higher than the percentages feeling that way in most European countries when a similar question was asked in 1982, on behalf of the Commission of the European Communities, in ten of them: Belgium, Britain, Denmark, France, Greece, Holland, Ireland, Italy, Luxembourg and West Germany.

Only in Holland, where 89 per cent said they worried 'a great deal' or 'a fair amount' about the problem, was there more widespread concern than in Canada – although the level in West Germany, 78 per cent, was only marginally lower than in Canada.

In France, it was 71 per cent and in Britain it was 69 per cent – with 12 in every 100 saying they were totally unconcerned. In Denmark it was 66 per cent, in Italy it was 64 per cent, in Luxembourg it was 63 per cent and in Ireland it was 61 per cent.

The countries least perturbed, with the worry level in both being 54 per cent, were Belgium and Greece. Twelve per cent of Belgians said they were completely unconcerned. So did 13 per cent of Greeks.

QUESTION THREE **With levels of concern about the future well-being of this planet varying from country to country – often reflecting purely national fears or self-interests – the Dutch and the British, in order to protect the environment, would be more prepared to sacrifice economic growth than the Italians or the French.** FALSE In this respect, the Italians and the French are keener to place top priority on the environment. Sixty-seven per cent of Italians would accept such a sacrifice. So would 58 per cent of the French. In Holland the proportion in favour is 56 per cent and in Britain it is 50 per cent.

That was established in 1982 by a survey, conducted on behalf of the Commission of the European Communities, in ten countries: Belgium, Britain, Denmark, France, Greece, Holland, Ireland, Italy, Luxembourg and West Germany.[10]

Concern about the environment is so high among the Danes that they are the most willing to accept its protection as being more important than economic growth – 75 per cent of them say so – while the converse view is held most strongly by the Irish. The 29 per cent of the Irish who would be prepared to make such a sacrifice are completely outnumbered by the 58 per cent who disagree. Thirteen per cent of the Irish give no opinion.

Environmental protection: preference over economic growth

		Percentage			Percentage
1	DENMARK	75	6	HOLLAND	56
2	ITALY	67	6	GREECE	56
3	WEST GERMANY	64	8	BRITAIN	50
3	LUXEMBOURG	64	8	BELGIUM	50
5	FRANCE	58	10	IRELAND	29

The Danes and the Irish also emerged at opposite ends of the opinion range on a related issue: 'Which is more important – protecting the environment or keeping prices under control?'

This question was based on the premise that environmental protection measures can be expensive and can 'sometimes oblige individuals to spend more money and hence increase their prices'.

The Danes were emphatically in favour of guarding the environment, even if that meant increases in the costs of goods or services, with 74 per cent saying so, nine per cent disagreeing and 17 per cent giving no opinion. The Irish were clearly more concerned about the cash than the environment – with 34 per cent favouring the environment, 53 per cent disagreeing and 13 per cent giving no opinion.

Environmental protection: preference over price control

		Percentage			Percentage
1	DENMARK	74	6	FRANCE	63
2	HOLLAND	72	7	BRITAIN	57
3	LUXEMBOURG	69	8	WEST GERMANY	54
4	GREECE	67	9	BELGIUM	50
5	ITALY	66	10	IRELAND	34

An October 1981 poll[11] showed that in America, with the recession biting more deeply, there was a swing away from environment protection – if it involved any escalation of prices.

Fifty-two per cent felt that priority should still be given to the environment, with 37 per cent preferring to safeguard price-levels and 11 per cent offering no opinion. However, an identical survey in June 1978 had shown that 60 per cent had then put the environment first, with 31 per cent regarding prices as more important and 9 per cent offering no opinion.

Another poll, in September 1981, invited Americans to consider the following statement: 'Protecting the environment is so important that requirements and standards cannot be too high, and continuing environmental improvements must be made regardless of cost.'[12] Forty-five per cent agreed, 42 per cent disagreed and 13 per cent gave no opinion.

QUESTION FOUR **Despite priding themselves on being a nation of animal-lovers, the British are six times as likely as the West Germans to be totally unconcerned by the fact that certain animals – and, indeed, plants – are threatened with extinction because of environmental changes.** TRUE Twelve Britons in every 100 told the 1982 Common Market pollsters that they were 'not at all worried or concerned' about this problem, compared with only 2 per cent of West Germans. In both countries, as in the other eight, there was a sizable majority who worried either 'a great deal' or 'a fair amount' about the issue but, here again, such concern was evidenced more strongly in West Germany than in Britain – being registered by 75 per cent there, compared with 73 per cent in Britain.[13]

Luxembourg was the country in which that feeling of anxiety was the most widespread, being expressed by 78 per cent, and only 5 per cent there indicated complete disinterest. The Dutch also emerged as having great empathy with endangered species, with 75 per cent indicating significant concern and only 7 per cent being totally uncaring.

Strength of feelings about possible loss of animal or plant species

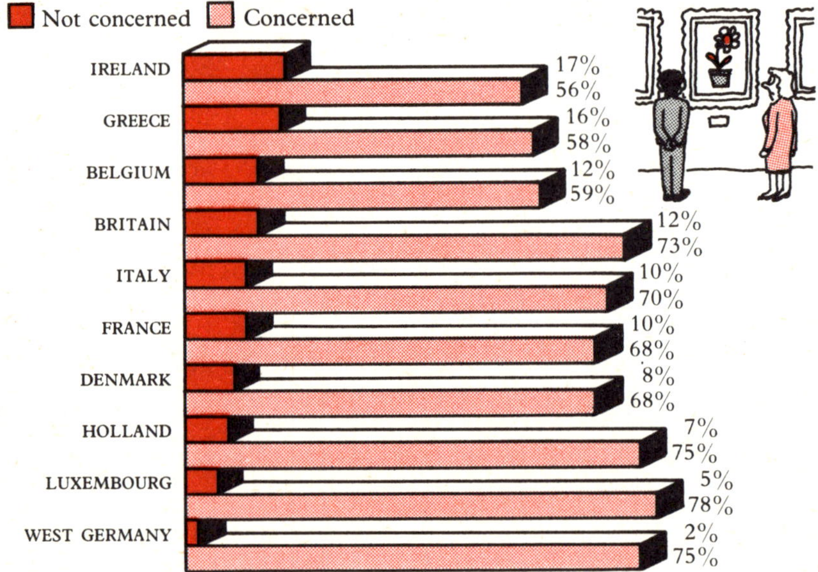

Greece was among the countries showing least interest in the possible loss of animal and plant species but right at the bottom of the list was Ireland. Only 56 per cent of the Irish, compared with 58 per cent of the Greeks, said they cared 'a great deal' or 'a fair amount' – and 17 per cent, compared with 16 per cent of Greeks, said they were not at all concerned.

The West Germans also express more concern than the British about the pollution of rivers and lakes. Eighty-two per cent, the highest proportion recorded in any of the countries, say that this problem worries them 'a great deal' or 'a fair amount', compared with 64 per cent of the British. One West German in every 100 says it does not worry them at all, compared to 15 Britons in every 100.

The people most concerned about 'pollution of rivers and lakes are the Dutch and those least worried are the Greeks – with 17 per cent saying they are totally unconcerned.

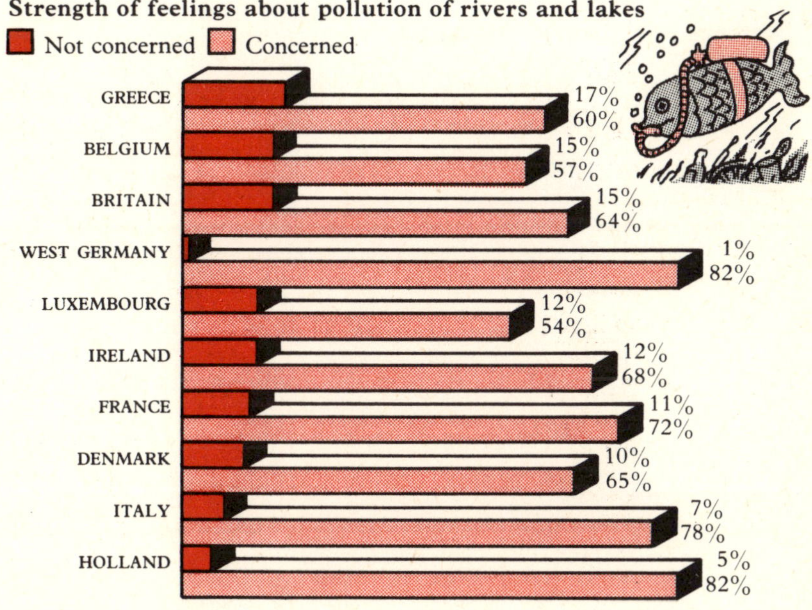

When Canadians were polled on the subject of water pollution in September 1983, by the Canadian Institute of Public Opinion, only 3 per cent felt there was no real cause for concern about the state of the Great Lakes. Twenty-nine per cent said the importance of clearing them was of 'some concern'. Sixty-six per cent said it was of 'critical concern' and in Ontario, where people were most familiar with the state of the lakes, that 'critical' vote climbed to 75 per cent.[14]

QUESTION FIVE **With the world becoming more reliant on nuclear power, there is increasing concern about the disposal of nuclear waste – and the level of such concern is higher in countries such as Belgium and Denmark than in France or Italy.** FALSE Although the majority of people in Belgium and Denmark are apprehensive about the disposal of nuclear waste, as the 1982 Common Market survey showed, these countries are still among the least-perturbed in Europe. In Belgium, 65 per cent worry 'a great deal' or 'a fair amount' about such disposal and in Denmark the proportion is 68 per cent. In France, it is 72 per cent and in Italy it is 77 per cent.[15]

The greatest worriers about this matter are the Dutch, with 83 per cent expressing fears, and the British are second with 77 per cent. Those least concerned are the Greeks.

Strength of feelings in European countries about the disposal of nuclear waste

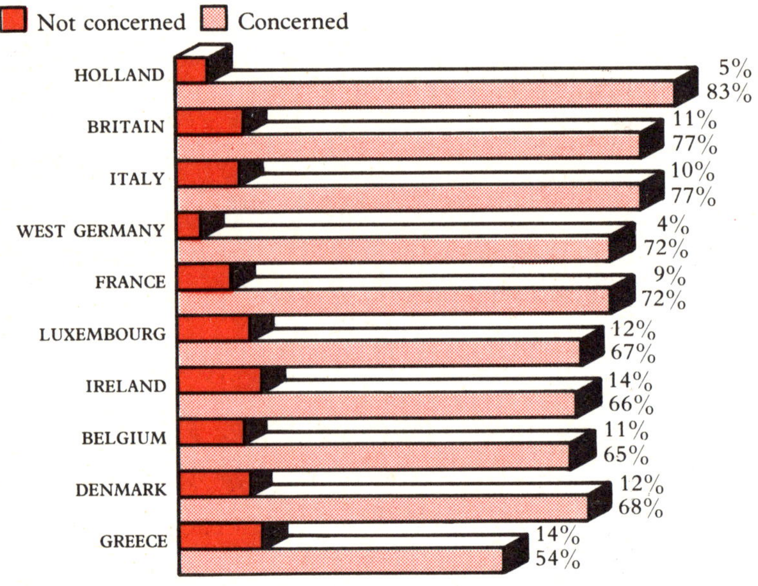

In America, attitudes against nuclear-power plants hardened considerably between 1979 and 1982. Most Americans, 62 per cent, were in favour of such plants in 1979, with only 38 per cent registering disapproval.[16] However, that was before the outcry about radiation at Three Mile Island which began on 28 March 1979, and was to create a dramatic reversal of public opinion. By November 1982, most Americans, 55 per cent, were opposed to the prospect of new nuclear-power plants and 45 per cent were in favour.

During that period, there was also a significant change of attitude towards the construction of additional coal-burning power plants. The 28 per cent who had been opposed to them in 1979 dropped to 24 per cent and the 72 per cent who had said they would not object to them increased to 76 per cent.

Pollsters asked: 'What effect, if any, do you think a great increase in the number of atomic/nuclear energy plants would have? Would our communities be more dangerous, less dangerous, or about the same as they are today?'

In 1973, 29 per cent of Americans said such plants would bring increased dangers. In 1982, the proportion was 54 per cent.

Enthusiasm for nuclear power-plants also waned significantly in Canada. In 1976, 41 per cent of Canadians favoured an increase in the generation of electricity through nuclear power and 14 per cent felt such generation should be stopped altogether.[17] By 1980, only 30 per cent wanted the nuclear-generating programme to be extended and 27 per cent wanted it scrapped.

In Japan also, public opinion has begun to turn against nuclear power-plants – although they have continued to win majority support. In 1979, 62 per cent of the Japanese were in favour of such plants and 21 per cent were against them. In 1981, 55 per cent were in favour and 29 per cent were opposed.[18]

QUESTION SIX **With public money often being in short supply, volunteers can play a major role in protecting or preserving the environment – through tasks such as clearing choked streams or helping to transform derelict land into gardens – and youngsters in America are more likely than those in France or Switzerland to join in free-time activities which contribute to improving society.** FALSE When it comes to being public-spirited in this way, youngsters in France are slightly ahead of those in America – and those in Switzerland are well ahead. In America, 4 per cent of young people aged 18–24 spend free time in activities which contribute to improving society – compared with 5 per cent in France and 6 per cent in Switzerland.

This was established during a survey for the Japanese government, published in 1984, which was conducted in 11 countries: America, Brazil, Britain, France, Japan, Korea, the Philippines, Sweden, Switzerland, Yugoslavia and West Germany.[19]

In Brazil, nearly 19 youngsters in every 100 do such activities, which puts their country at the top of the list, while the proportion in West Germany is 7 per cent and in Britain it is 5 per cent. At the bottom are the

Japanese – being nearly 4 times less likely to do such voluntary work as the Americans and more than 19 times less likely than the Brazilians.

Youngsters who join free-time activities to improve society

		Percentage			Percentage
1	BRAZIL	19	6	FRANCE	5
2	THE PHILIPPINES	13	8	AMERICA	4
3	YUGOSLAVIA	12	9	KOREA	3
4	WEST GERMANY	7	9	SWEDEN	3
5	SWITZERLAND	6	11	JAPAN	1
6	BRITAIN	5			

How did you fare with the questions? Take three marks for each correct answer. Scores of 0–6 show you are not qualified to judge national attitudes to pollution; 9–12 indicate that your instincts are sound; 15–18 demonstrate exceptional perception.

SECTION III

FAMILIES, ROYAL AND OTHER

11 A boy's best friend

Fathers are pushed into the back seat when youngsters have worries because, in most countries, a boy's best friend is his mother. So is a girl's.

In eight countries out of eleven, according to a Japanese Government survey,[1] she is the one they turn to with their troubles, while in none of the countries would youngsters turn to their fathers. In only four of the countries is poor old dad even in second place as confidante and in only three of the others does he manage third choice, trailing behind the mums and their children's friends.

Countries investigated in the survey, published in 1984, were: America, Brazil, Britain, France, Japan, Korea, the Philippines, Sweden, Switzerland, West Germany and Yugoslavia.

Among youngsters aged 18–24, mothers were the favourite confidantes in America, Britain, Brazil, France, the Philippines, Sweden, Switzerland and West Germany. Japanese youngsters preferred friends as their first choice. So did those in Korea and Yugoslavia.

But while in 1950 more than 60 per cent of American households were headed by a male breadwinner with a wife–mother at home full time, today less than 10 per cent of households fit this pattern. In 55 per cent of American households both adults work, either of necessity to make ends meet, or to raise the family's standard of living.[2] According to a Black Corp. poll in 1984 for *USA Today* almost 60 per cent of US men said their jobs cause stress in their lives, and 30 per cent said their wives' jobs cause them stress too. Many American men believe that they must reduce their own career goals if they have a wife with a career of her own; this includes 39 per cent of single men and 47 per cent of married men, 39 per cent of those 18–25, 44 per cent of 26–39-year-old men, 46 per cent of 40–64-year-old men and a thumping 59 per cent of those 65 or older. This 'role reversal' is leading men in America to spend an increasing amount of time with their kids. In a 1925 landmark survey of Muncie, Indiana, one father in ten said he spent virtually nil time with his children. In 1983, Gallup found that a quarter of fathers expected to be the primary parent after the mother returned to full-time employment. Eighty per cent were present at the birth of their children compared to 27 per cent a decade earlier. The Black Corp. poll for *USA Today* found that more than 90 per cent of men said being a husband/father was the most satisfying role in their lives; only 5 per cent said their work roles were the most important.[3]

In the 1984 Japanese Government survey Brazilian young people are apparently the most taciturn, or possibly the most secretive, because they have the highest proportion – 16 per cent – who insist they never discuss their problems with anyone.[4] That means they are more than twice as likely to bottle up their worries as the French and the Swiss (both 7 per cent) and more than three times as likely as the Americans (5 per cent), the West Germans (5 per cent) or the Swedes (4 per cent).

Japanese youngsters also tend to keep their troubles to themselves, with 10 per cent saying they do, and the most ready to talk about them are the British – with not one claiming to suffer in silence.

Some of the most universal worries among youngsters stem from relationships with the opposite sex and nowhere are boy–girl friendships more likely to cause anxiety than in Korea, where they are reported by 22 per cent of youngsters – a higher proportion than in Japan (19 per cent) or the United States (15 per cent).

Youngsters in West Germany and in Yugoslavia (11 per cent and 12 per cent, respectively) are slightly less likely to suffer from the traumas of adolescence, which puts them above youngsters in Switzerland and the Philippines in the adolescent agony tables (8 per cent each).

Young Britons (7 per cent) are half as likely as young Americans to have such problems.

France's liberated attitudes to sex are reflected by the fact that only 5 per cent of the country's youngsters rate boy–girl relationships as a significant source of anxiety, while in Sweden it is mentioned by only 2 per cent.

Youngsters with worries about boy–girl friendships

		Percentage			Percentage
1	KOREA	22	6	THE PHILIPPINES	8
2	JAPAN	19	6	SWITZERLAND	8
3	AMERICA	15	8	BRITAIN	7
4	YUGOSLAVIA	12	9	BRAZIL	6
5	WEST GERMANY	11	10	FRANCE	5
			11	SWEDEN	2

For most young people, however, worries about sex are dwarfed by those about money. Shortage of cash is seen as the biggest problem by youngsters in six of the countries – America, Brazil, Britain, France, the Philippines and West Germany.

It is listed second in Switzerland, being considered less onerous there than anxieties about academic studies, and in Sweden, where the chief worry among youngsters is finding a job.

In Yugoslavia, money problems are listed fourth – after worries about getting a job, academic studies and national issues. In Korea, it is also in fourth place – after worries about getting a job, academic studies, and securing a place in the best school or college.

Youngsters in the Philippines are the ones most acutely concerned about money, with 57 per cent saying so. Second are the Americans (53 per cent) and third are the British (45 per cent). Those least concerned are the Swiss (15 per cent).

Youngsters with worries about cash

		Percentage			Percentage
1	THE PHILIPPINES	57	7	WEST GERMANY	26
2	AMERICA	53	8	KOREA	25
3	BRITAIN	45	9	SWEDEN	24
4	FRANCE	30	10	YUGOSLAVIA	21
5	JAPAN	28	11	SWITZERLAND	15
6	BRAZIL	27			

Levels of seriousness with which youngsters view their problems also vary considerably from country to country. Those in France, Brazil and Korea are the most likely to wallow in despair and contemplate suicide. With approximately 3 per cent reporting such feelings in both countries, they are considerably more likely to consider killing themselves than the British, Japanese, Swedes, or Yugoslavs.

Thoughts of suicide occur to more young people in West Germany (3 per cent) than in Switzerland (2 per cent) or America (2 per cent), but the Americans are potentially still more at risk than the British (1 per cent).

Youngsters least likely to consider such drastic action live in the Philippines, where the thought has occurred to only a microscopic 0.3 per cent – fewer than 1 in every 300.

Youngsters who report having contemplated suicide

		Percentage			Percentage
1	FRANCE	3	7	BRITAIN	1
1	BRAZIL	3	7	JAPAN	1
1	KOREA	3	7	SWEDEN	1
1	WEST GERMANY	3	7	YUGOSLAVIA	1
5	SWITZERLAND	2	11	THE PHILIPPINES	0.3
5	AMERICA	2			

Although so many young people in France have considered killing themselves, most people live happier lives there than in Britain – according to popular opinion in America, Japan and West Germany.

In 1982, nearly 6,500 people surveyed in five countries – America, Britain, France, Japan and West Germany – were shown a list of seven countries:[5]

AMERICA BRITAIN CANADA FRANCE ITALY JAPAN WEST GERMANY

After being told they could not vote for their own country, they were asked: 'In which of those countries do people lead the happiest lives?'

Canada was voted the winner in each of the five countries – with the Americans giving it a resounding endorsement of 58 per cent, compared with one of only 3 per cent for Britain.

The American 'happiness quotient' vote

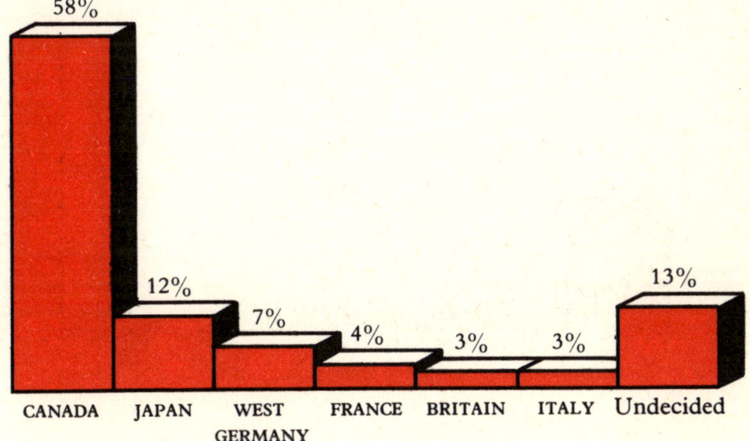

The British 'happiness quotient' vote

The French 'happiness quotient' vote

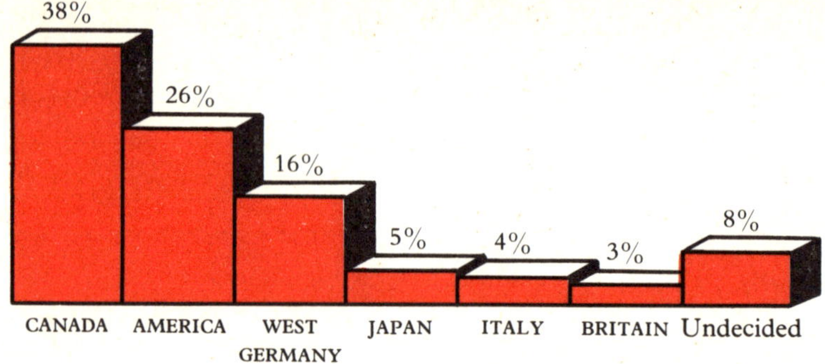

The Japanese 'happiness quotient' vote

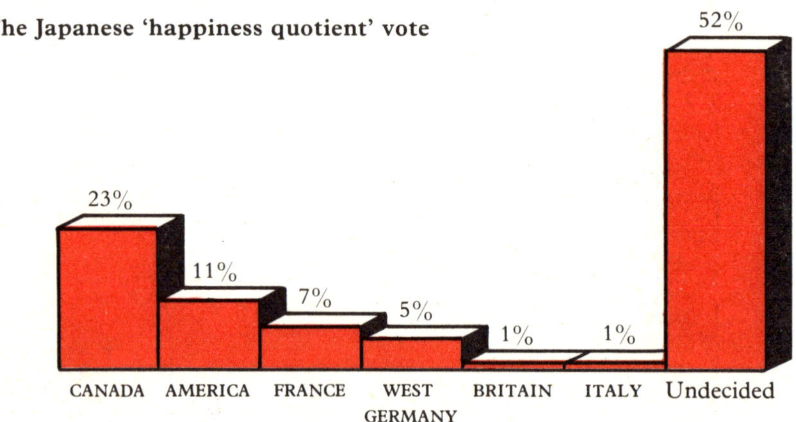

The West German 'happiness quotient' vote

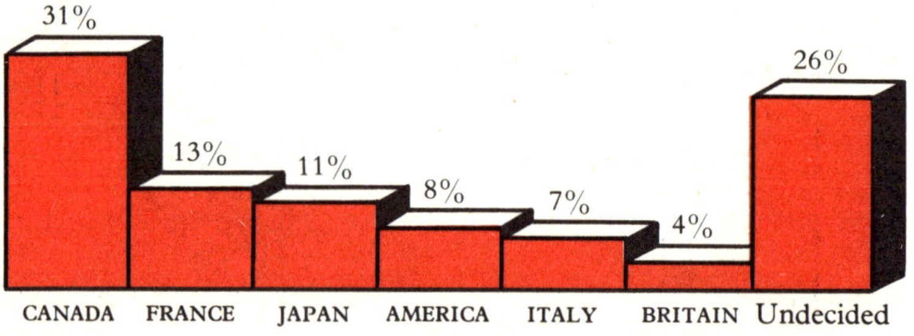

Maybe the British, who rather pride themselves on being cheerful, should start making more of an effort to smile!

12 Verdicts on babies – and on parents

Stockbrokers take longer to impregnate their wives after marriage than deckchair attendants or dustmen. Teachers are also slower than car mechanics.

A man's occupation gives a good guide to the number of months likely to elapse between his honeymoon and his wife's first pregnancy.

Ten years of British Government statistics[1] reveal distinctive variations between the social classes in the length of time women take to conceive.

In 1971, wives of professional men such as barristers and university professors gave birth, on average, 32 months after the wedding night. Wives of manual workers such as fitters and master bricklayers gave birth after 19 months. Wives of unskilled men such as labourers and road-sweepers did so after 9 months. All three groups were less impetuous by 1976 when the gaps were: wives of professionals 39 months, wives of manual workers 26 months, wives of unskilled men 12 months.

This trend continued in 1981 when the respective intervals were 42, 25 and 13 months. There were also plenty of couples, of course, who did not wait for marriage before becoming parents. In 1982 an illegitimate baby was born in the country about every five minutes, day and night, with such babies representing 14 per cent of the 626,000 live births.

The number of legal abortions peaked in England and Wales in 1980, with an average of one baby being aborted every four minutes. Thirty-four per cent of those abortions, in 1980 (129,000) and in 1982 (128,000), were performed on married women. In 1969, 50,000 abortions were performed in Britain.

Screeds have been written on the attitudes of adults to modern youngsters – and on those of youngsters to their parents and the world in general. Such attitudes vary enormously from country to country. Assess how in touch you are with international adult-youngster relationships by answering the following questions:

1 **More than half the people in France and Italy – double the British percentage – feel the world is no longer a fit place into which to bring babies.** TRUE OR FALSE?

2 **The British are more impressed by the joys of parenthood than the Germans or the Danes.** TRUE OR FALSE?

3 **Parents in Britain are more likely to over-indulge their children than those in Italy or France.** TRUE OR FALSE?

4 **Fathers in Japan are more sure of themselves on matters of discipline and education than fathers in America or Britain.** TRUE OR FALSE?

5 **Because of their traditional culture, Japanese youngsters are more likely to be willing to support aged parents eventually than youngsters in America or Britain.** TRUE OR FALSE?

6 **Young people in Germany are more satisfied with their home lives than those in France.** TRUE OR FALSE?

7 **There is twice as much dissatisfaction with places of work among working British youngsters as among working youngsters in Japan.** TRUE OR FALSE?

Now see below for the answers.

QUESTION ONE **More than half the people in France and Italy – double the British percentage – feel the world is no longer a fit place into which to bring babies.** TRUE More than 100 million parents in the European community agreed that society's future is too uncertain to risk bringing children into the world. They are the 42 per cent in nine countries who said so when questioned on behalf of the Commission of the European Communities.[2]

The Italians (57 per cent) and the French (51 per cent) were the most pessimistic. In Denmark and West Germany the percentage was 40.

Most optimistic were the British and the Irish – both with exactly a quarter of the population feeling that way.

QUESTION TWO **The British are more impressed by the joys of parenthood than the Germans or the Danes.** FALSE Despite the gloom described above, it was still universally agreed by all parents in the EEC – by 66 per cent to 27 per cent – that parenthood is the ultimate fulfilment of men and women.[3]

The British were in fact the most uncertain. Only 53 per cent agreed that parenthood was the 'ultimate fulfilment' and 38 per cent disagreed. The others did not know.

France was the nation which put parenthood on the highest pedestal – with a vote of 78 per cent – and in Luxembourg and Italy the percentages were 77 and 76, respectively. In Ireland, another Catholic country, it was 67.

In West Germany and Denmark the respective percentages were 63 and 56.

Women who had been students up to the age of 20 or more, were the most universally disenchanted by the prospect of being a parent. Only 48 per cent regarded parenthood as the 'ultimate fulfilment' and 47 per cent disagreed. Men in this category were more enthusiastic about babies – with 60 per cent agreeing and only 36 per cent disagreeing.

Feelings about the ideal number of children to have in a family also vary from country to country. Most Americans[4] and Europeans plump for two.[5]

The Australians have such vast expanses of land that it is hardly surprising that 54 per cent should favour three or four children in a family. However, the Japanese have space problems and so it is unexpected that 60 per cent of them want three or more.

And what of married couples unable to have their ideal number of babies? Should they be helped by test-tube methods? Here again, Australian enthusiasm is evident – with 69 per cent approving and 11 per cent disapproving.[6] In Britain, the percentage recorded in favour was 65 and that against was 21.[7] In Canada the percentages were 60 and 22.[8]

QUESTION THREE **Parents in Britain are more likely to over-indulge their children than those in Italy or France.** FALSE There is universal agreement in Europe that today's children are over-indulged but more people say it happens to a greater extent in Italy (69 per cent), in France and Belgium (67 per cent each) than in Britain (63 per cent).[9] Those regarded as the least indulgent are the Danes (43 per cent) and the Germans (42 per cent).

Sixty per cent of Europeans also feel that modern parents are not strict enough. The British are considered the most easy-going – with 78 per cent saying they are too lax – and the Germans (indicted by only 42 per cent) and the Danes (44 per cent) are seen as the best disciplinarians.

QUESTION FOUR **Fathers in Japan are more sure of themselves on matters of discipline and education than fathers in America or Britain.** FALSE On such matters, in the opinion of their children, Japanese fathers tend to lack confidence.

Youngsters aged 18–24 in eleven countries, polled for a Japanese

Government survey which was published in 1984, were asked this question: 'Is your father sure of himself on matters of discipline and education?'[10]

In America, 86 youngsters in every 100 said 'yes'. So did 78 youngsters in every 100 in Britain. The figure in Japan was only 61 – with 24 per cent saying 'no' and the others giving no answer.

The respect or awe with which fathers are regarded in the various countries may be assessed from this list which records the 'yes' percentages in descending order:

Fathers regarded with respect or awe

		Percentage
1	THE PHILIPPINES	97
2	AMERICA	86
3	YUGOSLAVIA	85
3	BRAZIL	85
5	BRITAIN	78
6	SWEDEN	75
6	KOREA	75
8	SWITZERLAND	71
9	FRANCE	70
10	GERMANY	64
11	JAPAN	61

The low position of German fathers in the list appears to emphasize that adults and children have conflicting views on this issue.

Japanese fathers have their honour redeemed by having a far higher rating from children when it comes to taking a lead on important family matters. Eighty per cent say they do – compared with America's 75, West Germany's 68, Britain's 53 and France's 50.

Which nation's fathers are most ready to take time to talk things over with the family? Well at the top of this list, with a vote of 90 per cent, were those in the Philippines – followed by the Yugoslavs (73) and the Swedes (71).

Fathers in America scored 69 – just ahead of French fathers (68 per cent), with those in Britain trailing behind (60 per cent). The Japanese managed a confidence vote of only 51.

Would children in these eleven countries like to have a mother who let them do as they wished? Or would they prefer one who made them do what she wanted?

Intriguingly, in five of the countries most children opted for strictness in a mother. They were the Philippines (74 per cent in favour and 24 against), Korea (50–41), America (49–36), Britain (40–31) and Sweden (38–28).

Heading the list of countries where children would prefer easy-going mothers was Japan – with 59 per cent in favour and 7 per cent against.

The others were France (54–28), Yugoslavia (51–35), Brazil (48–42), West Germany (41–25) and Switzerland (37–25).

QUESTION FIVE **Because of their traditional culture, Japanese youngsters are more likely to be willing to support aged parents eventually than youngsters in America or Britain.** FALSE Only 35 per cent of young people in Japan were prepared to state categorically: 'No matter what the circumstances, I will support my parents.' In Britain the percentage was 36 and in America it was 49.

More Japanese and British youngsters (5 per cent), compared with the Americans (3 per cent), also opted for an alternative: 'I would prefer that my parents support themselves or go on social welfare.'

Korea had the biggest percentage of youngsters (69) who said they would support aged parents in any circumstances. France, with 56, had the next biggest and the West Germans had only 31. The hardest-hearted were in Sweden, where only 15 per cent were prepared to make such a pledge. Sweden also had a higher percentage than any other European country of young people who vowed they would not support their parents under any circumstances.

QUESTION SIX **Young people in Germany are more satisfied with their home lives than those in France.** FALSE Ninety-one per cent of French youngsters report being 'satisfied' or 'more or less satisfied' with life at home. Eighty-five per cent of West Germans do so.

Among Europeans, no one is more satisfied with home life than the young Swedes (95 per cent), despite their avowed reluctance to show gratitude to their parents.

In Britain the percentage was 89 – the same as in America – and in Japan it was 76.

Tensions are apparently more rife in homes in Switzerland than in any of the other countries, with 73 per cent of dissatisfied youngsters there naming that as the reason for their feelings – compared with 32 per cent in Sweden and only 18 per cent in the Philippines.

In West Germany (65 per cent), tensions are reported as being higher than in France (49) and in Britain (48), while the Americans (40) and the Japanese (28) apparently have a lower level of tensions in the home than any of the other industrialized countries.

Squabbles with brothers and sisters are another major cause of dissatisfaction with life at home. Brazil tops the bickering league with 18 per cent, while Switzerland (13) and Britain (12) have second and third places. In Japan (8) there is more harmony on this issue and in America the rating is 10.

QUESTION SEVEN **There is twice as much dissatisfaction with places of work among working British youngsters as among working youngsters in Japan.** FALSE In fact, the converse is true. The percentage of youngsters expressing dissatisfaction with places of work in Japan is 35. In Britain it is only 15.

Japan is followed by France (27 per cent) and Korea (25 per cent). Yugoslavia and the Philippines tie for fourth place with 17 per cent and immediately below them is America with 16 per cent.

After Britain with 15, come Sweden and Brazil, both with 14, and then West Germany with 13. The country with the lowest level of work-place dissatisfaction among youngsters is Switzerland (9).

Pay being considered too low is the main across-all-frontiers reason for such dissatisfaction with that complaint coming from 68 per cent in America, 65 in France, 59 in Britain, 55 in Japan and 51 in West Germany.

Dissatisfied Japanese youngsters express stronger feelings than their contemporaries about working hours being too long and holidays too short. Forty-one per cent name that as a reason for dissatisfaction, compared with 28 per cent in France, 22 per cent in America, 19 in Britain and 18 in West Germany.

The comparatively high level of dissatisfaction expressed about places of work by young Japanese is mirrored by the level expressed by younger ones over life at school. Only 65 per cent are satisfied with school life, compared with 89 per cent of children in America.

Other national percentages for being satisfied with school include: Sweden 87, Britain 85, Brazil 84, West Germany and Yugoslavia 79, France 70 and Korea 67.

The main cause of dissatisfaction in schools in Japan (32 per cent say so) is the facilities and equipment, which are thought to be inadequate.

That grumble reaches a peak in the Philippines (89) and in Korea it is cited by 60 per cent of students. In Europe, it is highest in France (55). In West Germany it is 48 and in America it is 31.

Pupils with fewest complaints about facilities and equipment – only 13 per cent each – are the British and Swedes.

Many people pipe-dream of having so much money that they never again need to work. Youngsters in the eleven countries were asked what they would do if they had such money. Majorities, more than 70 per cent in some cases, said they would prefer to work.

Those in the Philippines (94 per cent) and in Sweden (86) were the most emphatic.

In descending order, here are the other national percentages in favour of continuing to work:

Those who, if wealthy enough to stop work, would favour continuing

		Percentage			Percentage
1	THE PHILIPPINES	94	7	JAPAN	75
2	SWEDEN	86	8	BRITAIN	70
3	KOREA	81	9	FRANCE	59
4	YUGOSLAVIA	80	10	WEST GERMANY	54
5	AMERICA	78	10	SWITZERLAND	54
5	BRAZIL	78			

One of the criticisms often levelled at youngsters is that they are so selfishly pre-occupied with their own interests that they are not prepared to pull their weight in order to help their communities or countries. In most of the eleven nations surveyed, such criticism would appear to be unjustified.

The youngsters were invited to give a 'yes' or 'no' to this statement: 'In order to serve [name of own country], I wouldn't mind sacrificing my own interests'.

More 'yes' replies came from the Yugoslavs (87 per cent) than from youngsters in any other country – with the Philippines (84) and Korea (73) being second and third.

In these findings, America takes fourth place with 70 and then comes Sweden with 56. Youngsters in Sweden, it might seem, have a higher regard for their country than for their parents.

Britain is sixth with 54, with Brazil (52) and West Germany (45) being seventh and eighth.

Then comes a dramatic drop. Only 23 per cent in France said 'yes' and the percentage was a dismal 17 in Switzerland.

Those with the least enthusiasm for putting their country's interests before their own are the Japanese where the in-favour vote in this Japanese-organized survey was only 16 – with a massive 65 per cent saying 'no' and the rest not answering.

This survey also shows that American and Japanese youngsters are more likely to be worried about their appearance than the West Germans or the British and twice as likely as the Swiss, four times as likely as the French and six times as likely as the Swedes.

It also shows that the Americans are more likely to be worried about sex than the Japanese, the West Germans, the Yugoslavs and the Koreans – twice as likely as the British, three times as likely as the French and the Swiss and six times as likely as youngsters in Brazil or the Philippines.

How did your judgment rate? Take two marks for each correct answer. Scores of 0–4 suggest you are completely out-of-touch with international adult–youngster relationships, 6–10 indicate an average awareness, 12–14 show an exceptional insight.

13 Britain's royal family

Without the royal family, Britain would be less stable politically – according to 68 per cent of Britons. Only 20 per cent disagree.

Sixty-eight per cent also feel that the country would have less influence in world affairs if it were not for the Queen.

And the importance of the work done by the royal family in promoting the interests of Britain abroad is recognized by a decisive 90 per cent of the nation – with the benefits being challenged by only 5 per cent.

A 1984 MORI poll reflects the immense popularity of the British royal family.[1] Seventy-two per cent of Britons say they are 'interested' in news about the royal family. The poll also confirms that the majority want the Queen to remain on the throne as long as possible, rather than abdicate in favour of Prince Charles. This shows a reversal of the national mood in 1981, when 48 per cent felt she should abdicate at some stage and only 45 per cent felt she should stay – and it emphasizes the country's increasing admiration for the Queen.

However, there is also agreement that Prince Charles could take over as monarch, if necessary, for he has the required qualities and experience. Sixty-seven per cent of Britons say so, with 26 per cent disagreeing.

More than 1,000 adults were asked which two or three members of the royal family are the most understanding of problems facing ordinary families. Here is the verdict:

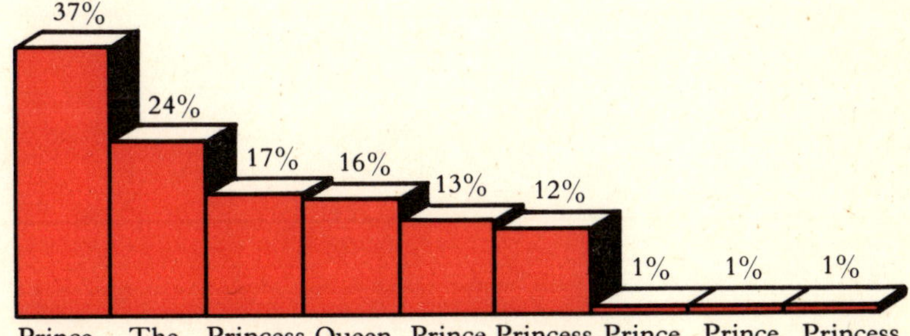

And which two or three are the country's best ambassadors? Here is that verdict:

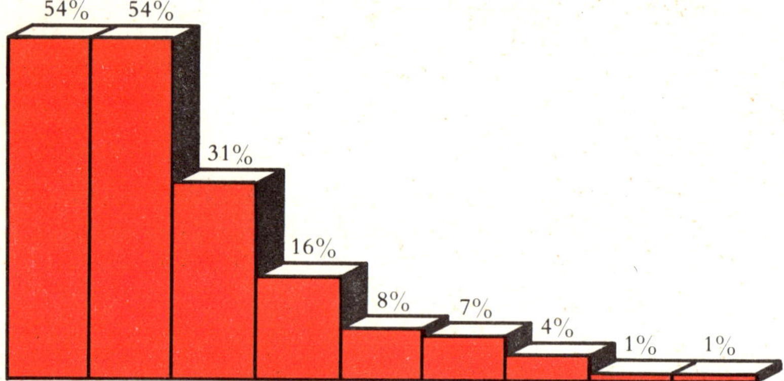

Prince Charles is also acclaimed as the most well-liked royal – beating the Queen by 4 per cent and his sister, Princess Anne, by 42 per cent. Once again, those polled were invited to nominate two or three members of the family. Here are the results:

Most well-liked members of the royal family

		Percentage			Percentage
1	Prince Charles	50	8	Princess Alexandra	5
2	The Queen	46	8	Princess Michael	5
3	Princess Diana	45	10	Prince Edward	3
4	Queen Mother	31	11	Prince William	2
5	Prince Philip	13	11	Princess Margaret	2
5	Prince Andrew	13	11	Duchess of Kent	2
7	Princess Anne	8	14	Mark Philips	1

A third accolade won by Prince Charles – not surprisingly in view of his renowned love of slapstick fun – is as the royal with the best sense of humour. Here he gets a vote of 62 per cent and his father, Prince Philip, comes a poor second with only 28 per cent. Both the Queen and the Queen Mother get a vote of 7 per cent for their sense of humour and Princess Margaret scores only 1 per cent.

Here is the 'humour' score-card:

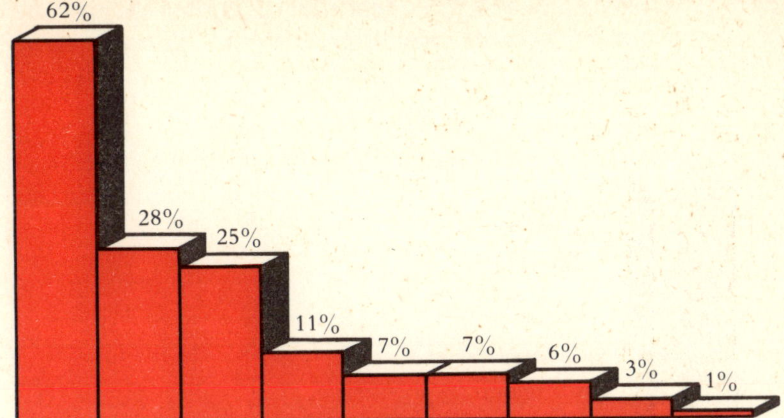

Britons have no doubt which member of the Royal Family gets most enjoyment out of life. Prince Andrew heads the list by a comfortable margin with a vote of 61 per cent and Prince Charles takes second place, a long way behind, with 27 per cent.

Incidentally, an earlier poll showed that 46 per cent of Britons approved of Prince Andrew's friendship with actress Koo Stark and only 29 per cent disapproved.[2] However, a poll in 1982 among women showed that only 6 per cent of British women would like to be a royal and only 2 per cent would like to marry a prince.[3] The Queen is considered to enjoy herself less than Prince Philip or the Queen Mother.[4]

Here is the 'enjoyment' score-card:

Prince Andrew is also rated as the best-looking man in the royal family. He gets a vote of 54 per cent and his closest rival, Prince Edward, gets only 13 per cent. Prince Charles trails in third place with 10 per cent.

Here is the 'best-looking' list:

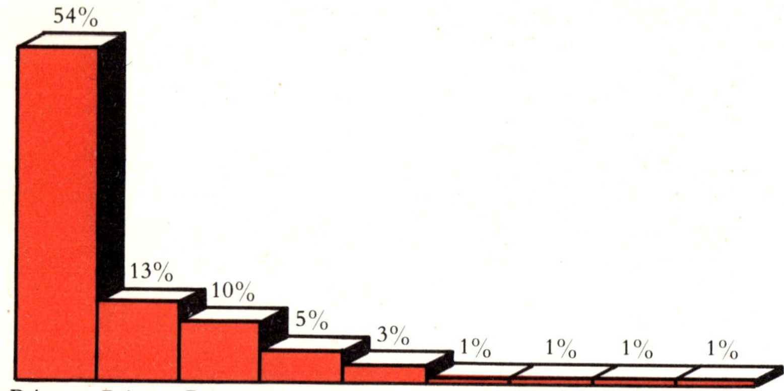

Princess Diana sweeps the board as the most attractive woman in the royal family – as well as being considered more than six times as glamorous as Koo Stark – and the second place is taken by Princess Michael of Kent.

Here is the 'most-attractive' list:

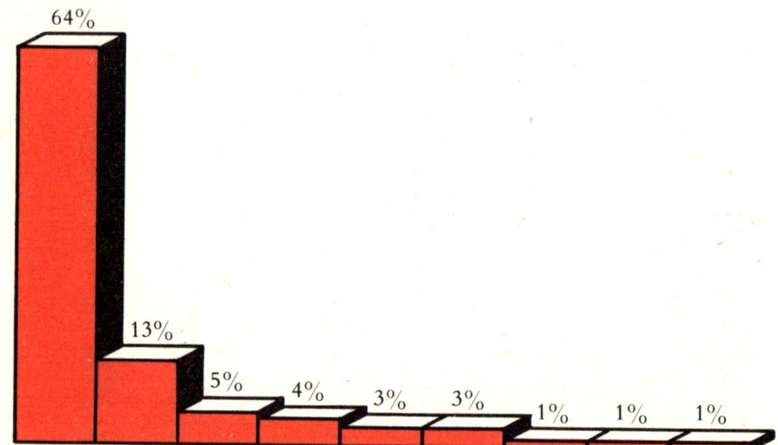

Princess Diana beats her husband by 1 per cent, in the opinion of the public, in having the most pleasant personality in the royal family.

Here is the 'pleasant personality' list:

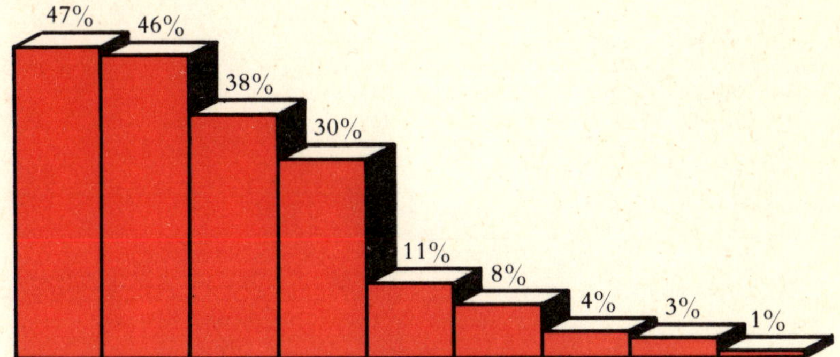

However, Princess Diana is also considered the shyest member of the family. Forty-three per cent say so, compared with the 35 per cent who named Prince Edward.

Here is the 'most shy' list:

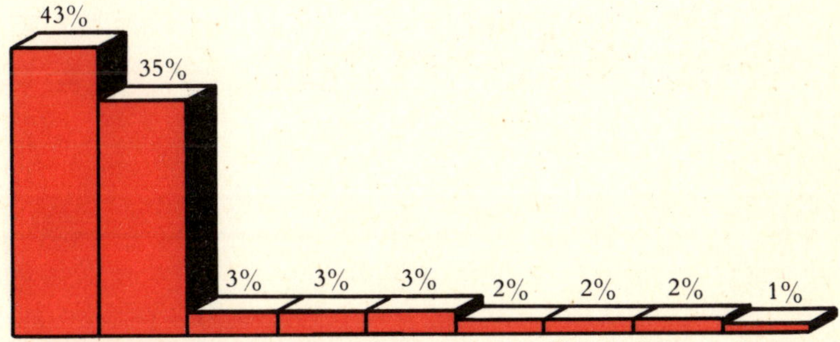

Prince Philip is the most outspoken member of the family. Fifty-five per cent say so. Thirty-nine per cent plump for Princess Anne, while Prince Charles is in third place with a vote of 25 per cent.

Here is the 'outspoken' list:

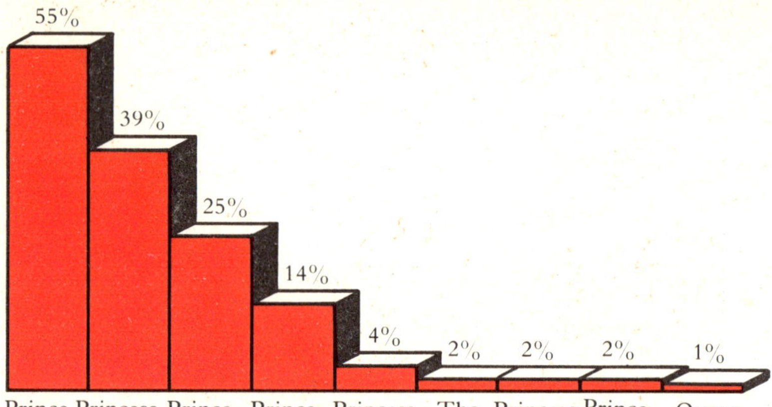

The royal regarded as being most ill-at-ease with ordinary people is Princess Anne, with Princess Diana and Prince Edward being together in second place. The one seen as being least ill-at-ease with ordinary people is the Queen Mother.

Here is the 'ill-at-ease' list:

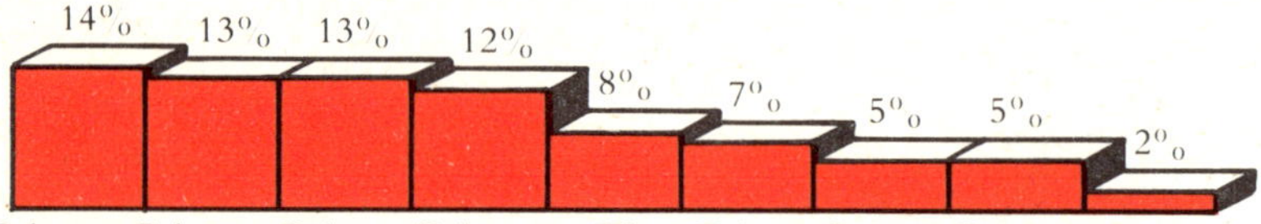

Although Britons get great pleasure out of following the activities of the royal family through television and newspapers, most feel that the media intrude too much into the family's private life (61 per cent), and opinion has not altered since 1979 (when 63 per cent said there was too much coverage). A decisive 77 per cent say there is too much coverage of private holidays, and only 15 per cent feel the balance is about right. Sixty-three per cent consider there is too much tittle-tattle reporting of alleged wrangles between members of the family but 19 per cent, who presumably savour suggestions of personal difference, say the balance is about right.

Princess Anne is regarded as the royal who is treated most unfairly by the media and her aunt, Princess Margaret, is also widely believed to get a raw deal.

Here is the 'treated unfairly' list:

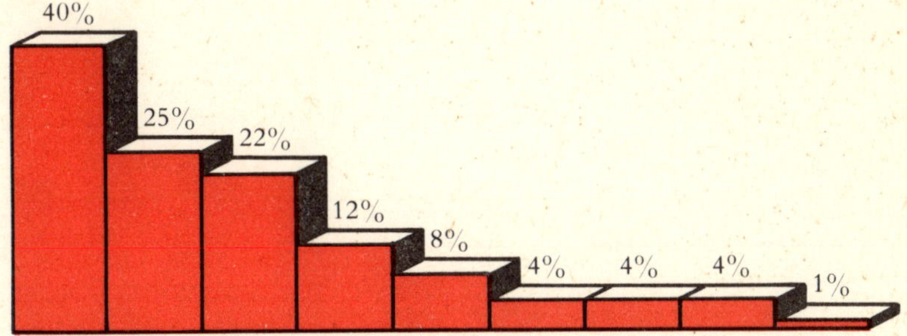

Prince Charles is seen as the royal who is best at dealing with journalists – with more than twice as many votes as Prince Philip.

This list reads:

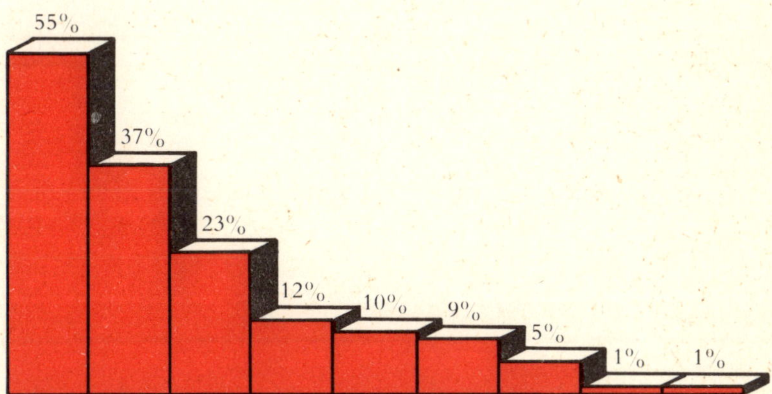

And who are the most hard-working royals?

Fourteen per cent say the Queen Mother and 16 per cent say Prince Philip. Twenty-five per cent say Princess Anne and 44 per cent say Prince Charles.

The far-ahead champion, with a vote of 69 per cent, is the Queen.

In 1982 a third of Britons thought that the royal family had a lot of say in the country's future – over twice as many as identified the same power in the Church (15 per cent), but less than half as many as identified it in the Prime Minister (78 per cent). The number saying the royal family has considerable influence, however, has increased since the mid 1970s: in 1976 the figure was only 17 per cent.[5]

SECTION IV

HEALTH, WEALTH AND HAPPINESS

14 Which countries are the healthiest?

Are you in good health? That question can bring a richly intriguing variety of replies, depending on the country in which it is asked, for attitudes to health are coloured by national characteristics.

For instance, the Spanish and the West Germans have a tendency to enjoy hypochondria. They are more likely to complain that their health is 'poor' or 'very poor' than the French, the Japanese or the Italians – and more than twice as likely to do so as the British.

Thirteen per cent of them offer this gloomy opinion of their own health, the highest proportion recorded in a survey of ten nations – Britain, Belgium, Denmark, France, Holland, Ireland, Italy, Japan, Spain and West Germany.[1]

A similar view is expressed by 12 per cent of the French, 10 per cent of the Japanese, 9 per cent of the Italians and 6 per cent of the British.

The most cheerful, in this respect, are the Dutch (3 per cent) and the Irish (4 per cent). However, the Irish win the overall prize for optimism about their health – with a runaway 78 per cent saying it is 'good' or 'very good'. Only 70 per cent of the Dutch voice such confidence.

Seventy-two per cent of Danes describe their health as 'good' or 'very good' but, as a nation, they have tumbled down the league by having 7 per cent who regard it as 'poor' or 'very poor'.

By subtracting all the 'negative' replies from the 'positive' ones, we get a picture of how national attitudes affect self-assessments of health. On this basis, the Irish are cheerfully at the top with 74 per cent, while the British and the Dutch, both with 67 per cent, tie in second place. The most resolutely despondent about their health are the Japanese with 32 per cent.

Optimism about health

		Percentage
1	IRELAND	74
2	BRITAIN	67
2	HOLLAND	67
4	DENMARK	65
5	BELGIUM	64
6	FRANCE	47
7	WEST GERMANY	41
8	ITALY	40
9	SPAIN	35
10	JAPAN	32

One per cent of the Belgians, Danes, Italians, Spaniards and West Germans did not know whether they were in good or bad health. Nor did 2 per cent of the Japanese and 3 per cent of the Dutch.

In America, nine in ten rate their own health as 'excellent' (36 per cent) or 'good' (53 per cent) and these fortunates are more likely to be men than women, as well as younger rather than older. Some 13 per cent of households report someone in situ who is chronically sick.[2]

How would you rate your general health?

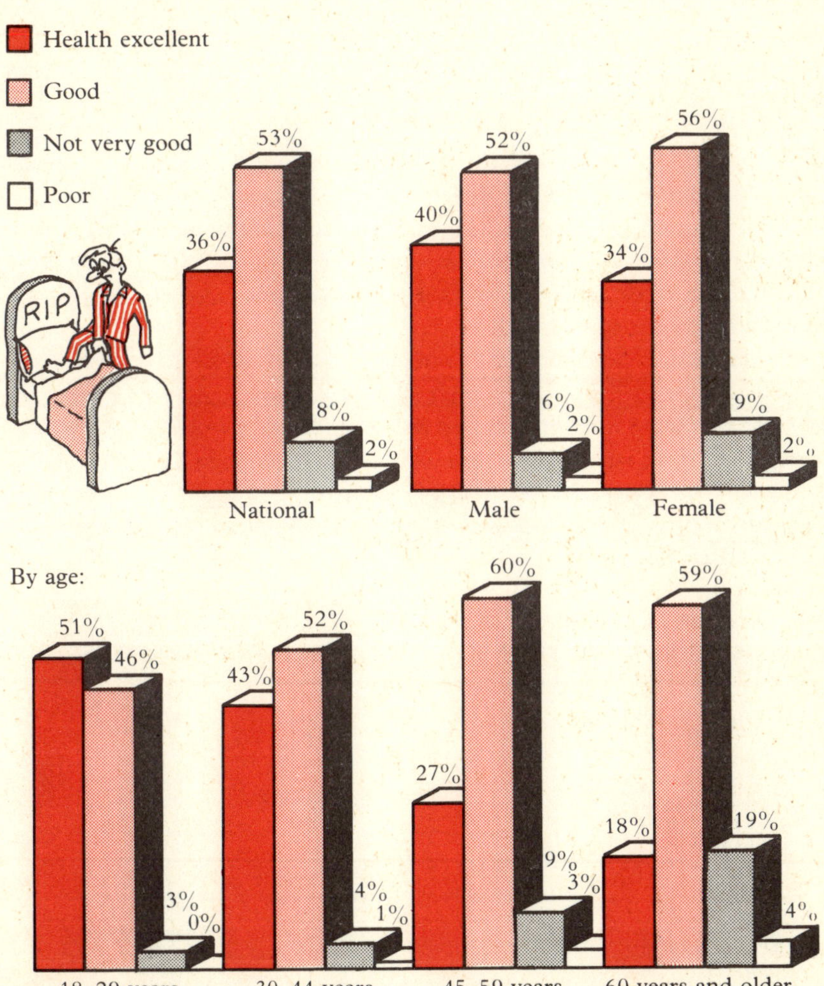

Is there anybody in your household who is chronically sick (someone who needs serious medical treatment or hospitalization fairly often)?[3]

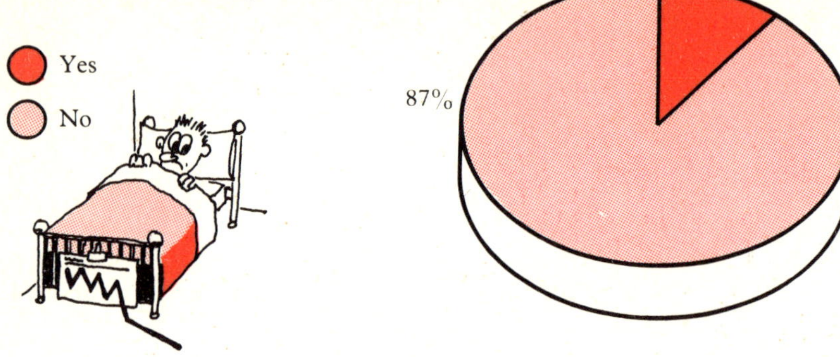

Moods affect health, just as health affects moods, and further questions revealed that the West Germans are also the most depressed (46 per cent say they feel that way), the most restless (45 per cent say so) and the most likely to be upset by criticism (25 per cent say so). They are also the most prepared to describe themselves as 'very lonely' – being more than twice as likely to do so as the British or the French, and more than three times as likely as the Dutch or the Danes.[4]

Paradoxically, despite their low place in the overall health assessment table, the Japanese score high marks for happiness in each of these four categories. Only 17 per cent report depression – a far smaller proportion than in countries such as Britain and Italy – and they are less likely to be restless or upset by criticism than any of the other nationalities. Only 13 per cent describe themselves as 'very lonely', which places them eighth in the loneliness list.

Those who describe themselves as depressed or very unhappy

		Percentage
1	WEST GERMANY	46
2	BRITAIN	25
2	ITALY	25
4	FRANCE	18
4	HOLLAND	18
6	SPAIN	17
6	IRELAND	17
6	JAPAN	17
9	BELGIUM	16
9	DENMARK	16

Those who describe themselves as restless

		Percentage
1	WEST GERMANY	45
2	BRITAIN	36
3	HOLLAND	33
4	SPAIN	29
5	ITALY	28
6	BELGIUM	27
7	IRELAND	26
8	FRANCE	20
9	DENMARK	19
10	JAPAN	16

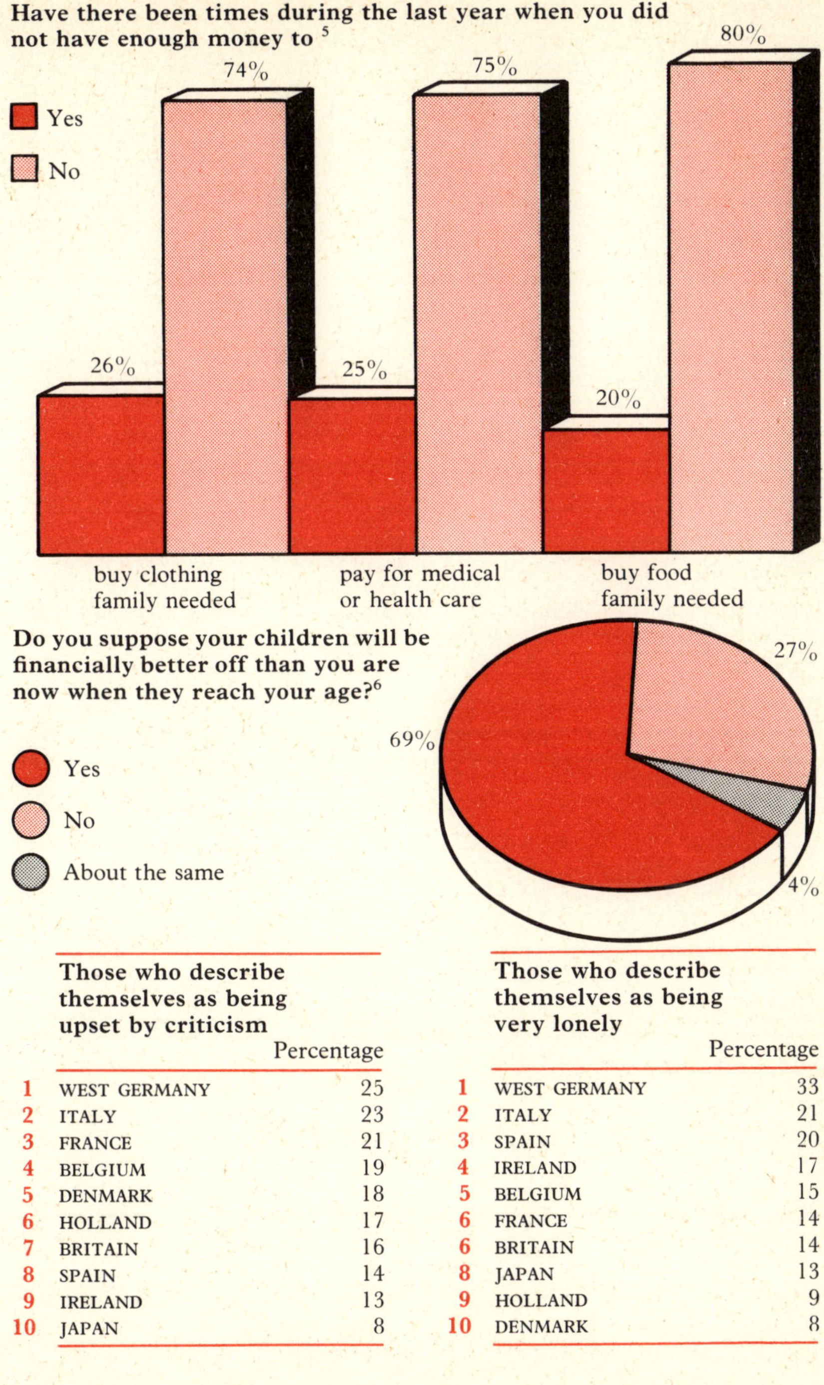

Those who describe themselves as being upset by criticism

		Percentage
1	WEST GERMANY	25
2	ITALY	23
3	FRANCE	21
4	BELGIUM	19
5	DENMARK	18
6	HOLLAND	17
7	BRITAIN	16
8	SPAIN	14
9	IRELAND	13
10	JAPAN	8

Those who describe themselves as being very lonely

		Percentage
1	WEST GERMANY	33
2	ITALY	21
3	SPAIN	20
4	IRELAND	17
5	BELGIUM	15
6	FRANCE	14
6	BRITAIN	14
8	JAPAN	13
9	HOLLAND	9
10	DENMARK	8

The most easily bored people are the Italians, with 33 per cent complaining of boredom, while the British, with 31 per cent, are second. Both nationalities have twice as much boredom, per head of population, as the Belgians or the Dutch and three times as much as the Danes. The poor West Germans also have an abundance of boredom – being in third place, with 27 per cent of the population citing it as a complaint.

In this category the Japanese again have a low 'black mark' rating of only 16 per cent – lower than the French, the Irish or the Spanish. So how do the Japanese qualify for their place at the bottom of the health-optimism league? Keys to the answer are provided by answers to supplementary questions.

In each of the countries, people were asked: 'During the past few weeks, did you ever feel on top of the world?' Now that, surely, is a question which begs a cheerful response. It got one in Denmark, where there was an affirmative answer from 65 per cent of the populace – so putting Denmark top of this particular list.

Ireland is apparently another good place for feeling on top of the world. Forty-four per cent there said they had felt that way, which put the country in second place – just ahead of Britain (43 per cent) and West Germany (42 per cent).

Emotionally, Spaniards clearly do not often bounce high in that way, with only 15 per cent answering 'yes'. But the country where such a sense of joyous exhilaration is most rare is Japan. There it was acknowledged by only 8 people in every 100. Which suggests that in the Land of the Rising Sun, for the great majority, it is a rarely experienced curiosity.

A similar result was recorded in Japan in response to a complementary question: 'During the past few weeks, did you ever feel things were going your way?'

	Those who felt on top of the world	Percentage
1	DENMARK	65
2	IRELAND	44
3	BRITAIN	43
4	WEST GERMANY	42
5	HOLLAND	40
6	BELGIUM	34
7	ITALY	28
8	FRANCE	26
9	SPAIN	15
10	JAPAN	8

	Those who felt things had been going their way	Percentage
1	IRELAND	61
2	BRITAIN	60
3	WEST GERMANY	54
4	BELGIUM	50
5	ITALY	45
6	FRANCE	42
6	SPAIN	42
8	DENMARK	37
9	HOLLAND	30
10	JAPAN	15

Only 15 per cent of Japanese would admit to having had such a comfortable feeling – compared with 54 per cent of West Germans, 60 per cent of Britons and 61 per cent of the Irish.

Satisfaction with life in America is high, with dissatisfaction levels of close to one in five only on career choice, success and the amount of money you have to live on. Moral codes, parental treatment and marital situation top the satisfaction scales in the USA.[7]

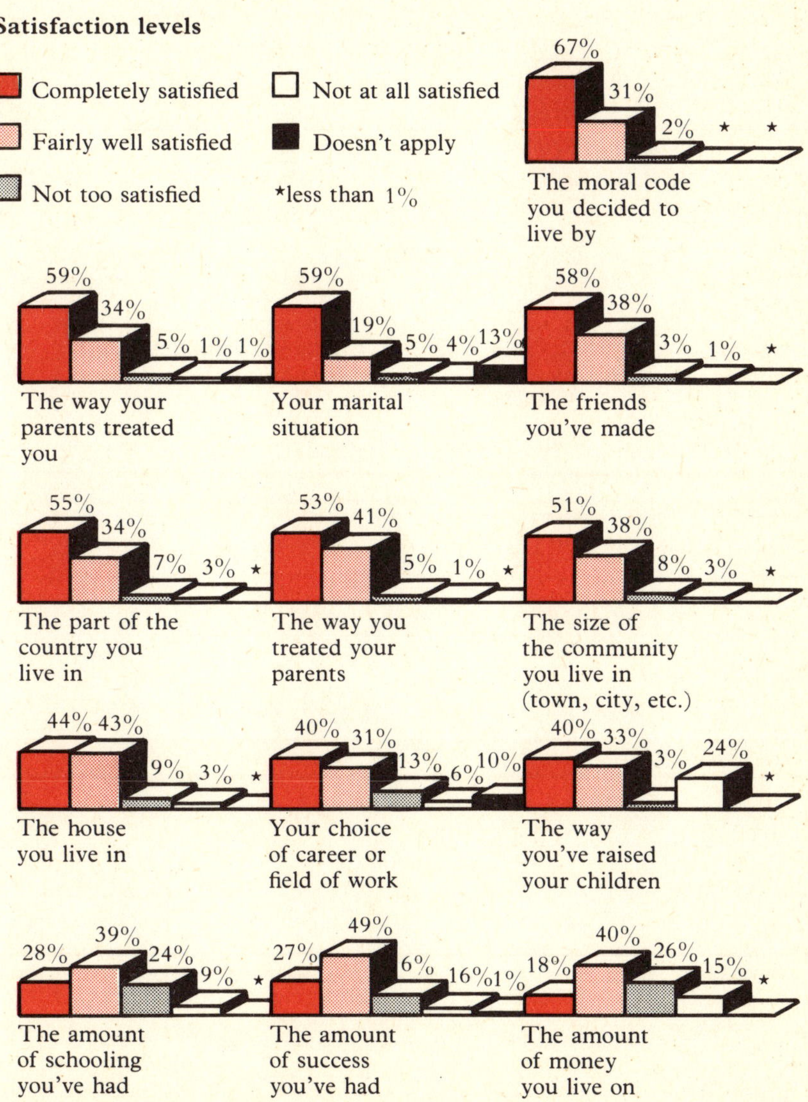

Yet one in four Americans polled by Gallup in 1984 felt that during the last year there were times when they did not have enough money to buy necessary family clothing or to pay for medical or health care; and one in five told Gallup that in the previous year there were times when they couldn't afford to buy food the family needed.[8] Further, a discouraging 27 per cent felt their children wouldn't be better off financially when they reached the age of their parents.[9]

Advances in medical science will probably make even cancer curable by about 1990 – in the view of 56 per cent of West Germans.

In West Germany, such advances are rated as being more important than the elimination of fears about atomic weapons.[10] Those poll findings confirm, yet again, the universal dread of cancer. Through the decades, it has consolidated its position as the most-feared disease in the world.

In 1947, when it was given far less publicity, it headed the list in Britain. Twenty-nine per cent of Britons then told Gallup it was the illness they most dreaded – followed by tuberculosis (13 per cent) and polio (11 per cent).[11]

By 1976, 58 per cent of Americans were identifying it to Gallup as their most-dreaded affliction – with 21 per cent naming blindness and 10 per cent saying heart disease.[12]

By 1982, 67 per cent of Japanese were citing it as such – strokes and heart disease taking second and third places with, respectively, nine and five per cent.[13]

Across the world, about a fifth of all deaths are caused by cancer but in certain countries – as World Health Organization statistics show – the risks appear to be disproportionately high.

Seventeen-nation surveys in 1974 and 1975 pinpointed the Dutch as being the most vulnerable to cancer, with 25.8 per cent of the population dying from it, while the Spaniards, with 17.3 per cent of such deaths, are apparently the least prone to cancer.[14]

National cancer-death statistics

		Percentage			Percentage
1	HOLLAND	25.8	9	ITALY	20.4
2	SWITZERLAND	24.1	9	CANADA	20.4
3	DENMARK	23.8	11	JAPAN	20.3
4	SWEDEN	22.3	12	AUSTRIA	20.2
5	FRANCE	21.7	13	NORWAY	19.3
6	WEST GERMANY	21.4	14	AMERICA	18.9
7	BELGIUM	21.1	15	IRELAND	17.6
8	BRITAIN	20.8	16	AUSTRALIA	17.4
			17	SPAIN	17.3

America is near the bottom of the risk-list with 18.9 per cent, below Japan (20.3 per cent), Britain (20.8 per cent) and West Germany (21.4 per cent). Other countries where the cancer risk is at its lowest are Ireland (17.6 per cent) and Australia (17.4 per cent).

Links between cigarette-smoking and ill-health are being recognized more clearly each year across the world.

Out of every 100 West Germans – during a typical three-month period in 1980 – 7 used medications to soothe their nerves, 5 used them to get rid of pimples and blackheads, and 1 used them to stop smoking.[15]

Like most other nationalities, the West Germans were by then immensely alert to the dangers of smoking. Only 40 per cent were smokers, compared with 46 per cent in 1965 and 51 per cent in 1950. And even a high proportion of smokers – 28 per cent – felt smoking should be banned in places of work.

This steady drop in West German smoking was entirely due to men giving up the habit, or never starting it, for, during the 30-year period, the proportion of females who smoked increased significantly – being 21 per cent in 1950, 24 per cent in 1965 and 29 per cent in 1980. The levels for male smokers during that period were: 1950 – 88 per cent, 1965 – 74 per cent, 1980 – 53 per cent.

Although 39 per cent of the Japanese were smokers in 1982, 71 per cent said they were 'aware' or 'somewhat aware' of the relationship between cigarettes and lung cancer.[16] A fifth of Japanese smokers said they 'hoped to stop one day' and 45 per cent, being more emphatic, said they 'intended to stop'. The other 35 per cent 'did not intend stopping' but all affirmed, perhaps significantly, that they 'hoped to smoke less'.

In Britain, smokers had clearly become a minority by 1984. Only 39 per cent of Britons were then smokers, compared with 49 per cent in 1964 and 56 per cent in 1958. During this great tumble in the popularity of smoking, Gallup discovered in 1975 that 62 per cent of Britons would favour a total ban on cigarette advertising and 29 per cent would favour a similar ban on sales.[17]

By 1983, the Office of Population Censuses and Surveys was able to report that 70 per cent of British smokers had tried and failed to give up the habit in the previous ten years. The most commonly given reason was the high cost, mentioned by 36 per cent, and 20 per cent had tried specifically because they were afraid of future illness.[18]

Awareness of the dangers of smoking increased similarly in America and Canada. Gallup established that in 1958 less than half of Americans – 44 per cent – accepted there was a connection between lung cancer and smoking. By 1974 that proportion had increased dramatically to 70 per cent, and it had increased again to 81 per cent by 1977.[19]

By that year, 19 per cent of Americans felt that cigarette sales should be banned – a view endorsed, intriguingly, by 11 per cent of smokers. Thirty-eight per cent of Americans were smokers by then, slightly less than the 40 per cent in 1974, and there were other poll signs which showed that even smokers were becoming more concerned about the effects – on themselves and on others. Twenty-eight per cent of American smokers favoured a complete ban on cigarette advertising – most, presumably, because they did not wish others to be tempted into the habit – and 8 per cent felt smoking should be outlawed in trains and buses, as well as in public places such as restaurants and offices.

In 1981, 54 per cent of Canadians favoured the banning of all cigarette advertising. By the following year, 42 per cent of Canadians were smokers, compared with 59 per cent in 1957.[20]

We have established that attitudes to health and emotional well-being can vary greatly between countries. So can the incidence of ill-health – together with the causes of it and the amount of medical expertise available to deal with it.

See how you would rate as an international diagnostician by answering these nine questions:

1 **Despite the pressures of living in a more fiercely competitive capitalist society, Americans are less likely to die of heart disease than Russians.** TRUE OR FALSE?
2 **Adults in West Germany are more than twice as likely to seek medical help for headaches as those in America.** TRUE OR FALSE?
3 **Toothache victims are more likely to get speedy relief in Norway than in Britain because, as a percentage of the population, Norway has three times as many dentists.** TRUE OR FALSE?
4 **Renowned for their huge steaks and gigantic Outback appetites, the Australians consume more unnecessary calories than people in Britain, Japan and West Germany.** TRUE OR FALSE?
5 **As one of the most health-conscious nations in the world, America has more doctors for every 100,000 people in the population than countries such as Russia, Italy, Hungary and Spain.** TRUE OR FALSE?
6 **Because over-crowded living conditions can create tensions which are detrimental to health, Singapore, with a packed**

population of 10,549 people to the square mile, has a higher percentage of suicides and self-inflicted injuries than America (64 people to the mile) or Russia (31 people to the mile). TRUE OR FALSE?

7 **The West Germans drink more alcohol than the Americans who, in turn, are heavier drinkers than the Russians.** TRUE OR FALSE?

8 **Possibly because of their enthusiasm for food and drink, the French and the Italians are more than twice as likely to die from digestive troubles or liver diseases as the British or the Australians.** TRUE OR FALSE?

9 **With psychiatry being such big business in America – which has more than 23,000 psychiatrists, about ten times as many as Britain, France or West Germany – a higher percentage of people in America are admitted as mental-hospital patients than in Britain, France or West Germany.** TRUE OR FALSE?

Answers start below.

QUESTION ONE **Despite the pressures of living in a more fiercely competitive, capitalist society, Americans are less likely to die of heart disease than Russians.** TRUE Only 435 Americans in every 100,000 are likely to die from heart disease, compared with 500 Russians.

This was shown by figures, gathered in 23 countries in 1980, which were analyzed by the World Health Organisation.[21]

Hungary emerged as the heart-disease centre of the world – with this disease killing 718 people in every 100,000 – and Sweden, with 603 such deaths, was second in the list. West Germany took third place with 584 and Britain was just behind with 579.

Australians are less prone to heart-disease deaths than the Americans, with a total of 391, but more prone than the French who have a total of 380.

Americans who want to avoid heart-disease death might consider moving over the border into Canada where the total – 343 – was 92 fewer in every 100,000. They would do even better if they went south of the border. In Mexico, the level is only 109.

The country with the lowest incidence of heart-disease deaths, only 70 in every 100,000, is Kenya. However, in Kenya, as different figures show, other causes inflict premature death on a high percentage of the population.

Number of deaths from heart disease

		Per 100,000 people			Per 100,000 people
1	HUNGARY	718	13	SAUDI ARABIA	320
2	SWEDEN	603	13	ISRAEL	320
3	WEST GERMANY	584	15	JAPAN	266
4	BRITAIN	579	16	CHINA	250
5	RUSSIA	500	17	SINGAPORE	176
6	ITALY	466	18	INDIA	175
7	SWITZERLAND	448	18	SRI LANKA	175
8	AMERICA	435	20	BRAZIL	110
9	AUSTRALIA	391	21	MEXICO	109
10	FRANCE	380	22	BAHAMAS	72
11	SPAIN	361	23	KENYA	70
12	CANADA	343			

QUESTION TWO **Adults in West Germany are more than twice as likely to seek medical help for headaches as those in America.**
TRUE Compared with Europeans, Americans either suffer very few headaches or are commendably stoic about them. Only 13 per cent consult doctors because of throbbing heads, compared with 28 per cent of West Germans and 39 per cent of Italians. Part of the explanation, of course, could be the size of the bills – startling enough to cause the most violent of headaches – which are presented by doctors in America.

A survey of troubled brows in 14 countries which was published in *Euromonitor* – prepared with material from the 1975 *Statistics Year Book*, and a confidential industry source – showed that the headache league was topped by Britain and Spain.[22]

Despite the vast range of over-the-counter remedies on offer, 42 per cent of Britons and Spaniards took their headache complaints to doctors, compared with 40 per cent of Belgians and 39 per cent of the French.

The sombre Swedes were more prepared to suffer in private, with only 27 per cent complaining to doctors about sore heads, but that is still more than double the percentage in America.

Men and women who seek headache relief from doctors

		Percentage			Percentage
1	BRITAIN	42	9	DENMARK	34
1	SPAIN	42	10	NORWAY	31
3	BELGIUM	40	11	WEST GERMANY	28
4	FRANCE	39	12	SWEDEN	27
4	ITALY	39	13	AMERICA	13
6	HOLLAND	38	14	JAPAN	0.47
7	AUSTRIA	36			
7	SWITZERLAND	36			

Bravest of all are the Japanese. Or maybe they're just the luckiest. Anyway, only an astonishing 0.47 per cent of them considered their headaches justified a visit to the doctor. But how much oriental torment is there, we wonder, behind that splendid inscrutability?

QUESTION THREE **Toothache victims are more likely to get speedy relief in Norway than in Britain because, as a percentage of the population, Norway has three times as many dentists.** TRUE In Norway, there is one dentist for every 1,090 people, while Britain has one for every 3,270 people. That percentage put Norway at the top of a 16-nation dental-service survey conducted in 1972/3/4 by the World Health Organization.[23]

Britain was eleventh in the list, below West Germany (one dentist for 1,960 people), America (one for 1,970 people) and France (one for 2,090 people), but ahead of Holland (one for 3,290), Belgium (one for 4,550) and Austria (one for 4,950).

It would seem that the worst place to pick to have toothache while on holiday would be Spain. The long-suffering Spaniards – who, incidentally, complain of toothache most frequently than other Europeans – have to share one over-worked dentist between every 9,650 of them.

Here are the national ratings, showing the numbers of people for each dentist:

People per dentist

		Number			Number
1	NORWAY	1,090	9	CANADA	2,650
2	SWEDEN	1,160	10	JAPAN	2,740
3	DENMARK	1,310	11	BRITAIN	3,270
4	WEST GERMANY	1,960	12	HOLLAND	3,290
5	AMERICA	1,970	13	BELGIUM	4,550
6	FRANCE	2,090	14	IRELAND	4,570
7	AUSTRALIA	2,460	15	AUSTRIA	4,950
8	SWITZERLAND	2,510	16	SPAIN	9,650

QUESTION FOUR **Renowned for their huge steaks and gigantic Outback appetites, the Australians consume more unnecessary calories than people in Britain, Japan and West Germany.** FALSE Like most people, Australians eat more calories than they need, but their appetites are modest when compared with those of the British, the Japanese and the West Germans.

A 1980 United Nations' survey in 23 countries investigated the number of calories eaten daily by the average person – as a percentage of the minimum requirement, as prescribed by the UN's Food and Agriculture Organization.[24]

Daily calories intake per person as percentage of number required

		Percentage
1	ITALY	150
2	AMERICA	139
3	SPAIN	135
4	FRANCE	134
4	HUNGARY	134
4	SINGAPORE	134
7	WEST GERMANY	133
7	SWITZERLAND	133
9	BRITAIN	132
9	RUSSIA	132
11	BAHAMAS	130
12	CANADA	127
13	JAPAN	124
14	MEXICO	121
15	SAUDI ARABIA	120
16	SWEDEN	119
17	ISRAEL	118
18	AUSTRALIA	117
19	BRAZIL	109
20	CHINA	107
21	SRI LANKA	102
22	KENYA	88
23	INDIA	87

Top of the gluttony list for calories were the Italians, with a daily consumption of 150, and the Americans were second with 139. Despite their much-vaunted reputation as formidable steak-eaters, the Australians, with 117, figured near the bottom of the list – below Sweden (119) and Israel (118), and well below Japan (124), Britain (132) and West Germany (133).

With a score of 127, Canadians were more restrained than their neighbours in North America but keener on calories than Mexicans (121) and Brazilians (109).

The Russians have a daily calorie intake of 132 – seven less than the Americans – and the level in Saudi Arabia is 120.

Those closest to being right on the minimum target for health were in Sri Lanka (102), while daily calorie counts of only 87 and 88, respectively, reflected the plight of people in India and Kenya.

QUESTION FIVE **As one of the most health-conscious nations in the world, America has more doctors for every 100,000 people in the population than countries such as Russia, Italy, Hungary and Spain.** FALSE Russia has a far higher proportion of doctors – 357 for every 100,000 people – than America or other countries in the West. Italy (294 doctors per 100,000), Hungary (250) and Spain (217) all have more as a percentage of the population than America, which has 192.[25]

A 22-nation survey by the World Health Organization showed that in 1980 America was also lagging behind Israel (270), Switzerland (244),

West Germany (222) and Sweden (204) in its percentage of doctors – being ninth in the international league table.

Canada (182), Australia (179) and France (172) were tenth, eleventh and twelfth, respectively. Britain was in thirteenth place with 154 – 26 more to each 100,000 people than Japan.

Kenya was the most badly served, with only 9 doctors to the 100,000 – a proportion three times smaller than that in India.

Doctors per 100,000 people

		Number			Number
1	RUSSIA	357	12	FRANCE	172
2	ITALY	294	13	BRITAIN	154
3	ISRAEL	270	14	JAPAN	128
4	HUNGARY	250	15	SINGAPORE	87
5	SWITZERLAND	244	16	BAHAMAS	66
6	WEST GERMANY	222	17	SAUDI ARABIA	61
7	SPAIN	217	18	BRAZIL	59
8	SWEDEN	204	19	CHINA	52
9	AMERICA	192	20	INDIA	27
10	CANADA	182	21	SRI LANKA	14
11	AUSTRALIA	179	22	KENYA	9

That preponderance of doctors does not ensure longevity for the Russians. Their average life-span of 72 years is shorter than those of Americans (75), Britons (74) and West Germans (73).

People in Sri Lanka, averaging 69 years, can expect to live two years longer than those in China and three years longer than Brazilians.

Longest-living are the Japanese and the Swedes, both with an expectancy of 77 years, while in Kenya, Saudi Arabia and India the respective average spans are only 56 years, 55 years and 52 years.

Life expectancies

		Age			Age
1	JAPAN	77	13	RUSSIA	72
1	SWEDEN	77	13	SINGAPORE	72
3	FRANCE	76	15	HUNGARY	71
3	SWITZERLAND	76	16	SRI LANKA	69
5	AMERICA	75	17	CHINA	67
5	CANADA	75	18	BAHAMAS	66
7	BRITAIN	74	19	BRAZIL	64
7	AUSTRALIA	74	20	KENYA	56
7	ITALY	74	21	SAUDI ARABIA	55
7	SPAIN	74	22	INDIA	52
11	WEST GERMANY	73			
11	ISRAEL	73			

Babies are twice as likely to die soon after birth in Russia as in countries such as Australia, Canada and France – and nearly three times as likely as in Japan or Sweden. They are also more likely to die young, perhaps surprisingly, in America, Britain and West Germany than in Spain.

The most horrifying statistics on infant mortality come from India, where in 1981 more than 12 per cent of babies – 121 in every 1,000 – died before their first birthdays. The situation was only marginally better in Saudi Arabia, where baby deaths were 111 in every 1,000. In Kenya, the figure was 85 in every 1,000 and in Brazil it was 75.

As well as having the greatest longevity, Japan and Sweden had the lowest rate of infant mortality – 7 in 1,000.

Infant mortality rates per 1,000 live births

		Number			Number
1	INDIA	121	12	WEST GERMANY	13
2	SAUDI ARABIA	111	13	AMERICA	12
3	KENYA	85	13	BRITAIN	12
4	BRAZIL	75	13	SINGAPORE	12
5	CHINA	71	16	FRANCE	10
6	SRI LANKA	43	16	CANADA	10
7	BAHAMAS	25	16	SPAIN	10
8	HUNGARY	21	16	AUSTRALIA	10
9	RUSSIA	20	20	SWITZERLAND	9
10	ISRAEL	15	21	JAPAN	7
11	ITALY	14	21	SWEDEN	7

QUESTION SIX **Because over-crowded living conditions can create tensions which are detrimental to health, Singapore, with a packed population of 10,549 people to the square mile, has a higher percentage of suicides and self-inflicted injuries than America (64 people to the mile) or Russia (31 people to the mile).**
FALSE Despite being so jam-packed, Singapore has exactly the same ratio of suicides and self-inflicted injuries, 11 in every 100,000, as Australia, which has only 5 people to the square mile. That is slightly less than America (12 in every 100,000) and considerably less than Russia (45 in every 100,000).[26]

These facts were established by surveys which investigated levels of self-injury and population crowding in 23 countries.

In general, crowding does not appear to be a key factor in motivating people to harm or kill themselves. In fact, in many cases, the evidence would seem to suggest the reverse. Canada, for instance, has only 6 people

Suicide/self-injury and population gradings

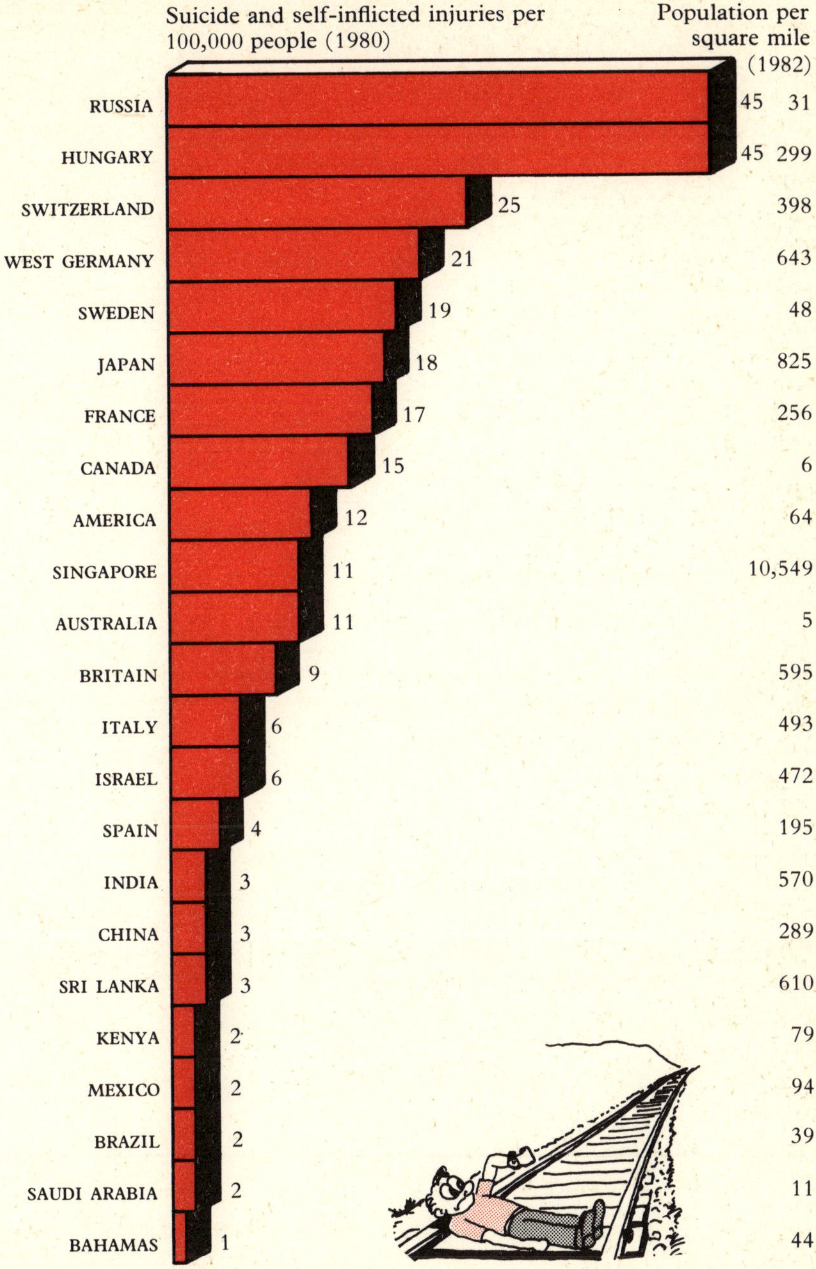

to the square mile but, with a suicide/self-injury level of 15 in every 100,000, has a higher incidence than Britain (9 in every 100,000), where there are 595 people to the square mile.

Japan has 825 people to the square mile, but a suicide/self-injury rate of 18 in 100,000 – compared with the 19 in 100,000 in Sweden, where there are only 48 people to the square mile.

There are 643 people to the square mile in West Germany but the suicide/self-injury level there, 21 in 100,000, is lower than in Switzerland, which has 398 people to the square mile and a suicide/self-injury level of 25 in 100,000. Israel has 472 people to the square mile and a suicide/self-injury level of 6 in 100,000, while France, with only 256 people to the square mile, has a level of 17 in 100,000.

Obviously, religious beliefs and national characteristics, together with economic and domestic pressures, have significant roles in shaping attitudes to suicide and self-injury and, in Europe, the incidence is strikingly lower in the Roman Catholic countries of Italy (6 in 100,000) and Spain (4 in 100,000).

The people least likely deliberately to do themselves a mischief live in the Bahamas.

QUESTION SEVEN **The West Germans drink more alcohol than the Americans who, in turn, are heavier drinkers than the Russians.**

TRUE Many stories have been circulated about how strong liquor is used as an antidote to the bleakness of life in the Soviet Union – and, indeed, to the harshness of the winters – but the Russians are comparatively abstemious when measured against the Americans and the West Germans. They also drink less than the British, the Australians, the Swiss and the Spanish. However, another Iron Curtain country, Hungary, is near the top of the high-drinking league.

These facts were established through a 23-nation survey in 1981.[27]

The most enthusiastic imbibers, not unexpectedly, are the French. Each of them quaffs, on average, 24.1 pints of pure alcohol a year – nearly twice as much as the British (12.5 pints) and almost six times as much as the Mexicans (4.2 pints).

Although the Italians have a reputation as wine-lovers, their alcohol intake of 19.2 pints is slightly lower than that of the Swiss (19.4 pints) and certainly lower than that of the West Germans (22 pints).

The Americans consume a more modest 14.6 pints, which is less than the Canadians (16 pints) or the Australians (17.6 pints). The Japanese restrict themselves to 9.9 pints, while the annual level per person is only five pints in China and India.

Statistics reflect the fact that – officially, at least – there is absolutely no drinking in Saudi Arabia.

The drinking league table, per person, per year

		Pints			Pints
1	FRANCE	24.1	13	ISRAEL	12.0
2	SPAIN	22.9	14	RUSSIA	10.9
3	WEST GERMANY	22.0	15	SINGAPORE	10.0
4	HUNGARY	20.4	16	JAPAN	9.9
5	SWITZERLAND	19.4	17	SWEDEN	9.5
6	ITALY	19.2	18	KENYA	5.0
7	AUSTRALIA	17.6	18	INDIA	5.0
8	CANADA	16.0	18	CHINA	5.0
9	BRAZIL	15.0	18	SRI LANKA	5.0
10	AMERICA	14.6	22	MEXICO	4.2
11	BAHAMAS	14.0	23	SAUDI ARABIA	—
12	BRITAIN	12.5			

Only four in ten Americans drink wine – and those who do don't drink much; in the USA the average per capita consumption of wine is 2.2 gallons a year, less than a tenth of the 25 gallons per person in France and Italy.

According to National Family Opinion, a majority of American men polled in 1983 said they preferred coffee, soft drinks, milk, fruit juice, distilled spirits and malt beverages (beer) to wine.[28]

QUESTION EIGHT **Possibly because of their enthusiasm for food and drink, the French and the Italians are more than twice as likely to die from digestive troubles or liver diseases as the British or the Australians.** TRUE With the Italians topping the international table for over-eating and the French heading the one for heavy drinking, it seems hardly surprising that they should also head the problem-stomach league – with 6.2 per cent in each country succumbing to diseases of the stomach or liver. Only 2.6 per cent of Australians do so and the level in Britain is a mere 2.5 per cent.

This emerges from a 17-nation survey in 1974 and 1975 by the World Health Organization.[29]

Although the Americans have more of a tendency to over-eat than the West Germans, they drink considerably less and this could explain why, with 3.8 per cent of their population dying of stomach/liver problems, they are lower down the list than the West Germans, where the level is at a disturbing 5.6 per cent.

Curiously, however, the Japanese – more modest than either the Americans or the West Germans in their eating and drinking – are even nearer the top of the list, with 5.7 per cent. Could this be as a result of inner tensions generated by enduring secret headaches with such oriental stoicism?

Although Canadians drink more than the Americans, they eat less and, possibly as a result, they figure slightly lower in the table than the Americans.

The people with the happiest stomachs are the Irish.

Deaths from digestive and liver troubles as a percentage of total deaths

		Percentage			Percentage
1	FRANCE	6.2	9	AMERICA	3.8
1	ITALY	6.2	10	CANADA	3.7
3	AUSTRIA	5.8	11	BELGIUM	3.5
4	JAPAN	5.7	12	HOLLAND	3.1
5	WEST GERMANY	5.6	12	DENMARK	3.1
6	SPAIN	5.5	14	AUSTRALIA	2.6
7	SWEDEN	4.2	15	BRITAIN	2.5
8	SWITZERLAND	4.0	16	IRELAND	2.2

QUESTION NINE **With psychiatry being such big business in America – which has more than 23,000 psychiatrists, about ten times as many as Britain, France or West Germany – a higher percentage of people in America are admitted as mental-hospital patients than in Britain, France or West Germany.** FALSE Maybe all those expensive analysts earn their fees by keeping Americans comparatively sane – or maybe most are not really necessary but are merely fashionable extras – for Americans are less likely to need mental-hospital beds than people in those three European countries.

That was established in a 1970 survey, embracing ten countries, by the World Health Organization – which also exploded beliefs about any obvious link between population-crowding and mental ill-health.[30]

Top of the list for admissions to mental hospitals was Sweden (48 people to the square mile), where nearly 1 person in 100 was becoming a patient each year. (The precise figure was 99.7 in every 10,000.)

Second was France (256 people to the square mile), where admissions were running at 50.8 per 10,000 people.

With a population more than twice as packed as France (595 to the square mile), Britain took third place, with admissions being 31.9 per

10,000. Although West Germany's population is even more congested (643 to the square mile), its proportion of admissions was marginally lower – 31.6 per 10,000.

Then came America, with 64 people to the square mile, which had an admission rate of 30.4 per 10,000.

Mental-hospital admissions and population gradings

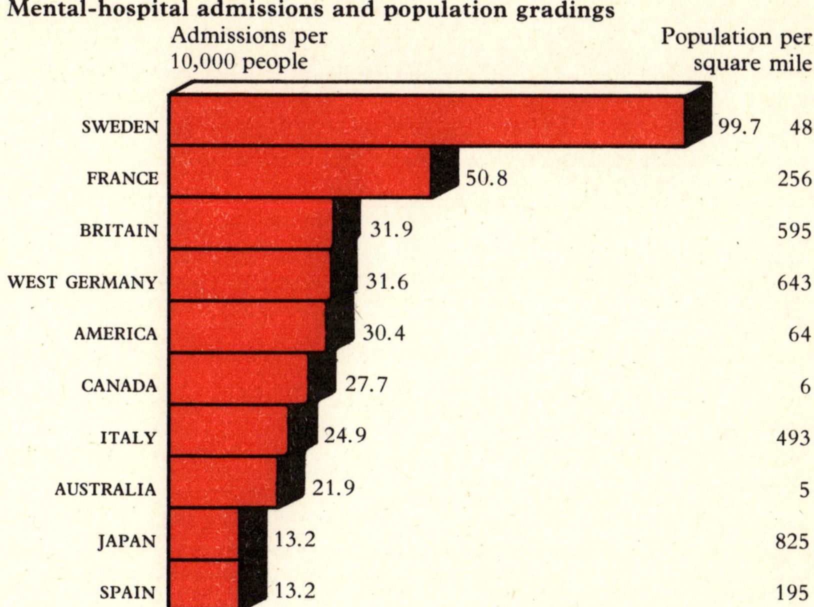

The people with the most crowded country were the Japanese (825 people to the square mile), but they shared bottom place with comparatively empty Spain – both of these countries having admission rates of 13.2 per 10,000.

How did you fare with the questions? Take three marks for each correct answer. Scores of 0–9 suggest that, on matters relating to heatlh, you are not particularly worldly wise; 12–18 show you have sound average understanding of the subject; 21–27 indicate exceptional insight.

15 Keeping fit

Two Britons out of every three claim that they can touch their toes without bending their knees.[1]

Similar awareness of the value of keeping fit and supple has been growing fast in most parts of the world – with great increases in the numbers of people exercising and participating in sports.

In America, for instance, sporting prowess has become so admired that 22 per cent of the population, if given the chance, would like to be professional athletes – exactly double the 11 per cent who would like to be film stars.[2]

In West Germany, the proportion of the population participating regularly in sports multiplied by three between 1957 and 1976 – jumping from 7 per cent to 21 per cent.[3]

In Japan, there is just as much enthusiasm, with 24 per cent playing sports,[4] while in nearby Taiwan 4 per cent do Tai-chi every day and 39 per cent exercise regularly. Only 2 per cent of Taiwanese never consciously exercise.[5]

Back in 1977, the Gallup organization was able to report: 'One of the most dramatic changes in American lifestyles to take place during the last two decades is the increase in the numbers of Americans who regularly exercise. Today 47 per cent of Americans say they participate in some form of physical exercise daily – twice the percentage recorded in 1961.'[6]

Eleven per cent of those than exercising daily in America were joggers, with men being more than twice as keen as woman on this form of activity.

A tendency noticed in other parts of the world was also recorded by Gallup: 'Many behavioral and attitudinal trends in America follow the "trickle down" process; that is, they are taken up by the affluent and higher-educated groups and are later picked up by others, and the case of exercise appears to be no different. Those most likely to say they exercise daily are basically the "upscale" socio-economic group; that is, the college-educated, those in the upper- and upper-middle income brackets, and professionals, business people, and others in white-collar positions.'

As a group, more American professionals and managers exercise daily than adults in other categories:

Americans who exercise daily

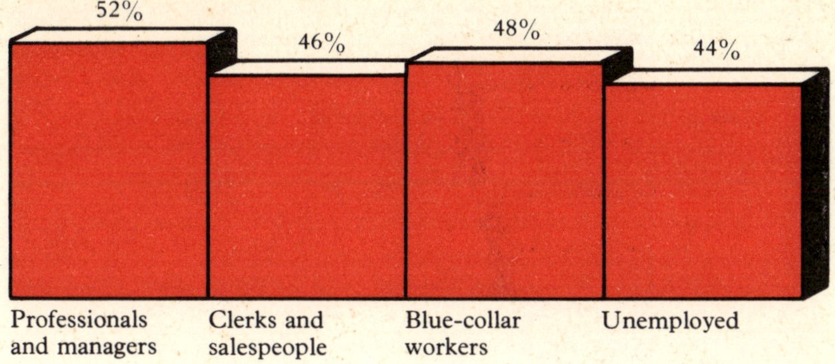

What sort of lead were 'up-market' people giving in Europe in 1984?

There is certainly no doubt in Sweden, where more than a third of business executives, 38 per cent, are enthusiastic joggers – compared with 21 per cent in West Germany, 18 per cent in Belgium, and only 9 per cent in Italy.[7]

Although many city streets often seem crowded with lunchtime joggers in Britain, the country has one of the lowest percentages of jogging executives in Europe (16 per cent).

Jogging executives

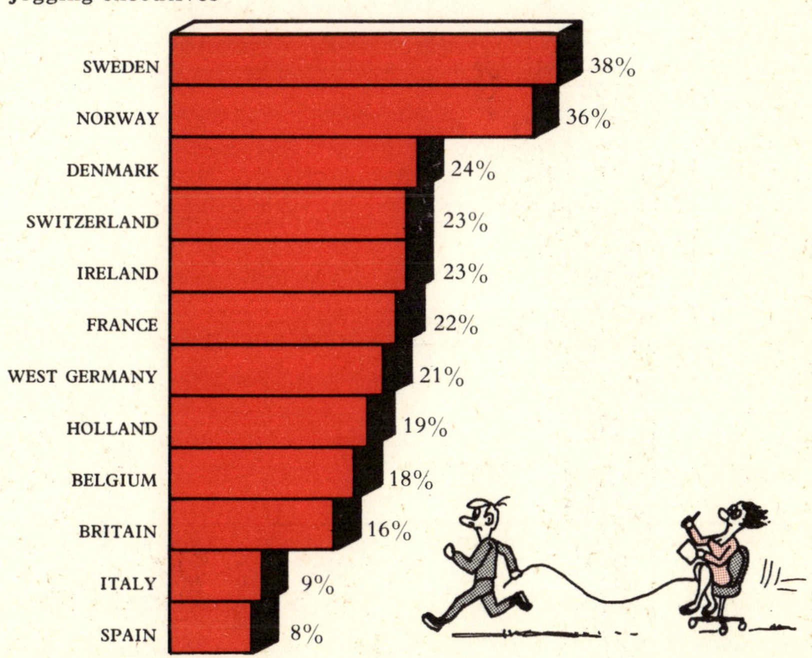

Footballing executives

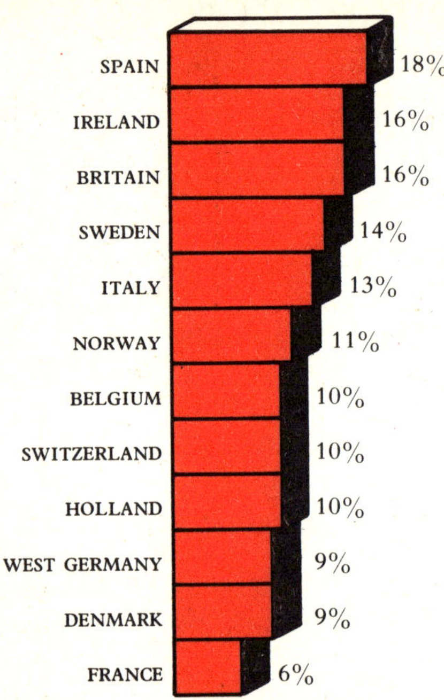

Hunting-and-shooting executives

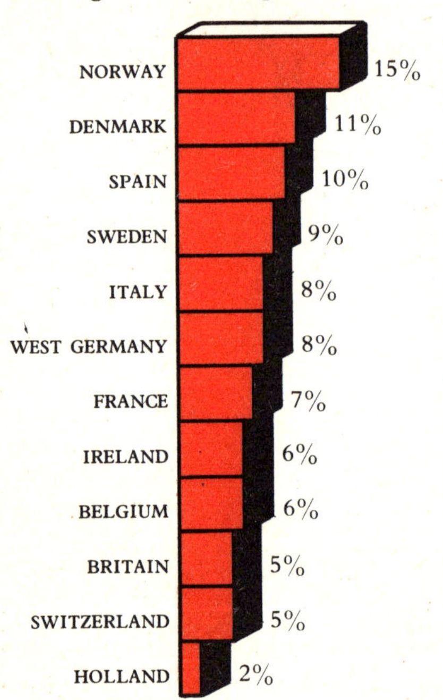

Golfing executives

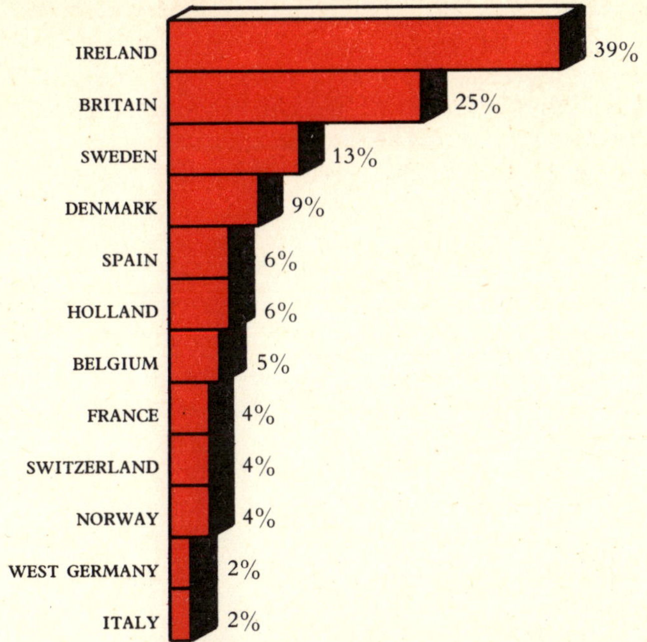

Swimming executives

Soccer is the sport in which Spanish executives lead the way. They are twice as keen on playing it as their counterparts in Denmark and three times as keen as those in France.

Norwegian executives are the ones most attracted to hunting and shooting, with those sports being enjoyed by 15 per cent there, compared with only 5 per cent in Switzerland and Britain.

As a sport for executives, golf hardly rates in West Germany and Italy where it is played by only 2 per cent. The sport really achieves widespread popularity among executives in Ireland and Britain, where it is played by 39 per cent and 25 per cent, respectively. The Swedes come third, with 13 executives out of every 100 being golfers.

Swimming is the most universally popular sport among executives, with an average of 42 per cent exercising through it in the twelve countries. The West Germans, 55 per cent, are the most enthusiastic, and the least enthusiastic are the Danes and Swedes, 24 per cent each.

Reasons for exercising vary from nation to nation. Nearly half the British who exercise regularly, 46 per cent, cite pleasure – a reason given by only 11 per cent of the people in Taiwan. Nearly three-quarters of the Taiwanese, 72 per cent, exercise 'to strengthen the body', with jogging being their most popular activity – followed by basketball, mountain-climbing and baton-twirling.[8]

In Britain, MORI established in 1984 that women are almost four times as likely as men to do keep-fit exercises, but men are nearly three times as enthusiastic as women about jogging. Nearly one British woman in five takes part in aerobics or dance and exercise – activities followed by only 1 man in 50.[9]

Class differences are also reflected by sporting and athletic preferences in Britain. The middle classes favour squash, badminton and tennis. The working classes are more likely to prefer cycling, weight-training and body-building.

However, the chase after fitness has also brought problems – according to a September 1984 survey conducted for Britain's Chartered Society of Physiotherapy – with the boom in aerobics and exercise dance classes having produced 'an appalling catalogue of injuries among women'.

Inquiries at 83 hospitals and among private physiotherapists and sport-medicine specialists revealed more than 1,600 cases of women, aged 16–24, who had been treated for injuries suffered in such classes. The average age of the injured was $27\frac{1}{2}$, with 648 suffering back injuries, 234 having Achilles' tendon or leg injuries – including 15 with ruptured Achilles' tendons – and 206 with knee injuries.

An official of the society, physiotherapist Ruth Doodson, commented: 'Alarming injuries are happening as a result of teachers instructing pupils to do exercises that are quite outrageous. It may be as many as one in ten taking part in these classes are suffering injuries.

'Women arrive clutching their latest fashion leotards, expecting tight Achilles' tendons, unused stomach muscles and weak backs to vanish by the end of their exercise session. It only multiplies the feeling of inferiority when this does not happen; even more so when they injure themselves.'

How important is it to win games of sport?

Forty-two per cent of Americans told pollsters from the Research and Forecasts organization in 1982 that they nearly always encourage their children to be aggressive in competition, and 66 per cent of them – 73 per cent of men and 58 per cent of women – added that, when playing themselves, they almost always try their best to win.[10]

Nearly a third of American parents, 32 per cent, always worry about their children being injured on playing fields and 6 per cent admit that, as spectators, they yell at referees – with 3 per cent also admitting that they argue with their children's coaches. However, the majority of Americans, 54 per cent, are against violence in sport, feeling that fights between players detract from the spectators' enjoyment – although 14 per cent consider that such fights generally add to the enjoyment of games.

Another intriguing fact which emerged from this survey was that 46 per cent of Americans either 'strongly agree' or 'somewhat agree' with the statement: 'International sports competition reduces the threat of war.'

Twenty-seven per cent 'somewhat disagreed'. Twenty-six per cent considered it was rubbish.

Fears of being embarrassed, MORI discovered in 1984, help turn exercises mainly into communal activities for the British. Only about three in ten (28 per cent), most of them older than 65, prefer to take exercise on their own. A similar percentage (30) say that doing so makes them feel embarrassed – with women being nearly three times as prone as men to being 'very embarrassed' (22 per cent compared to 8 per cent).[11]

A 1983 MORI poll for the *Daily Express* established the following Top Ten exercises and sports for men and women in Britain.[12] (Percentages shown are of those who were exercising in 1983)

Despite featuring so highly in that list, football had already been proved to have lost its huge pulling power as a spectator sport in Britain.

After nearly 2,000 people had been questioned about the professional game by MORI in 1982 on behalf of the *Daily Star*, it transpired that 78 per cent of British men – nearly four in five – did not go near a ground. Only 17 per cent went as often as once a year, and only 2 in 100 followed teams every week. Few women actually watch soccer – 96 per cent indicating that they do not.[13]

Top ten exercises and sports in Britain for men

		Percentage
1	Running/Jogging	26
2	Football	25
3	Swimming	20
4	Squash	19
5	Weight training/body building	13
6	Badminton	12
7	Golf	11
7	Keep-fit exercises	11
7	Bicycling	11
10	Tennis	9

Top ten exercises and sports in Britain for women

		Percentage
1	Keep-fit exercises	38
2	Swimming	26
3	Badminton	15
4	Bicycling	13
5	Yoga	10
5	Running/Jogging	10
7	Squash	9
7	Dance exercise/ballet/aerobics	9
9	Tennis	8
10	Basketball/netball	4

Fans who still went to live matches, as opposed to those who saw games only on television, had clear views about what was wrong with thc sport: sixty-six per cent complained of violence in the grounds, 54 per cent felt players were paid too much, 49 per cent considered that admission charges were too high. Only 5 per cent felt their local clubs gave good value for money and – potentially bleak news for the sport's future prospects – only 4 per cent considered that games were events to which it was suitable for them to take children.

Disillusionment with association football was not confined to Britain. In 1982, 45 per cent of Spaniards told Gallup they were 'not at all interested'.[14] Their country was then hosting the World Cup.

16 Alcohol – the pleasures and the perils

Alcohol is universally regarded as one of man's most welcome friends – and as one of his most treacherous enemies.

Across the world, there is an increasing awareness of the dangers presented by drink – more road accidents and violent crime, more ill-health and premature deaths – and vast numbers of people, including a significant proportion of Americans, would like it to be outlawed.

In France, 96 per cent of adults regard alcoholism as a 'very serious' or 'quite serious' national problem. A ten-nation survey showed similar anxieties being expressed in other countries – by 95 per cent of Italians, 94 per cent of the Irish, 93 per cent of the Danes and 89 per cent of the West Germans.[1]

In Britain and Holland, the same view was given by 88 per cent, in Belgium by 84 per cent and in Japan by 57 per cent.

After conducting an American survey in 1977, Gallup reported: 'The percentage of drinkers in the United States has reached a 38-year high point, while the proportion of families where liquor is cited as a cause of trouble has increased dramatically in just three years. The latest nationwide audit of drinking shows 71 per cent of adults 18 and older saying they use alcoholic beverages such as liquor, wine, or beer. Only 29 per cent are total abstainers. The percentage of drinkers in 1974 was 68 per cent.'[2]

In Canada at that time, incidentally, there was a smaller percentage of total abstainers. A CIPO survey showed that 75 per cent of Canadians drank alcohol in 1974 and 78 per cent were doing so in 1978. The level there dropped again to 73 per cent in 1983.[3]

The American Gallup report continued: 'The rise in the percentage of drinkers over the last three years has come about almost entirely among women. While the proportion of male drinkers has remained at about the same level, the proportion of female imbibers is up five points. Men, however, continue to be more likely to drink than women.[4]

'Approximately one American in five, 18 per cent, says alcohol has been a cause of trouble in his or her family. In 1974 the comparable figure was 12 per cent – the same as recorded in a survey in 1966.

'Social observers have expressed alarm at excessive drinking and alcoholism in American society, pointing to findings that show alcohol to be involved in about half of highway fatalities and in about half of all homicides.

'The latest survey shows that about one person in five, 19 per cent, favours a return to prohibition; that is, a law forbidding the sale of all beer, wine and liquor throughout the country.'

Anxiety continued to mount. In 1977, the year of that survey, 67 per cent of Americans regarded heavy drinking as a 'very serious' or 'moderately serious' national problem – compared with the 57 per cent who had felt that way in 1973.[5] By 1978 the proportion was 70 per cent and by 1979 it had grown again to 72 per cent.

Methods of tackling the problem of excessive drinking, which were less Draconian than total prohibition, have been explored by pollsters on both sides of the Atlantic. MORI collected the views of Britons in 1981 when conducting a survey for the Brewers' Society.[6]

How Britons would try to counter alcoholism

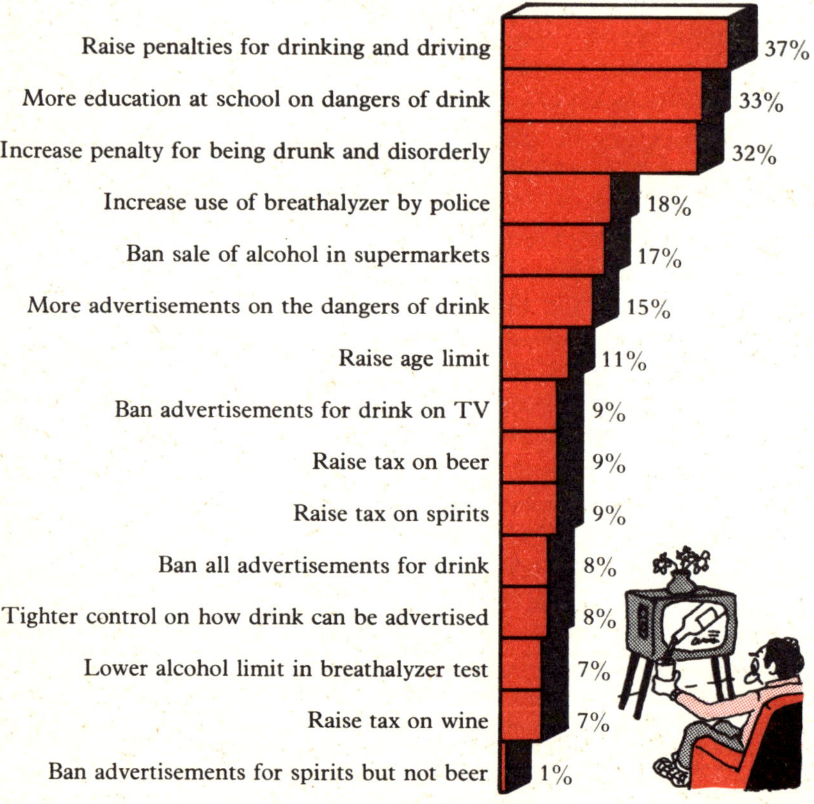

Now test your knowledge, or instincts, about international drinking habits by considering the following questions:

1 **The average American drinks far more beer than the average Swede – and more than twice as much as the average Japanese.** TRUE OR FALSE?
2 **The Italians drink more French champagne in a year than the combined populations of America, Australia, Austria, Canada, Sweden and Ireland.** TRUE OR FALSE?
3 **British executives are more likely to be abstainers from alcohol than their counterparts in Spain, Holland and Norway – and are three times as likely to abstain as those in Ireland.** TRUE OR FALSE?
4 **British and West German business executives are more enthusiastic about wine than those in France.** TRUE OR FALSE?
5 **Enough money to buy more than 400,000 averagely priced houses – or more than two million family cars – is spent annually on alcohol by Britons.** TRUE OR FALSE?
6 **As a percentage of their family budgets, the Americans spend about twice as much as the British on drink, tobacco and food.** TRUE OR FALSE?

Answers start below.

QUESTION ONE **The average American drinks far more beer than the average Swede – and more than twice as much as the average Japanese.** TRUE Americans drink an average of 151 pints of beer a year – about the same as the Canadians – according to a 17-nation comparison in 1975 by Britain's Brewers' Society.[7] That puts their intake well above that of the average Swede, who downs 103 pints, and makes it more than double that of the Japanese, who each restrict themselves, on average, to 62 pints a year.

The famed thirst of the Australians, quenched by an individual average of 250 pints a year, lags behind that of the West Germans, who each drink their way through an average of 259 pints.

The Belgians are third in the international beer-drinking league, with each consuming an annual average of 237 pints, and the British are sixth with 207 pints – 56 more than the Americans.

Although the Japanese are extremely modest in their beer-drinking habits, their average individual intake would last the average Italian, who drinks only 22 pints, for the best part of three years.

The beer-drinking table, per person, per year

		Pints			Pints
1	WEST GERMANY	259	10	HOLLAND	138
2	AUSTRALIA	250	11	SWITZERLAND	127
3	BELGIUM	237	12	SWEDEN	103
4	IRELAND	230	13	SPAIN	79
5	DENMARK	227	13	FRANCE	79
6	BRITAIN	207	13	NORWAY	79
7	AUSTRIA	182	16	JAPAN	62
8	CANADA	151	17	ITALY	22
8	AMERICA	151			

QUESTION TWO **The Italians drink more French champagne in a year than the combined populations of America, Australia, Austria, Canada, Sweden and ireland.** TRUE Together with the British, the Italians hold top place as foreign customers for champagne from France. French government figures for 1977, covering 14 countries, showed that Britain and Italy both bought 7.3 million bottles – 2.5 million more than the Americans and slightly more than the total bought by the 6 countries listed above. The Canadians drank 1.4 million bottles, a million more than the Australians and 14 times as many as the Irish.

France's worst customers in the countries surveyed were the Norwegians who drank only 70,000 bottles. However, that was more than balanced by the thirst of the French – who emptied a phenomenal 124.5 million bottles; this is more than 3 bottles per year for every adult in France!

The international league of French champagne drinkers

		Million bottles			Million bottles
1	FRANCE	124.5	8	CANADA	1.4
2	BRITAIN	7.3	9	AUSTRALIA	0.4
2	ITALY	7.3	10	SPAIN	0.3
4	BELGIUM	6.8	10	SWEDEN	0.3
5	AMERICA	4.8	12	AUSTRIA	0.2
6	WEST GERMANY	4.0	13	IRELAND	0.1
7	SWITZERLAND	2.3	14	NORWAY	0.07

QUESTION THREE **British executives are more likely to be abstainers from alcohol than their counterparts in Spain, Holland and Norway – and are three times as likely to abstain as those in Ireland.** FALSE Among executives in Britain, 3 per cent are completely abstemious. That is a smaller proportion than the 4 per cent in Spain, the 5 per cent in Holland and the 7 per cent in Norway – and it is dwarfed by the 11 per cent in Ireland. In fact, the Irish were shown to have by far the

Abstemious executives

		Percentage			Percentage
1	IRELAND	11	8	ITALY	3
2	NORWAY	7	8	BRITAIN	3
3	HOLLAND	5	8	FRANCE	3
3	SWITZERLAND	5	8	BELGIUM	3
5	SPAIN	4	12	DENMARK	1
5	SWEDEN	4			
5	WEST GERMANY	4			

How executives rate as spirit drinkers

	Brandy Percentage	Gin Percentage	Rum Percentage	Whisky Percentage
1	BRITAIN 43	SWEDEN 63	DENMARK 47	DENMARK 85
2	NORWAY 39	BRITAIN 62	SWEDEN 32	SWEDEN 83
3	SPAIN 38	DENMARK 58	NORWAY 26 BRITAIN 26	BRITAIN 79
4	W. GERMANY 37	NORWAY 47	—	NORWAY 78
5	DENMARK 36 FRANCE 36 SWEDEN 36	SPAIN 42	FRANCE 25 BELGIUM 25	FRANCE 77
6	—	BELGIUM 41	—	ITALY 73 IRELAND 73
7	—	IRELAND 40	W. GERMANY 24	—
8	ITALY 28	SWITZERLAND 33	SPAIN 23	BELGIUM 67
9	SWITZERLAND 27	FRANCE 28	SWITZERLAND 22	SPAIN 64
10	IRELAND 24	W.GERMANY 21	HOLLAND 20	HOLLAND 58
11	BELGIUM 12	HOLLAND 20	ITALY 14	SWITZERLAND 53
12	HOLLAND 7	ITALY 19	IRELAND 13	W. GERMANY 46

greatest proportion of executive abstainers in the Pan European Survey 3, which was published by Research Services Ltd in 1984.[8]

The least abstemious were the Danes, with only 1 per cent of them being abstainers.

The previous table points accurately to the fact that Europe's champion executive spirit-drinkers are the Danes. Although they rank third in the gin-drinking league and fifth equal in the one for brandy, they qualify for the top spot by being the most enthusiastic imbibers of rum and of whisky.

The British are the top brandy-drinkers, just ahead of the Norwegians, and the Swedes are the keenest on gin – with British gin-drinkers being second. The moderate Irish are in the bottom half of the tables, in respect of all four drinks, and the French, despite their reputation as *bon viveurs*, are also down the lists – being fifth as drinkers of whisky, fifth equal as rum- or brandy-drinkers, and ninth as gin-drinkers.

QUESTION FOUR **British and West German business executives are more enthusiastic about wine than those in France.** TRUE With the exception of champagne, which they drink in great quantities, French executives are less in favour of wine than their counterparts in Britain and West Germany. The Pan European Survey 3, published in 1984, showed that as wine-drinkers they were tenth equal with the Spanish – with less being drunk only by the Irish.[9]

Europe's top wine-drinkers are the Danes, with 95 per cent of them enjoying it, and the British and Swiss, with 93 per cent, are second. Although equal fifth in the list, with 89 per cent, West Germany has more executive wine-drinkers than France, where the proportion is 79 per cent.

How executives rate as wine-drinkers

		Percentage
1	DENMARK	95
2	BRITAIN	93
2	SWITZERLAND	93
4	BELGIUM	90
5	SWEDEN	89
5	WEST GERMANY	89
7	ITALY	83
8	HOLLAND	81
9	NORWAY	80
10	FRANCE	79
10	SPAIN	79
12	IRELAND	76

How executives rate as champagne-drinkers

		Percentage
1	FRANCE	79
2	DENMARK	62
3	BELGIUM	60
4	SPAIN	59
5	BRITAIN	55
6	NORWAY	50
7	ITALY	48
8	SWITZERLAND	45
9	SWEDEN	42
10	WEST GERMANY	41
11	IRELAND	34
12	HOLLAND	27

However, nearly 79 Frenchmen in every 100 drink champagne – so putting their country at the top of the executive champagne-drinking table. At the bottom is Holland, where the proportion of executive champagne-drinkers is only 27 per cent.

QUESTION FIVE **Enough money to buy more than 400,000 averagely priced houses – or more than two million family cars – is spent annually on alcohol by Britons.** TRUE In 1980, Britons spent £10,200 million on alcohol – more than three times the £3,329 million they spent on furniture.[10] That money would have bought 408,000 homes at an average price of £25,000 – or 2,040,000 cars at £5,000 each.

For years there had been a steady increase in expenditure on alcohol in Britain, which can be traced by comparing it over a 15-year period – as a percentage of the average family's budget – with money spent on food and clothing and footwear.

In 1966, 22 per cent of family spending was on food. That was 15 per cent more than on alcohol. Clothing and footwear accounted for 9 per cent – 2 per cent more than alcohol.

By 1980, the amount being spent on food was only 9 per cent more than that spent on alcohol – and the percentage being spent on clothing and footwear was marginally *less* than that spent on alcohol. In that year, Britons spent £292 million more on alcohol than on clothing and footwear – and £3,787 million more on alcohol than on fuel and light.

How percentages were spent

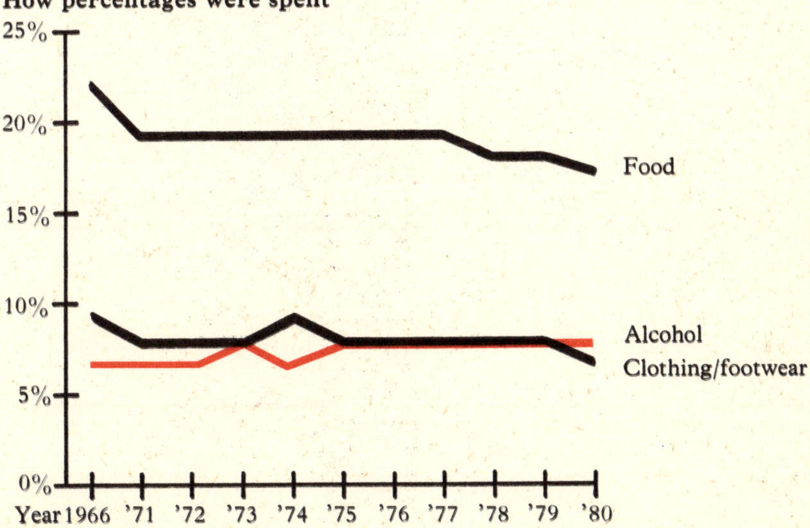

The qualities wanted by men and women in their ideal pub

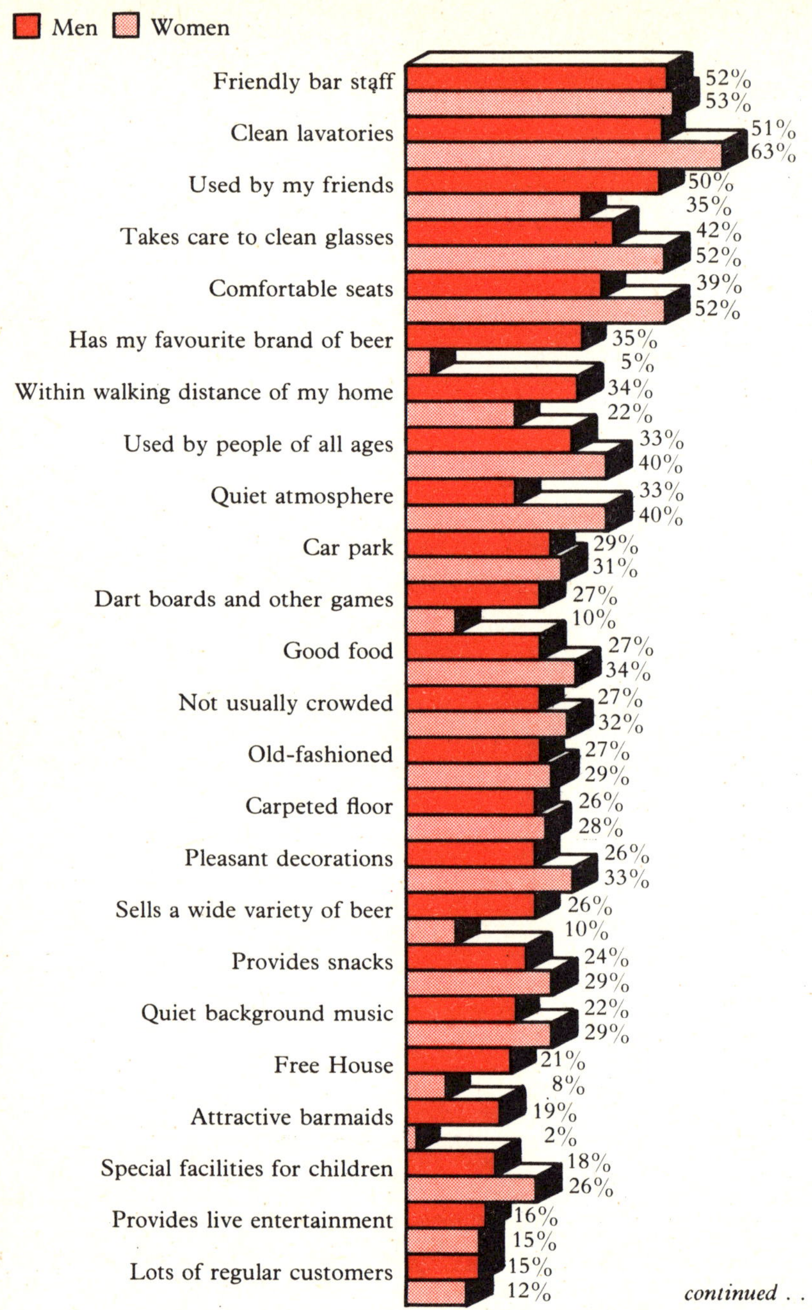

continued . . .

continued . . .

Nearly a third of the British, 32 per cent, were going to a public house at least once a week during 1981 and 4 per cent were going either every day or almost every day.

While establishing this with a survey on behalf of the Brewers' Society, MORI also found that most men, 86 per cent, preferred beer, while women tended to choose spirits (33 per cent), wine or sherry (24 per cent) or soft drinks (24 per cent).[11]

Further differences between the sexes were discovered when MORI asked men and women to rate the qualities they would want in the ideal pub.

Clean lavatories were considered the most important feature by the majority of women, 63 per cent, while men gave them a 51 per cent vote and rated them as being marginally less essential than 'friendly bar staff'. Women were keener than men on clean glasses and on comfortable seats, on carpeted floors and on good food. They were also rather more enthusiastic about juke-boxes and about quiet background music.

Modern pubs, rather than old-fashioned ones, appealed to men more than women, and they were seven times as insistent on their ideal pub having their favourite brand of beer – an attraction considered important by only 5 per cent of women.

Although men, not surprisingly, were more than nine times keener than women on a pub having attractive barmaids, such barmaids were regarded as being far less important than dartboards and a convenient car park.

QUESTION SIX **As a percentage of their family budgets, the Americans spend about twice as much as the British or the Danes on drink, tobacco and food.** FALSE In fact, the proportion spent on those items by the Americans is about *half* that spent by the British or the Danes.

A 1977 survey in 17 countries, published by Euromonitor, showed that the Americans were spending the smallest proportion, 15 per cent, on drink, tobacco and food. The proportions in Denmark and Britain were each 31 per cent.[12]

The French were well down the European table, with 26 per cent – 2 per cent less than the West Germans and 11 per cent less than the Italians.

Those spending the biggest proportion on drink, tobacco and food were the Irish, with those items absorbing 44 per cent of their money.

Most expensive category for the Americans was cars and other forms of transport which accounted for 30 per cent of their budgets – compared with 14 per cent for the British, 12 per cent for the West Germans, 11 per cent for the French and only 9 per cent for the Spanish.

Household expenditure on drink, tobacco and food

		Percentage			Percentage
1	IRELAND	44	9	BELGIUM	28
2	ITALY	37	9	WEST GERMANY	28
3	SPAIN	34	9	AUSTRIA	28
4	DENMARK	31	12	HOLLAND	26
4	BRITAIN	31	12	FRANCE	26
4	JAPAN	31	14	SWITZERLAND	25
4	NORWAY	31	14	AUSTRALIA	25
8	SWEDEN	29	16	CANADA	19
			17	AMERICA	15

How did you fare with the questions? Take three marks for each correct answer. Scores of 0–6 indicate either that there are great gaps in your knowledge or that, on this subject, your instincts are well off-beam; 9–15 reflect a good grasp of the subject; 18 identifies you as an expert.

17 Gadgetry

Although most of us regard the telephone as a necessity in the home, it is still a comparative novelty for the majority of people in several countries.

In China, for instance, there was only 1 telephone for every 125 people in 1981 – compared with 1 for about every 2 people in European countries such as Britain, France and West Germany, and in Japan, and 1 for every 1.3 people in America.[1]

In Russia there was 1 for every 11.2 people, in Saudi Arabia there was one for every 40 people, and in India there was one for every 250 people.

Even in the highly developed capitalist countries of the West, it is not so long since only a minority of people had home telephones. In 1966, for example, only a quarter of the households in Britain and in West Germany had telephones. By 1984, the proportion had risen to 78 per cent in Britain,[2] the same figure that was reached in West Germany in 1980[3] – and in both countries, as in others, it was continuing to rise.

Now the trend is for more telephonic gadgetry, such as answering machines, and more sophisticated receivers, such as the mobile phones which can be taken out and used away from the home.

The Norwegians are the keenest on having telephone chats while driving – or while on walk-about – with 11 per cent of their executives owning mobile telephones. This puts them well ahead of the Swedes and Danes, who are in second and third place with 7 and 6 per cent, respectively.

This was established by Pan European Survey 3, published in 1984, which was conducted in twelve countries by Research Services Ltd.[4]

At the bottom of the table were Ireland, Belgium, Holland, Britain and France, each with 1 per cent. However, French executives are the most likely to dismay their friends with telephone answering machines. These machines are owned by 12 per cent of them. Britain is at the bottom of the table, along with the Norwegians, Swedes and Irish.

Britain is the European country in which home computers have made the biggest impact on executives. With 17 per cent owning one, the British are twice as likely to have one as the Irish or the Danes and three times as likely as the French. Italian executives are the least enthusiastic about home computers. Only 2 in every 100 own one.

Executives who own mobile telephones and telephone answering machines

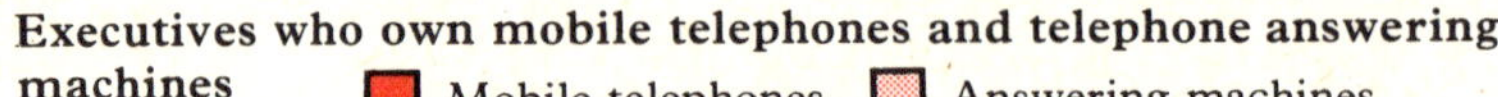

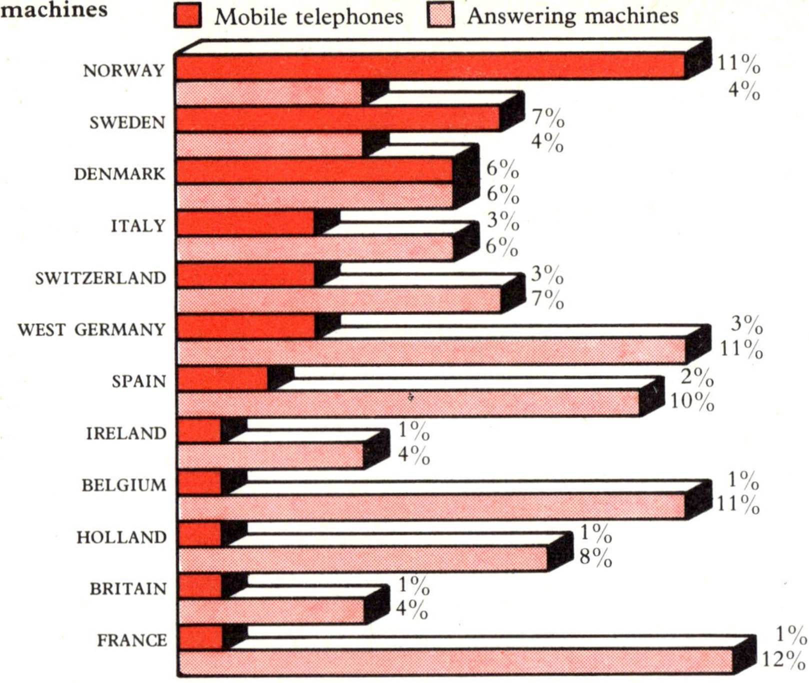

Executives owning home computers

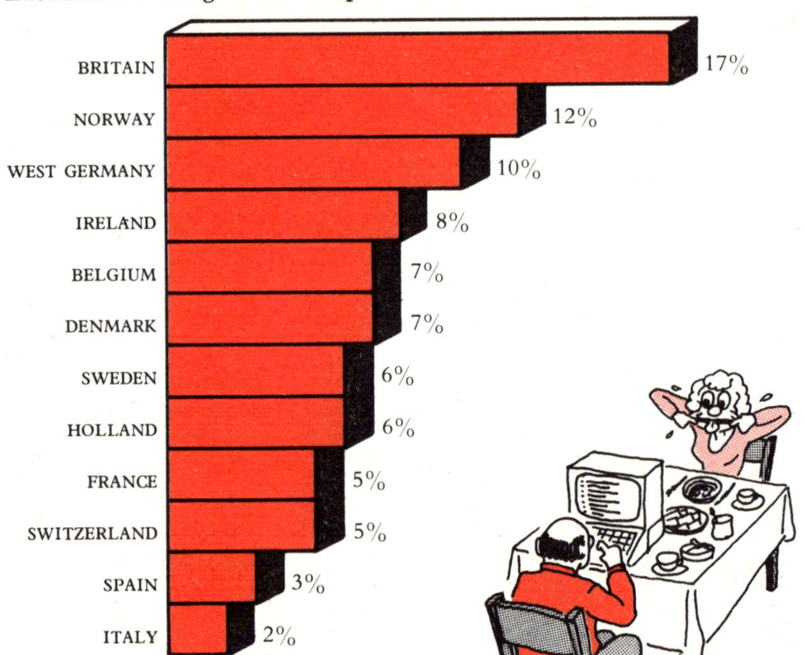

Our rapidly growing reliance on gadgets in the home was demonstrated through surveys conducted in 1953 and 1980 by the Institut für Demoskopie Allensbach.[5] Between those years, the proportion of West Germans who had refrigerators grew from 9 per cent to 97 per cent. The proportion with vacuum cleaners jumped from 26 per cent to 96 per cent.

Even in the shorter period from 1975 to 1980, as the same pollsters discovered, there were significant increases. In 1975, for instance, 14 per cent of homes had radio alarm clocks. By 1980, the proportion was 56 per cent. In 1975, 48 per cent had a freezer. By 1980, the proportion was 70 per cent.

An insight into the wide range of gadgets popular in the home was provided by a 1981 Roper Organization survey in America. Seventy-one per cent of American households then had a blender, 57 per cent had an automatic coffee-maker, 47 per cent smoke-alarm systems, 39 per cent push-button telephones and 25 per cent had special pulsating shower-head attachments.[6]

By that time, however, Americans were becoming progressively more disenchanted about the level of value-for-money represented by major household appliances. A 1982 survey by Trendex, for General Electric, showed that the proportion regarding them as poor value had increased from 7 per cent in 1965 to 20 per cent.[7]

More than twice as many Americans, incidentally, were then expressing dissatisfaction with car repairs – with 48 per cent describing them as 'poor value'. That was almost as high as the 53 per cent who felt the same way about Federal taxes.

Items per 1,000 inhabitants[8]

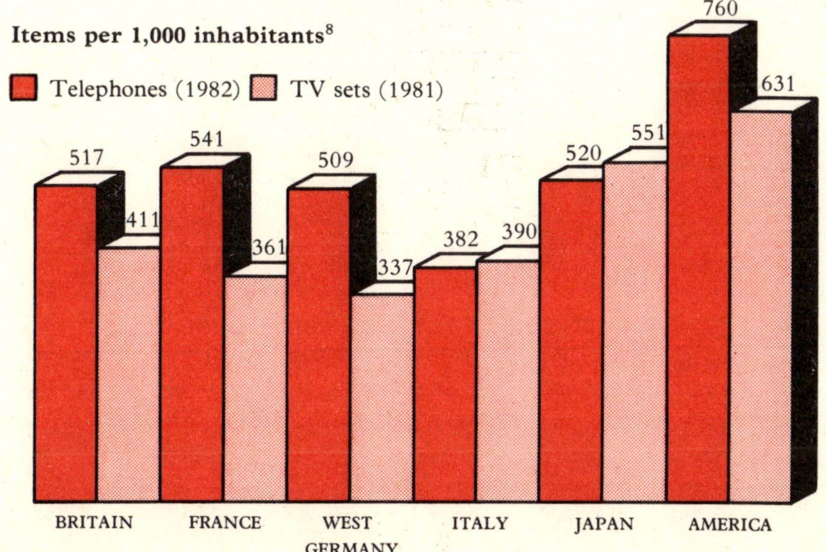

Americans were half as much again as likely to regard their car as a necessity as their television set in 1983. In a Roper survey of that year 91 per cent of Americans said that their automobile was essential and 87 per cent gave their washing machine the same importance. The television was regarded by over a third (36 per cent) as a luxury item, as many regarding their toaster as a necessity as the television. A quarter (26 per cent) of Americans even regarded a *second* automobile as a necessity, but only 4 per cent put a home computer in the necessity category.[9]

Necessity or luxury?

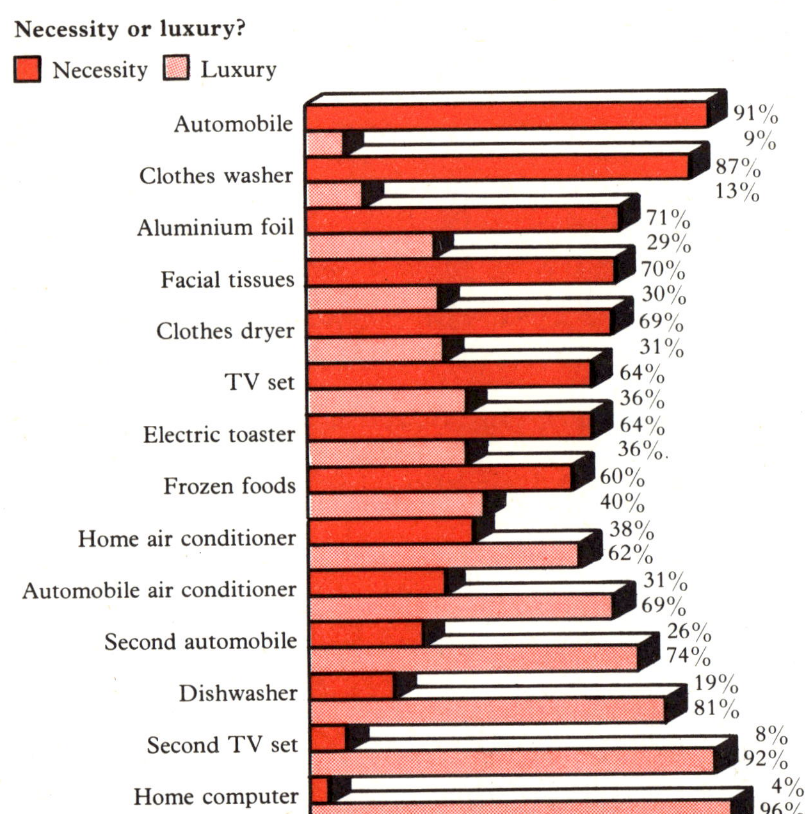

Personal computer owners in America constitute a pretty élite fraternity: according to a reader survey of *Personal Computing Magazine* subscribers.[10] About 90 per cent are college graduates, 47 per cent have postgraduate education, 69 per cent earn more than $35,000 a year and 28 per cent more than $50,000. Another study, by Yankelovich, Skelly and White, found that the printers and plotters are the most popular computer extras to buy.[11] After these come floppy disc drives, monitors, games equipment and modems (telephone links). Top uses include word processing, entertainment, file maintenance, business and accounting, education and training, and personal finance.

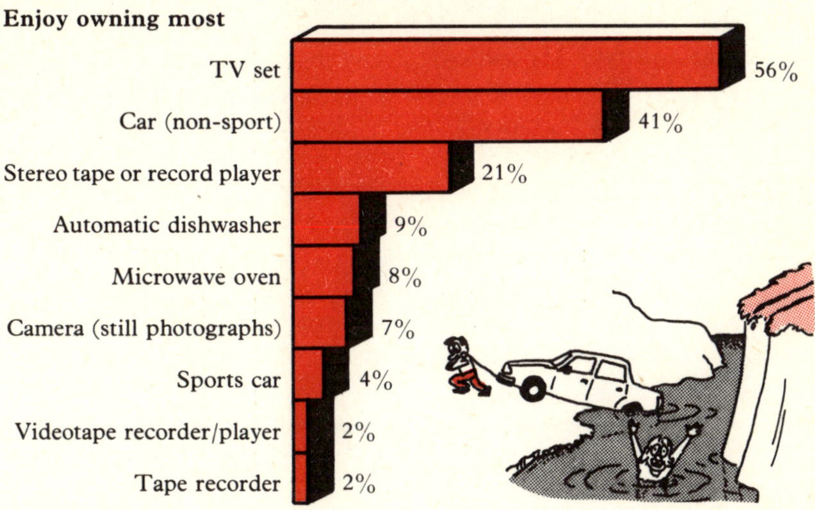

Of affluent Americans who do possess things that most people regard as luxuries, after the television and car, the stereo was most enjoyed. Few mentioned a home computer, movie or video camera or electronic TV games.

18 Cars – the great ownership race

As a nation of car-owners, the British are lagging more than 30 years behind the Americans – and have been overtaken in dramatic style by other Europeans, such as the French, the West Germans and the Italians.

In 1982, there was 1 car for every 3.5 people in Britain[1] – the ratio in America in 1953. By 1982 the Americans had surged ahead to have 1 car for every 1.8 people, the highest ratio in the world.[2]

In 1953, although so far behind America, Britain was leading its neighbours in Europe – with 1 car for every 18 people. France then had 1 for every 21 people, West Germany had 1 for every 45 people, and Italy had only 1 for every 77 people.[3]

By 1982, the European situation was reversed. While Britain then had 1 car for every 3.5 people, Italy had 1 for every 2.9 people, France had 1 for every 2.7 people, and West Germany had 1 for every 2.6 people.[4]

Canada, with 1 car for every 2.3 people, was second in the league of car-owning nations in 1982, and Australia, with one for every 2.4 people, was third.

Although Japan exports such vast numbers of cars, it had comparatively few in its home market – 1 for every 4.6 people. The Russians, perhaps not unexpectedly, were less well served, having to share each car between 27.8 people. At the bottom end of the scale, India had 1 car for every 1,000 people and China had 1 for every 2,000.

Cars are often regarded as status symbols and executives in Britain are more likely to have such a symbol in triplicate than their counterparts in other European countries.

They are more than three times as likely to own as many as three cars or more as executives in Holland, and more than five times as likely as executives in Sweden.[5]

West German managers and executives are the leading multi-car owners in Europe, with 16 per cent of them owning at least three. Italy's top men come second with 13 per cent and the British are third with 12 per cent. Bottom of this list are the Swedes with 2 per cent.

The relatively high esteem accorded to cars in West Germany was also obvious when the Institut für Demoskopie Allensbach investigated matters of style and taste in 1976.[6] Pollsters discovered that nearly a quarter of West Germans, 23 per cent, felt their style or taste was reflected in their choice of cars. Presumably to help enhance their images as owners, 25 per cent had fitted fur seat-covers by 1980 and 6 per cent had invested in racing-style steering wheels.

Executives who own at least three cars

		Percentage			Percentage
1	WEST GERMANY	16	8	SPAIN	6
2	ITALY	13	9	NORWAY	5
3	BRITAIN	12	10	HOLLAND	4
4	BELGIUM	11	10	DENMARK	4
5	SWITZERLAND	10	12	SWEDEN	2
6	FRANCE	7			
6	IRELAND	7			

A more significant pointer came in 1978 when West Germans were invited to list things they regarded as sacred. Fifteen per cent picked the New Testament and 17 per cent picked the crucifix. Twenty-four per cent picked 'being able to watch television undisturbed in the evenings' and 27 per cent picked 'being able to drive my own car any time'.[7]

What sex is your car? That may seem a curious question but, it was discovered in 1983 that British drivers are three times as likely to regard their cars as female, rather than male.[8] One in ten gives the car a personal name – with the favourite, by far, being Betsy. The most popular name in Britain for 'male' cars is Fred.

Vast numbers of these Betsies and Freds are driven illegally fast and nearly one driver in five admits to routine flouting of the 70 mph speed limit on motorways. The 11 per cent who consider that limit is too high are outnumbered, almost by two to one, by those insisting it is too low. More than a quarter of British motorists claim to have driven at 100 mph and 6 per cent claim speeds of more than 120 mph. A survey in 1982 established that exactly a quarter of British drivers had been stopped for speeding.[9]

The West Germans are also keen on speed. On freeways, 24 per cent drive at 130 km/h (just over 80 mph), 12 per cent drive at 140 km/h, 8 per cent at 150 km/h, and 6 per cent at 160–170 km/h.[10]

Women are more enthusiastic than men about motoring for pleasure in West Germany. Fifty-two per cent say they enjoy driving, compared with 43 per cent of men.

(In 1975, incidentally, 7 per cent of West Germans described their own driving as 'very good' and 45 per cent as 'good'. Forty-one per cent described it as 'mediocre'.)

Eighty-two per cent of Americans in 1977 said that there should be stricter laws regarding drinking and driving. Eighteen per cent disagreed or offered no opinion. Perhaps coincidentally, 18 per cent also said they had driven after drinking too much for safety![11]

Costs of new cars vary astonishingly across the world – a fact emphasized by a 1976 survey conducted in 17 capital cities by the Union Bank of Switzerland.[12]

Although prices have risen universally since that time – when a Ford Cortina cost only £2,130 in Britain – the basic pattern remains significant as an indication of international variations.

UBS based the investigation on the costs of popular, medium-sized cars, comparable with the Cortina, in each of the 17 countries – such as a Chevy Nova Standard in America, a Holden Kingswood in Australia and a VW Passat TS in West Germany.

New York emerged as one of the cheapest cities for new cars. The calibre of vehicle which could have been bought there for £2,320 would have cost £2,950 in Düsseldorf, £3,056 in Toronto, £3,549 in Sydney and £4,451 in Copenhagen. However, all these prices were low in comparison with the £6,421 which would have been charged in Oslo.

Cheapest place to buy such a car was Madrid, where the price of £1,915 was £14 lower than in Tokyo.

Prices of comparable cars

		Pounds			Pounds
1	MADRID	1,915	10	DÜSSELDORF	2,950
2	TOKYO	1,929	11	TORONTO	3,056
3	LONDON	2,130	12	ZÜRICH	3,100
4	NEW YORK	2,320	13	SYDNEY	3,544
5	DUBLIN	2,591	14	AMSTERDAM	3,700
6	VIENNA	2,819	15	STOCKHOLM	4,030
7	BRUSSELS	2,849	16	COPENHAGEN	4,451
8	MILAN	2,850	17	OSLO	6,421
9	PARIS	2,938			

However, price is far from being the most important factor in determining the choice of a vehicle. That was proved in 1983 when MORI questioned nearly 2,000 Britons about which considerations influence them when they are buying a new car.[13]

After being invited to choose four or five 'good points' out of a list of 24, respondents voted 'not too expensive' as being eighth in importance – placing it after good all-round visibility, low servicing costs, and driving comfort.

Important considerations for car buyers

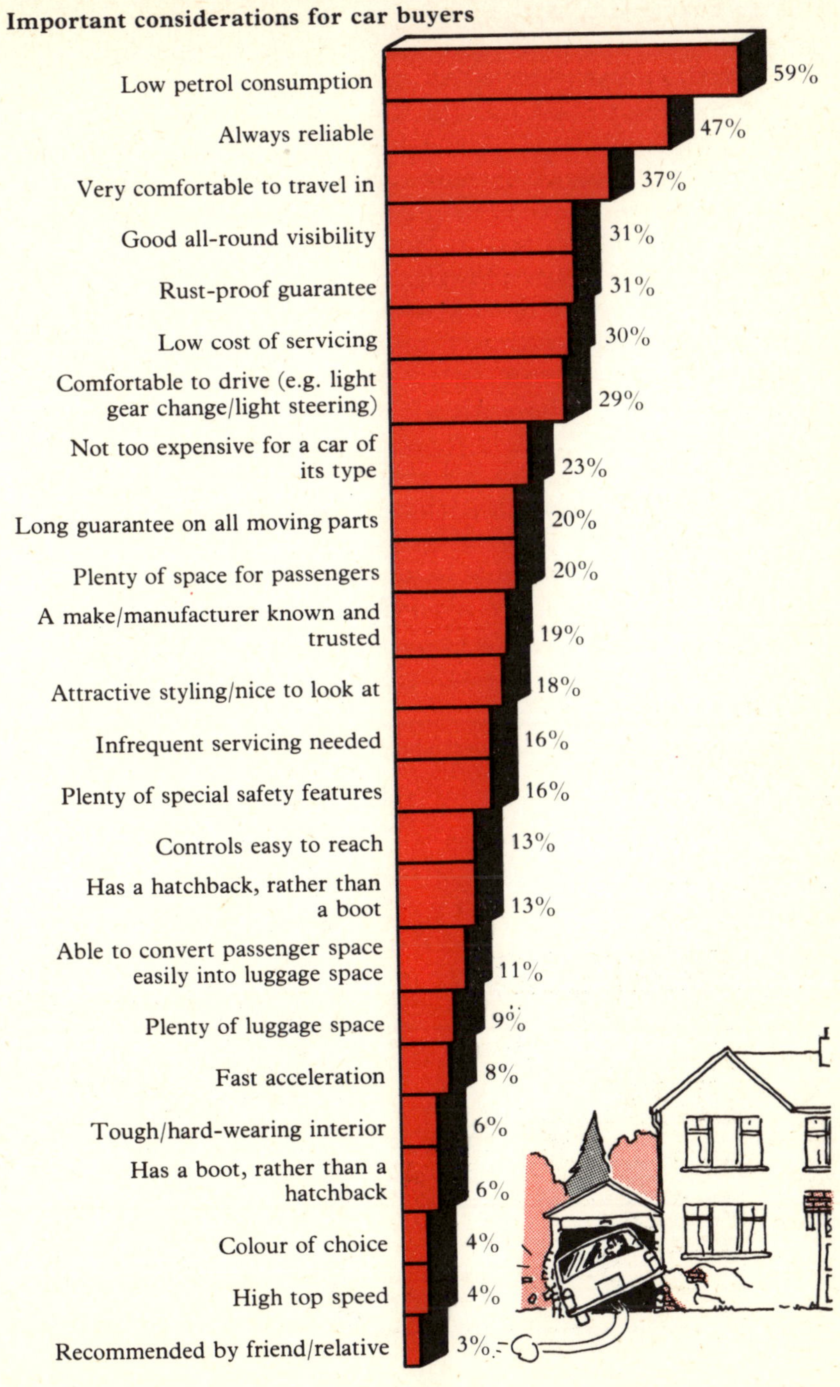

The most important consideration, with 59 per cent saying so, is low petrol consumption, and only 3 per cent put great store on recommendations by relatives or friends.

This poll also showed that the British regard Britain – ahead of countries such as Japan, France and West Germany – as the country producing cars which are the most reliable, best-looking and longest-lasting. However, Japan is seen as the country making cars which are the 'most economical to run' and the 'best value for money'.

Although six out of seven British drivers, 83 per cent, consider it is 'essential' or 'very important' to have cars serviced regularly, 30 per cent get their cars serviced only when they feel something needs doing. When driving 'hates' were investigated by the Institut für Demoskopie Allensbach in 1979, it was established that the most detested annoyance among West Germans, with 61 per cent agreeing, was getting caught in rush-hour traffic, while 56 per cent hated traffic jams generally. Seventeen per cent got angry about traffic lights staying 'too long' on red, 13 per cent about their newly washed cars being splashed, and 5 per cent about 'never being served immediately at gas stations'.[14]

While driving a car isn't as much feared by Americans as snakes, mice or dogs, 8 per cent of Americans admitted to the Roper Organization's interviewers that they are bothered at least somewhat by the thought of driving a car.[15]

Fears and phobias

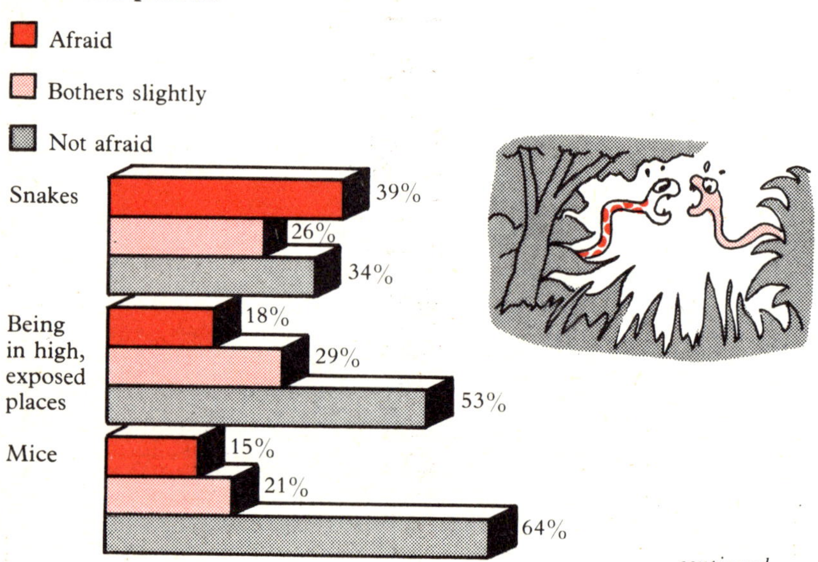

continued . . .

continued . . .

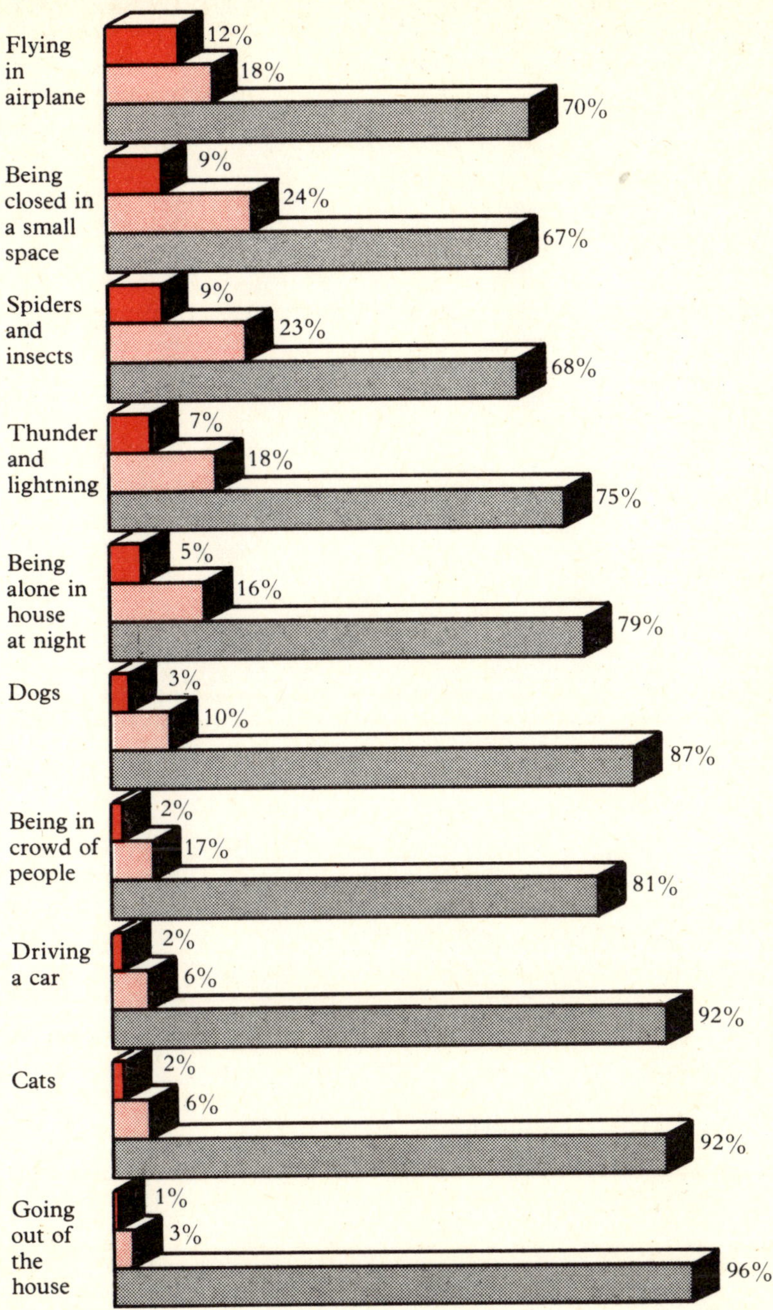
Flying in airplane
12%
18%
70%
Being closed in a small space
9%
24%
67%
Spiders and insects
9%
23%
68%
Thunder and lightning
7%
18%
75%
Being alone in house at night
5%
16%
79%
Dogs
3%
10%
87%
Being in crowd of people
2%
17%
81%
Driving a car
2%
6%
92%
Cats
2%
6%
92%
Going out of the house
1%
3%
96%

19 The impact of television

Television so dominates modern life that it is often difficult for people, particularly younger ones, to realize that it is still a comparative newcomer.

Imagine a Britain, for example, in which 63 people out of every 100 had never seen television pictures. That is how it was as recently as 1949.

Even in the limited areas of the country where transmissions could then be received, only 8 per cent of families had a set. And, as Gallup discovered, the service did not inspire widespread enthusiasm.[1] Twenty-nine per cent of people living in the transmission areas said they did not want a set and a further 32 per cent said they could not afford one.

As a domestic priority, the television set also had a low rating in 1950. Only 2 per cent of Britons said they wanted one when asked which items they would like to buy for themselves. Three per cent said they would prefer to buy underwear and the biggest proportion – 33 per cent – told Gallup they would sooner have a new suit or dress.

However, it was not long before television began to tighten its grip on fast-growing audiences across the world and was being regarded as a necessity.

By 1974, for instance, West Germans considered that having the best possible television set was twice as important as having the best brandy – and five times as important as having expensive socks.[2] They also told pollsters then that they would be more inclined to pay extra for top quality when buying a television set than when buying a washing machine, a carpet, or even toys for the children.

Eleven per cent said they would plump for best quality when buying sports equipment, 33 per cent would do so when buying a watch, and 52 per cent would do so when buying a television.

By then, only 4 per cent of households in West Germany did not have a set.

By 1976, college examination marks had tumbled dramatically in America. Why? Nearly half the people asked by Gallup, 49 per cent, blamed 'too much television viewing' – completely outvoting the 16 per cent who preferred to believe the examinations were 'not reliable'.[3]

By 1977, 70 per cent of Americans felt there was a direct link between violence on television and the country's rising crime rate.[4]

By 1979, West Germans considered that too much viewing was as bad for health as oral contraceptives – with 12 per cent saying so – and was almost as bad as petrol fumes at filling stations (cited by 13 per cent).[5]

Television addiction was by then solid and almost universal. In 1981 Americans were admitting that they got more personal satisfaction or enjoyment from their sets than from their friends, their meals or their hobbies.[6]

With the average American then watching television for nearly 3 hours each day – although 42 per cent were complaining about programmes which were an 'insult to intelligence' – pollsters from the Roper Organization showed respondents a card listing 15 activities.

Respondents were then invited to pick the three or four which gave them the most personal satisfaction or enjoyment.

The league table which resulted showed that television came second only to the family. It was more than twice as important as work and more than three times as important as physical exercise.

When it comes to deciding which television programmes are most worth watching, the American man is usually the boss in his own home. He has the final word if there is a clash of opinion. At least, he has it in 44 per cent of homes – according to a 1978 Roper survey – and the woman has it in 20 per cent. In the other 36 per cent of homes there is apparently no clearcut pattern and the choice of programme is a matter for negotiation.[7]

In theory, of course, such negotiation should hardly be necessary, as most American families have more than one set – 51 per cent did in 1981 – and the country has more sets per head of population than any other.

An international survey in 1981[8] showed that in America there are 624 sets for every 1,000 people – compared with 404 in Britain, 354 in France, 337 in West Germany and 303 in Russia.

In China there are 5 sets for every 1,000 people. In Kenya there are 4. In India and Sri Lanka there are 2.

Most Americans say that they enjoy watching television. One American adult in 20 admits to being glued to the box 7 hours or more a day, and 2 in 100 to 9 hours a day plus!

Nearly all Americans (94 per cent) watch television every day, while only a bare majority (56 per cent) read a newspaper daily. A little more than three-quarters (77 per cent) of Americans, and the same percentage of British adults, are 'regular' (at least a few times a week) readers.[9]

Average hours per day spent watching television

How often do you read the newspaper?

Every day

A few times a week

Once a week

Less than once a week

Never

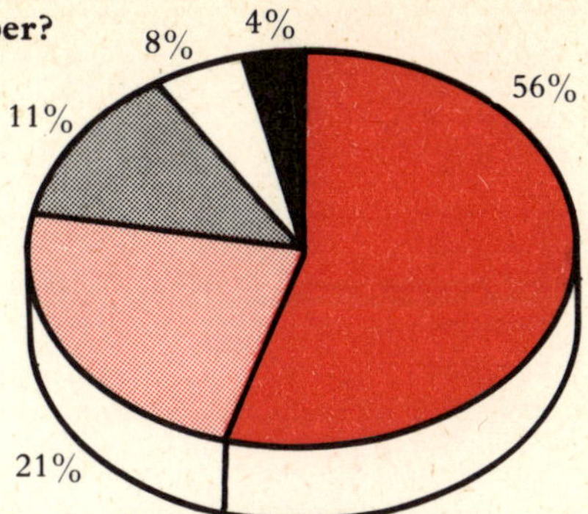

20 Crime and punishment

Crime has now soared to such startling levels that in many countries – including America, Britain, Holland and Italy – it is a greater cause for concern than the proliferation of nuclear weapons.

In seven out of nine countries surveyed, including Japan and West Germany, it dwarfs anxieties about inflation and the energy crisis. Across the world, people are apprehensive about the economic future – and about the spectre of a military holocaust – but they are even more fearful about the escalation of muggings and burglaries, of kidnaps, rapes and murders.

In March 1983, the Atlantic Institute for International Affairs assessed the seriousness of sources of worry in the following countries: America, Britain, France, Holland, Italy, Japan, Norway, Spain and West Germany.[1]

Cross-sections of the populations were asked which of the following were the greatest concerns for themselves and their countries:

1. The threat of war
2. The energy crisis
3. Inflation
4. Inadequate defence
5. High unemployment
6. Social injustice
7. Crime
8. Nuclear weapons
9. Excessive government spending
10. Poor political leadership

Spain gave crime the lowest priority, and Norway placed it fourth, and that probably reflects the comparatively low incidence of crime reported in those countries.

Interpol figures for 1974, for instance, showed that Spain had less than 1 murder or attempted murder for every 100,000 people in the population, compared with Britain's $2\frac{1}{2}$ and West Germany's $4\frac{1}{2}$. FBI figures showed that America had nearly 10 murders or attempted murders for every 100,000 people.[2]

A similar situation was seen in respect of sex offences and major larcenies.

Spain had 12 reported sex offences for every 100,000 people. Britain had 50, West Germany had 77. Apart from all other types of sex offences, America had 26 rapes for every 100,000 people.

Spain had 360 major larcenies for every 100,000 people. Britain had 1,074, West Germany had 1,611, America had 1,744.

So perhaps it is hardly surprising that the Spaniards should be the only ones to regard crime as a lesser concern than social injustice.

Except in Japan, each national list was headed by unemployment and in four countries – America, Britain, Holland and Italy – the second place was taken by crime.

In Japan, which has the lowest level of worry about unemployment, crime tied in first place with the threat of war.

The Americans were the people who laid the greatest emphasis on poor political leadership as a cause for concern. That was third on their worry list. In Britain, Italy and Holland it was sixth, in West Germany and Norway it was eighth, in France and Japan it was ninth. The people least concerned about their nation's political leadership were the Spaniards. That worry was at the very bottom of their list, along with 'inadequate defence'.

Here is how the 9 countries rated the worries:

	America		Britain
1	High unemployment	1	High unemployment
2	CRIME	2	CRIME
3	Poor political leadership	3	Nuclear weapons
4	Inflation	4	Threat of war
5	Excessive government spending	5	Inflation
6	Threat of war	6	Poor political leadership
7	Social injustice	7	Social injustice
8	Nuclear weapons	8	Excessive government spending
9	Energy crisis	9	Inadequate defence
10	Inadequate defence	10	Energy crisis

	France		Holland
1	High unemployment	1	High unemployment
2	Inflation	2	CRIME
3	Threat of war	3	Nuclear weapons
4	CRIME	4	Threat of war
5	Social injustice	5	Excessive government spending
6	Excessive government spending	6	Poor political leadership
7	Nuclear weapons	7	Social injustice
8	Energy crisis	8	Inflation
9	Poor political leadership	9	Energy crisis
10	Inadequate defence	10	Inadequate defence

	Italy
1	High unemployment
2	CRIME
3	Threat of war
4	Inflation
5	Nuclear weapons
6	Poor political leadership
6	Social injustice
8	Energy crisis
9	Excessive government spending
10	Inadequate defence

	Japan
1	CRIME
1	Threat of war
3	Inflation
4	Nuclear weapons
5	Energy crisis
6	Excessive government spending
7	Social injustice
8	High unemployment
9	Poor political leadership
10	Inadequate defence

	Norway
1	High unemployment
2	Nuclear weapons
3	Threat of war
4	Inflation
4	CRIME
6	Social injustice
7	Excessive government spending
8	Poor political leadership
9	Inadequate defence
10	Energy crisis

	Spain
1	High unemployment
2	Threat of war
3	Nuclear weapons
4	Social injustice
4	Inflation
6	CRIME
7	Energy crisis
8	Excessive government spending
9	Inadequate defence
9	Poor political leadership

	West Germany
1	High unemployment
2	Nuclear weapons
3	Excessive government spending
4	CRIME
5	Social injustice
6	Inflation
7	Threat of war
8	Poor political leadership
9	Energy crisis
10	Inadequate defence

One major source of widespread international concern, the future of the environment, was not considered in this survey. Is the despoiling of natural life a greater threat, or a lesser one, than the rise in crime and terrorism? That question was explored during a survey in ten nations – Britain, Belgium, Denmark, France, Greece, Holland, Ireland, Italy, Luxembourg and West Germany.[3]

In only two of those countries, Denmark and West Germany, was the future of the environment rated higher than crime as a source of concern. In Britain, there was almost exactly twice as much anxiety about crime as about the environment.

Would tougher punishments reduce the levels of crime? Are courts harsh enough with criminals? Polls on both sides of the Atlantic confirm that most people would favour more severe penalties.

Eighty-one per cent of Americans told NORC in 1982 that the courts did not deal harshly enough with criminals. Three per cent felt sentences were too harsh. The others did not know or felt the balance was about right.[4] In 1977 a MORI survey for the *Daily Express* found that more than 9 Britons in 10 believed 'There should be harsher penalties to combat crime and violence in Great Britain'.

Fifty per cent of Canadians told CIPO in 1982 that conditions in penal institutions were too liberal. Seven per cent felt they were too harsh. The others did not know or felt the balance was about right.[5]

(The French, incidentally, favour their prisons being more liberal in one respect. Fifty per cent of them told the Institut Français d'Opinion Publique in 1983 that they felt male prisoners should be allowed to have sexual intercourse with their wives or mistresses. Thirty-seven per cent disapproved and 13 per cent were undecided.)[6]

Sixty-seven per cent of Britons told Gallup (1982) that courts were giving sentences that were too short. Five per cent felt sentences were too long. The others did not know, or considered that the level of sentencing was about right.[7]

Similar views are expressed in other countries. Seventy-seven per cent of the people in Taiwan, for instance, told CPO in 1982 that they approved of punishments being more severe. Only 11 per cent disapproved and 12 per cent offered no opinion.[8]

This international wish for tougher punishments grows steadily stronger. The trend was charted by CIPO in Canada. In 1966, 43 per cent of Canadians felt courts were not dealing harshly enough with criminals. Here is how that feeling has mounted since then:[9]

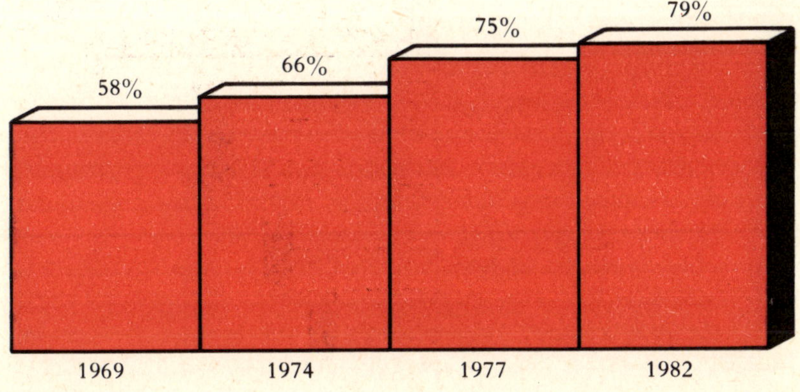

Support is also increasing for the death penalty. NORC figures show that 63 per cent of Americans were in favour of it in 1974. Sixty-six per cent favoured it in 1978 and 74 per cent favoured it in 1982.[10]

In 1982, 70 per cent of Canadians wanted the death sentence[11] and 78 per cent of Britons wanted it for terrorist murders – 6 per cent more than in 1981.[12]

But are executions wanted as a deterrent – or as displays of society's vengeance? One of the arguments often offered against capital punishment is that it is not more effective than long prison sentences in keeping people from crimes such as murder. If that could be proved to be true, would the majority still be in favour of the death penalty?

Americans were asked that question by HS in 1973, 1976 and 1983. Their answers showed that vengeance was clearly a prime motivation. Even while accepting that the death sentence was not the best deterrent, 35 per cent were in favour of it in 1973. Forty-six per cent were in 1976. Fifty-two per cent were in 1983.[13]

Variations in public approval of the death penalty reflect attitudes to different types of crime. Here are the percentage of Britons who told SSLT in 1982 that they would favour the death penalty for certain categories of crime – with the 1981 percentages also shown:[14]

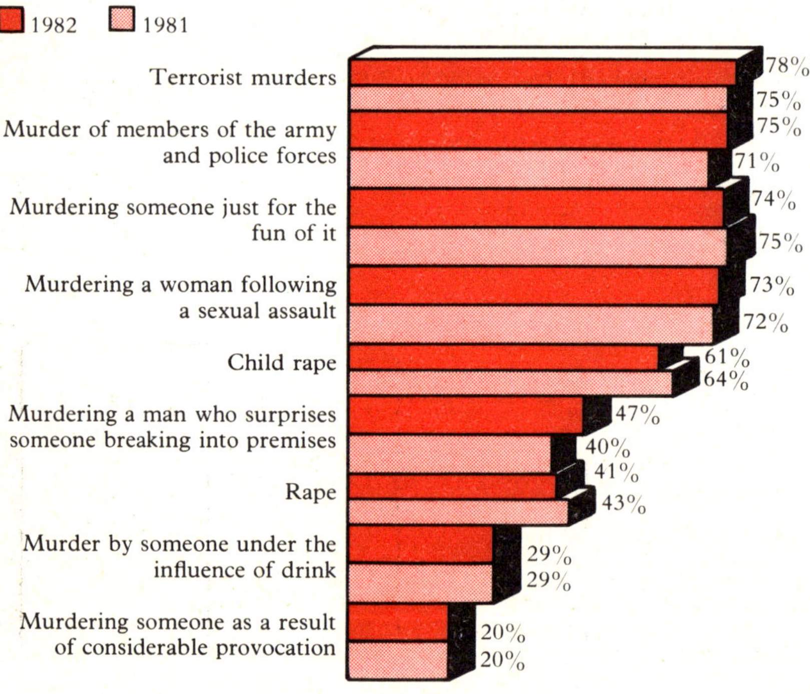

Confirmation that a dominant factor is revenge, on behalf of the victims and society, came in replies to a further question:

What should be the first concern of the courts in sentencing a criminal?

Sixteen per cent said 'to reclaim him as a good citizen'. Thirty-eight per cent said 'to punish in order to stop others following the criminal's example'. A decisive 41 per cent said bluntly: 'To punish him for what he has done to others.' The other 5 per cent offered no answer.

Burglary worries about half of Americans, according to a survey by ABC News in 1982, when they found three Americans in ten admit they worry 'a great deal about being burgled'. Women were more worried than men, and blacks more than twice as anxious as whites.[15]

Is America a violent society? Is it ever! One American in five has been threatened with a gun or shot at, and two in five (over half – 60 per cent – of men) have been punched or beaten by another person.[16]

Attitudes to crime vary from nation to nation and can often seem surprising. So can the raw facts. See if you can identify the truths by answering these questions:

1 **Intentionally hitting a victim with a lead pipe – so savagely that he needs hospital treatment – is regarded by Americans as a more severe crime than knowingly lying under oath during a trial.** TRUE OR FALSE?
2 **Cheating on Federal income-tax returns is regarded by Americans as a more severe crime than getting customers for a prostitute.** TRUE OR FALSE?
3 **In European countries such as Britain, France and West Germany, taking and driving away a car illegally is considered less excusable than a political assassination.** TRUE OR FALSE?
4 **Police investigating major larcenies are about four times as likely to get their man in Japan as in West Germany.** TRUE OR FALSE?
5 **In Britain, 4 per cent of males found guilty of, or cautioned for, sex offences are aged 10–13.** TRUE OR FALSE?
6 **Youngsters regard the influence of bad friends as a more significant cause of juvenile crime than the lack of parental supervision.** TRUE OR FALSE?

Answers start on the next page.

QUESTION ONE **Intentionally hitting a victim with a lead pipe – so savagely that he needs hospital treatment – is regarded by Americans as a more severe crime than knowingly lying under oath during a trial.** FALSE Lying under oath is considered more serious than hitting a person with a lead pipe. So is stealing property worth $10,000 from outside a building. People at the wrong end of lead pipes may not be too delighted, but those facts were established by America's National Survey of Crime Severity, published in October 1983.[17]

The object was to measure how Americans rank the severity of crimes by asking them to assess 204 illegal events. Planting a bomb which kills 20 people heads the eventual 'severity list' with a score of 72, compared with playing hookey from school, which qualifies for less than half a point.

The second most serious crime is raping a woman so forcibly that she dies. That earns 53 points, ten more than killing a victim while robbing at gunpoint.

A woman who stabs her husband to death is not behaving as badly as a man who stabs his wife to death. Americans give his crime a rating of 39 and hers only 28 – six less than that of a person who runs a narcotic ring.

In fact, women victims in general get more sympathy than men. Teenage boys who may feel like beating up parents, for instance, would be well advised to concentrate on their fathers, rather than their mothers. A boy who punches his mother so hard that she needs hospitalization is guilty of a 16-point crime. Doing the same to dad rates a mere 8 points.

Any American who finds tonight that his home has been broken into – and that $1,000 has been stolen – may be comforted by the knowledge that his fellow-countrymen, with rather puzzling logic, regard such a crime as being marginally more acceptable than that of a man who steals property worth $1,000 after breaking into a school or a museum.

However, that level of housebreaking does merit a severity rating of 10 points and so is considered more serious than the 7-point crime of breaking into a department store and stealing merchandise worth $1,000.

Among Americans, sex inspires more indignation than cash. A man who exposes himself in public is rated as being 1 point more of a bad hat than one who knowingly passes a dud cheque.[18]

A man who runs his hands over the body of a female victim and then flees is committing a 5-point crime – 1 point more severe than that of a man who steals $100 from a victim's pocket.

What if that same man drags the woman into an alley and tears her clothes – but runs off before she is physically harmed or sexually attacked? His crime then becomes worth 17 points. That is 1 point more serious than attempting to kill a victim with a gun – as long as the gun misfires and the victim escapes unharmed.

Killing a person by recklessly driving a car has a severity rating of 19 – 5 more than the crime of breaking into a bank at night and stealing $100,000.

An employer who illegally threatens to fire workers if they join a labor union rates only 3 black points and is therefore regarded as behaving twice as well as the person who gets 6 points for using heroin.

QUESTION TWO **Cheating on Federal income-tax returns is regarded by Americans as a more severe crime than getting customers for a prostitute.** FALSE With a rating of 6 black points in the National Survey of Crime Severity, pimping is considered 2 points less acceptable than cheating on income tax. Being a prostitute, however, is regarded far more favourably. That gets a disapproval rating of only 2 points – slightly lower than that awarded to people who run illegal gambling joints.

Forcible rape which involves no other physical injury is seen as being as severe a crime as skyjacking an aircraft – both rate 26 points – but kidnapping, with a rating of 21 points, is considered less serious.

Americans are comparatively relaxed over obscene phone calls and over men having sex with willing under-age girls. Both crimes have a rating of only 2 points – and are therefore marginally less severe than that of knowingly carrying an illegal knife.

A store-owner who sells cooking oil, although he knows the shipment is bad, is committing an 8-point crime – on a level with selling marijuana to others for resale, but less severe than the 9-point crime of performing an illegal abortion.

A real estate agent who refuses to sell a house to a person because of that person's race is a 5-point criminal. A person who activates a false fire alarm is a 4-point criminal. One found firing a rifle for which he knows he has no permit is a 2-point criminal.

A legislator who takes a bribe from a company before voting for a law favouring that company is committing a 14-point crime. A factory boss who knowingly gets rid of industrial waste in a way that pollutes a city's water supply is committing a 13-point crime. A police officer who knowingly makes a false arrest is committing a 10-point crime.

Taking bets on the numbers and disturbing the neighbourhood with noisy behaviour are seen as little more than token crimes – worth only 1 point each – but both are considered more serious than being drunk in public or being a vagrant.

QUESTION THREE **In European countries such as Britain, France and West Germany, taking and driving away a car illegally is considered less excusable than a political assassination.** TRUE Some may feel that the general public in Europe is as surprising as that in America in its judgments on matters of crime. However, 'borrowing' a car is certainly considered more reprehensible than a political assassination in those three countries. And the same applies in others, such as Denmark and Holland.

This intriguing fact was established during a nine-nation survey for the European Values Systems Study Group.[19]

People in each country were asked to consider 22 types of antisocial behaviour – some of which were criminal and others, rather than being offences, were more a reflection of permissiveness. They were then asked the degree to which each of those 22 types could be justified – always, sometimes or never? Analysis of the replies produced an international guide to attitudes on morality and on crime – one which shows clearly the type of actions considered most inexcusable.

We have extracted 12 categories of behaviour out of the original 22, in order to focus more closely on criminal actions, and to show how they are regarded in the five countries mentioned above.

In each of these countries, taking and driving away a car is regarded as the most inexcusable of the 12 crimes – with 'political assassination' managing to get into second place only in West Germany.

In Denmark and Holland, 'political assassination' is third and in France it is fourth. In Britain, it is fifth – apparently being considered more excusable than taking a car, threatening workers who refuse to strike, taking marijuana, or fighting with the police.

Murder in self-defence is regarded as the most excusable of the 12 listed acts in all countries.

Cheating on tax is seen as being comparatively justified in all countries, particularly in France, and is even more excusable than keeping money which has been found in the street.

In view of their liberal attitudes to sex, it is interesting to note that the French are marginally the toughest on prostitution – being the only nation to feel that it is less forgivable than tax-dodging.

The French judgment on people who fight with the police is lighter than in other countries. They rate such behaviour eighth in the scale of inexcusability – seeing it as more forgivable than travelling on public transport without paying the fare or failing to report damage to a parked vehicle.

In West Germany and Holland, 'fighting with the police' is seventh in the list. In Denmark, it is fifth. In Britain, it ties in third place with using marijuana.

Anyone who threatens workers for refusing to go on strike can expect less sympathy from the public in Britain and France than in West Germany, Holland or Denmark.

Here are the national ratings – with the most inexcusable acts at the top and those most justifiable at the bottom:

Britain

1 Taking and driving away a car
2 Threatening workers who refuse to strike
3 Taking marijuana
4 Fighting with police
5 Political assassination
6 Receiving stolen goods
7 Travelling without paying fare
8 Failing to report damage to a parked car
9 Keeping money you have found
10 Cheating on tax
11 Prostitution
12 Murder in self-defence

Denmark

1 Taking and driving away a car
2 Receiving stolen goods
3 Political assassination
4 Failing to report damage to a parked car
5 Fighting with police
6 Travelling without paying fare
7 Threatening workers who refuse to strike
8 Taking marijuana
9 Keeping money you have found
10 Cheating on tax
11 Prostitution
12 Murder in self-defence

France

1 Taking and driving away a car
2 Threatening workers who refuse to strike
3 Taking marijuana
4 Political assassination
5 Receiving stolen goods
6 Failing to report damage to a parked car
7 Travelling without paying fare
8 Fighting with police
9 Keeping money you have found
10 Prostitution
11 Cheating on tax
12 Murder in self-defence

Holland

1 Taking and driving away a car
2 Receiving stolen goods
3 Political assassination
4 Threatening workers who refuse to strike
5 Taking marijuana
6 Failing to report damage to a parked car
7 Fighting with police
8 Travelling without paying fare
9 Keeping money you have found
10 Cheating on tax
11 Prostitution
12 Murder in self-defence

West Germany

1 Taking and driving away a car
2 Political assassination
3 Taking marijuana
4 Receiving stolen goods
5 Threatening workers who refuse to strike
6 Failing to report damage to a parked car
7 Fighting with police
8 Travelling without paying fare
9 Cheating on tax
10 Keeping money you have found
11 Prostitution
12 Murder in self-defence

QUESTION FOUR **Police investigating major larcenies are about four times as likely to get their man in Japan as in West Germany.** TRUE International crime statistics for 1974, provided by Interpol, emphasize the remarkable efficiency of the police in Japan. They solved 80 per cent of all reported major larcenies – compared with the 21 per cent success rate in West Germany.[20]

One major reason for this huge gap was almost certainly the differences in crime levels between the two countries. In Japan, there were only 2 reported major larcenies for every 100,000 people. In West Germany, there were 1,611.

Police in Sweden and France were even less successful than in West Germany – solving only 15 per cent and 18 per cent, respectively. In Australia, the rate was 20 per cent, in Denmark it was 25 per cent, and in Holland it was 29 per cent.

Police forces in Britain were more successful than others in Europe but even in Britain the success rate was only 33 per cent – indicating that 67 per cent of crooks were finding that crime really did pay.

In fact, crimes such as burglary have become even more successful in recent years in Britain. In England and Wales, the 'clear-up' rate for burglary in 1971 was 37 per cent. In 1980, it was only 31 per cent. In Scotland, during the same period, it fell from 26 per cent to 22 per cent. In Northern Ireland, it fell from 27 per cent to 20 per cent.

During the ten years, a similar pattern was seen with other types of crime. In 1971, 42 per cent of robberies were solved, but only 29 per cent were in 1980. In 1971, 34 per cent of criminal-damage offences were solved, but only 28 per cent were in 1980.

Criminals also used guns more and more during that period. In 1971, there were 1,734 serious crimes – including burglary, robbery and sex offences – in which firearms were used. In 1980, there were 6,587.

QUESTION FIVE **In Britain, 4 per cent of males found guilty of, or cautioned for, sex offences are aged 10–13.** TRUE Nineteen per cent of male sex offenders are aged 10–16 – with 4 per cent being in the 10–13 group.[21]

The percentage of young girls who commit sex offences, when compared with older females, is still more startling. Thirty-three per cent are committed by girls aged 10 to 16 – and 6 per cent by those aged 10–13.

Burglars of both sexes start young. Forty-eight per cent of burglaries by males are committed by boys aged 10–16 – and 15 per cent by boys aged 10–13. Fifty-two per cent of burglaries by females are committed by girls aged 10–16 – and 21 per cent by girls aged 10–13.

Other forms of theft – and handling stolen goods – are also popular with the young. Twenty-seven per cent of such crimes by males are committed by boys aged 10–16 and 40 per cent of those by females are committed by girls aged 10–16.

They are also ready to use violence against people – with 17 per cent of male violence being by boys aged 10–16 and 33 per cent of female violence being by girls in the same age-group.

Many of these children commit fraud and forgery – with the boys being responsible for 8 per cent of such crimes committed by males and the girls for 9 per cent of those by females.

QUESTION SIX **Youngsters regard the influence of bad friends as a more significant cause of juvenile crime than the lack of parental supervision.** FALSE More blame rests with parents. That is the verdict in eight countries out of eleven.

Young people aged 18–24 were questioned on behalf of the Japanese Government in the following countries: America, Brazil, Britain, France, the Philippines, Japan, Korea, Switzerland, Sweden, West Germany and Yugoslavia. The results were published in 1984 and show that the failure of parents is seen as the *principal* reason for juvenile crime in America, Britain, Brazil, France, Sweden and the Philippines.[22]

In West Germany, the mass media are cited as the principal culprits, followed by the influence of friends. Mistakes by parents are rated third.

The mass media also attract most of the blame in Switzerland. In Yugoslavia and Korea, the main cause is seen as the influence of friends. In Japan, it is seen as 'lack of self-control in the youth'. In each of these four countries, lack of parental supervision is regarded as the second most important contributory cause.

The youngsters were invited to gauge the relative importance of six causes of juvenile crime.

Here is how they were listed:

	Britain
1	Parents/lack of supervision by parents
2	Influence of friends
3	Influence of mass media such as TV, newspapers and magazines
4	Lack of self-control in the youth
5	Influence of adult society/society is too permissive
6	Education in school

West Germany	Japan
1 Influence of mass media	1 Lack of self-control in the youth
2 Influence of friends	2 Lack of supervision by parents
3 Lack of supervision by parents	3 Influence of mass media
4 Lack of self-control in the youth	4 Education in school
5 Influence of society	5 Influence of friends
6 Education in school	6 Influence of society

Among the countries surveyed, Sweden is the most permissive. So it is hardly surprising that the influence of the permissive society is considered a more important contributory cause of juvenile crime there than in countries such as America, Britain and West Germany.

Although 'education in school' gets a low rating as a cause of crime in most countries, there is mounting anxiety about schoolroom discipline. In 1969, a Gallup survey showed that 49 per cent of American adults felt such discipline was not severe enough. By 1970, that view was expressed by 53 per cent, and by 1978 by an amazing 84 per cent.

A significant proportion of American youngsters aged 13–18 were also acknowledging the failure of schoolroom discipline by 1978. Thirty-one per cent believed it was 'about right'. Thirty-one per cent felt it was 'too strict' and the biggest group – 38 per cent – said it was 'too lenient'.

How accurate was your judgment? Take 2 points for each correct answer. Scores of 0–4 indicate a poor understanding of crime and attitudes to crime; 6–8 show a sound awareness; 10–12 reflect an exceptional insight.

21 Who cares about the Ten Commandments?

Religious faith is regarded more lightly in France than in other European countries, including Britain, West Germany and Spain. So are the Ten Commandments.

Most Frenchmen are ready to respect the fourth and fifth Commandments – about honouring parents and not killing – but are less enthusiastic about foregoing adultery or the coveting of neighbours' wives.

A 1981 poll[1] established what percentages of people in each of five countries – Britain, France, West Germany, Italy and Spain – consider the Commandments still apply to them.

The third Commandment – 'Thou shalt keep the Sabbath holy' – is the least respected. Even in Catholic Italy, where religious ethics are most valued, Sundays are considered inviolate by only 51 per cent of the people. The percentages fall to 38 in Spain, 35 in Britain, 29 in West Germany and 20 in France.

The sixth Commandment – 'Thou shalt not commit adultery' – has majority support in each country except France, while the Spanish are the ones most reluctant to concede that the bearing of false witness or the coveting of neighbours' goods are crimes in the sight of God.

Most people in Britain and France are not perturbed about the name of the Lord being taken in vain. In Germany, opinion is split 50–50 over this Commandment. In Italy and Spain, the majority say that it should be obeyed.

Failure to honour parents is seen as a more serious breach than adultery or the bearing of false witness in Britain, West Germany, Italy and Spain.

See overpage for the full findings, with the percentages of those who feel that the individual Commandments are applicable to them.

Pollsters have also discovered that politeness is exactly twice as important as religious faith to Europeans – and tolerance is considered three times as important.

During a nine-nation survey in 1981, a cross-section of Europeans was shown a list of 17 qualities – ranging from honesty and loyalty to thrift and patience – before being invited to choose the 5 most important.[2]

'Religious faith' finished thirteenth, well below qualities such as independence, self-control and 'a sense of responsibility'.

Those who feel that the individual Commandments are applicable to them

I
I am the Lord thy God, thou shalt have no other gods before me.

II
Thou shalt not take the name of the Lord Thy God in vain.

III
Thou shalt keep the Sabbath holy.

IV
Thou shalt honour thy mother and thy father.

V
Thou shalt not kill.

VI
Thou shalt not commit adultery.

VII
Thou shalt not steal.

VIII
Thou shalt not bear false witness.

IX
Thou shalt not covet thy neighbour's wife.

X
Thou shalt not covet thy neighbour's goods.

	I	II	III	IV	V	VI	VII	VIII	IX	X
BRITAIN	48%	43%	35%	83%	90%	78%	87%	78%	79%	79%
FRANCE	30%	24%	20%	67%	80%	48%	69%	67%	52%	62%
GERMANY	45%	50%	29%	72%	88%	64%	81%	73%	62%	70%
ITALY	68%	66%	51%	91%	96%	62%	93%	88%	64%	73%
SPAIN	48%	52%	38%	75%	81%	58%	78%	56%	65%	61%

The universally selected 'top five', with the percentages voting for them, were: honesty (73), tolerance (51), good manners (49), sense of responsibility (46), politeness (34).

Religious faith scored only 17, being marginally lower than perseverance (18) and not far ahead of imagination (13).

Countries which rated religious faith particularly low were Britain and Holland (14), France (11) and Denmark (8). In West Germany and Belgium it rated 17, while in Italy and Spain it rated 22.

Ireland was the only country in which religious faith was fairly strong – with a vote of 42 per cent that placed it fourth in the list of desirable qualities. Ireland's top three were honesty, good manners and tolerance.

In Britain – where good manners are more prized than in the other countries – religious faith is considered less important than patience, perseverance and self-control. It also has a lower priority than obedience, independence and hard work but, by margins of 3 and 5 per cent, respectively, faith is valued more highly than imagination and thrift.

So how Christian are the Christian countries?

Intriguing facts were established by MORI in 1981. Eleven per cent of Britons did not know if someone called Jesus was born about 2,000 years ago. Twelve per cent did not know if He was born in Bethlehem. Seventeen per cent did not know if He was visited, soon after His birth, by wise men and shepherds.[3]

Only 8 per cent of German Protestants went to church regularly in 1980, compared with 15 per cent in 1963,[4] and a 1981 NOP survey showed that in Britain only 6 per cent of Anglicans were going to church as often as once a week.[5]

On both sides of the Atlantic, surveys have indicated that religion is losing its influence. In 1982, 46 per cent of Canadians said so, while 33 per cent considered its influence was growing.[6] The same year, 67 per cent of Britons said so, with only 14 per cent claiming an increase of influence.[7]

These findings followed a trend shown by a 1978 Gallup survey in America. Fifty-one per cent of Americans then felt religion was losing influence and 39 per cent felt it was increasing its influence.[8] Between 1965 and 1978 the number of Americans who dismissed religion as 'not very important' doubled from 7 per cent to 14 per cent.

However, religion is still regarded as being far more important among youngsters in America than among those in Britain or other European countries such as France and Switzerland.

A survey published in 1984 by the Japanese government shows that religion is considered 'very important' or 'somewhat important' by 93 per cent of young people in America, compared with 46 per cent in Sweden,

45 per cent in Japan, 36 per cent in Switzerland and West Germany and 35 per cent in France.[9]

The percentage in Britain is only 33 and Britain also has the highest percentage – 24 – of those saying religion is 'not at all important'. Only 2 per cent of youngsters do so in America.

Among young people, enthusiasm for religion has climbed in America, Japan and West Germany since a similar survey was conducted in 1977. It has dropped in Britain, France and Switzerland.

Some measure of how religion is losing its appeal in Britain can be gained by comparing the modern situation with that reflected through a 1957 survey by Gallup.[10]

On a typical Sunday in 1957, 4 Britons in every 100 played sport, 8 went to a cinema, 11 worked in the garden and 14 went to church.

Ninety-two per cent felt children should go to Sunday School – although the majority did add, 'providing they want to' – and only 4 per cent were against children going to Sunday School.

At that time, incidentally, 20 per cent felt divorce should be made easier, 18 per cent felt it should be made more difficult, and 18 per cent felt it should not be allowed at all.[11]

Sixty-two people in every 100 were also against horse-racing being allowed on Sunday.

Vast numbers of people in various countries do *intend* to go to church more often.

In 1949, 17 per cent of Britons resolved to cut down on smoking, 10 per cent resolved to cut down on gambling, 5 per cent resolved to get up earlier and 2 per cent resolved to go to church more often.[12]

In 1979, 39 per cent of Germans resolved to take life less seriously, 18 per cent resolved to eat less sweets, 13 per cent resolved to be less curt and 10 per cent resolved to go to church more often.[13]

In both countries, church attendances continued to fall.

Even though Catholics go to church more often than Protestants – a 1981 NOP survey showed that nearly half of them go at least once a week in Britain – they are less confident than Protestants about their chances of eventually getting to Heaven.[14]

In fact, they are less certain than Protestants about the existence of Heaven or of Hell.

These facts emerged from an American Gallup survey in December 1980.

Seventy-three per cent of Catholics believe there is a Heaven but 77 per cent of Protestants do so. Only 48 per cent of Catholics believe there is a Hell, but 61 per cent of Protestants do so.[15]

Forty-eight Protestants in every 100 feel they have an 'excellent' or 'good' chance of going to Heaven, but only 46 per cent of Catholics are so optimistic.

Yet a 1980 German survey has shown that more Catholics, 52 per cent, believe in some form of life after death than Protestants, 33 per cent.[16] Such belief is also more common among women (46 per cent) than men (34 per cent).

What sort of life awaits beyond the grave?

One in which people continue to love each other, according to 53 per cent of Americans, and in which there is humour (25 per cent say so).

Twelve per cent of Americans anticipate that, after embarking on that new life, they will still be able to contact friends and relatives on earth. Five per cent fear it will be boring.

Humans may be sharing that afterlife with the souls of flowers and vegetables, for a quarter of Germans believe that plants have souls – and nearly 70 per cent believe that animals have souls.

Sixteen per cent also consider it is possible that, after physical death, human souls move to take up lodgings in other bodies.

22 Being charitable

Are people really becoming more selfish and self-centred? Is life increasingly developing into a rat-race – with less consideration for others and their problems?

Both answers, according to popular belief, are 'yes'.

Seventy-two per cent of Americans told pollsters in 1981 that people were less willing to help neighbours than they had been 25 years earlier.[1] Sixty-one per cent said people were less willing to help their elderly parents, and 58 per cent said they were less willing to volunteer for youth activities such as scouting and coaching.

That, then, is the popular view. But are such majority opinions justified?

Surveys suggest that they may be more true about attitudes in Europe than in America.

In West Germany, for instance, there is certainly a growing awareness of the need to help others. That was demonstrated in 1979 when a question that had initially been put in 1960 was asked again: 'How important are voluntary charity groups for us today?'[2]

In 1960, 55 per cent of West Germans considered them 'very important' or 'important', while 8 per cent saw them as being 'rather superfluous'. In 1979, 89 per cent considered them 'very important' or 'important' and only 1 per cent saw them as being 'rather superfluous'.

So the need was clearly recognized. However, when it came to personally helping to meet that need, there was a marked decrease in enthusiasm.

In 1962, 49 per cent said they could 'imagine helping' with charity work. Only 37 per cent said so in 1979. In 1962, 47 per cent said that the idea of helping in charity work, if they had the time, was 'out of the question'. In 1979, 59 per cent said so.

This trend was confirmed by others.

In 1978, when asked to evaluate what was most 'sacred' to them, 23 per cent said 'doing my part for progress and a better society'. Twenty-five per cent said 'being able to stop work punctually' and 35 per cent said 'being able to go on vacation regularly'.[3]

In 1974, nearly a quarter of West Germans, 24 per cent, felt that one of the key things in their own life was 'helping others'. Only 15 per cent were prepared to say that in 1979. In 1974, nearly half of them, 46 per cent, were keen on 'helping to create a better society'. Only 25 per cent were in 1979.[4]

In America, a very different attitude was reported in 1977: 'Volunteerism, the spirit of helping others that played such a vital role in building America, is still alive and flourishing more than 200 years later. Despite claims by some social observers that Americans are becoming increasingly alienated from one another, one person in four, 27 per cent, reports being engaged in volunteer activities, such as helping the poor, sick or elderly.[5]

'Traditionally, the church has been near the center of much of the charitable activities and social volunteerism of Americans and, not surprisingly, some of today's spirit of helping appears to be religiously motivated.'

By 1981, Gallup was able to report that even more Americans, 29 per cent, were engaged in voluntary work. That percentage represented more than 40 million adults.[6]

Why did these people volunteer?

Why Americans are engaged in voluntary work

How they learned about the activities for which they volunteered

Ten per cent of Americans in 1981 believed that: 'Volunteer workers take jobs away from those who need them.' Eighty-five per cent said: 'Even if there is enough money to pay people to provide services, it is still important for community life that a lot of useful work is done by volunteers.'[7]

A question asked by MORI in Britain found that about 30 per cent of adults say they have helped on fund-raising drives during the 1980s.

The strength of the charitable urge in Britain in 1983 was glimpsed when Gallup asked: 'What would you do if you won £100,000 in the Pools?' Twenty-six per cent said they would buy or improve homes or pay off mortgages, 21 per cent said they would travel, 14 per cent said they would give some to friends or relatives, and 8 per cent said they would make a donation to charity.[8]

Oh yes . . . and 4 per cent said they would refuse the money as they did not gamble.

All countries are reliant, to some degree, on the goodwill of others – allies, neighbours, trading partners – and this leads us to the subject of charitable attitudes on an international scale. The strength of such attitudes in Europe was tested in October 1982, when people in ten Common Market countries were asked this question: 'Are you, personally, prepared or not to make some sacrifice, for example, paying a little more taxes, to help another country in the European Community experiencing economic difficulties?'[9]

The Community's combined vote involved 33 per cent saying 'yes', 54 per cent saying 'no', and 13 per cent saying they did not know. However, there were fascinating fluctuations in attitudes between the countries.

On the basis of this survey, it appears that the Dutch are more generously inclined towards this form of international charity than the French or West Germans – and nearly twice as much so as the British. The Italians emerge as the most generous, while the most reluctant to part with their cash in this way are the Belgians.

How countries rate for warmth of feeling about individuals helping other nations

		'Yes', percentage			'Yes', percentage
1	ITALY	48	6	WEST GERMANY	30
2	HOLLAND	41	7	DENMARK	26
3	GREECE	40	8	IRELAND	23
4	LUXEMBOURG	37	9	BRITAIN	22
5	FRANCE	31	10	BELGIUM	20

The country with one of the lowest 'don't know' votes and by far the most emphatic 'no' – 71 per cent – was Britain. Only 38 per cent said 'no' in Italy – the only country in which, discounting the 'don't knows', giving had majority support.

23 Daydreams

Nearly all of us occasionally escape from reality into the comfort of daydreams and, as surveys have shown, there are great similarities in dream content on the two sides of the Atlantic.

Sixty-four per cent of West Germans enjoy being able temporarily to cast aside financial worries, for instance, when they drift into daydreams about having great wealth. So do 53 per cent of Americans.

Fifty-three per cent of West Germans happily travel around the world in their daydreams. So do 57 per cent of Americans.

Fancy hearing that great roar of approval from the crowd as you perform some great athletic feat? Twelve per cent of West Germans hear it for their own prowess. So do 16 per cent of Americans.

These complementary polls were conducted in America in 1979[1] and in West Germany in 1980.[2] The results provide tables of the most popular daydreams in America and in West Germany.

Americans daydream about

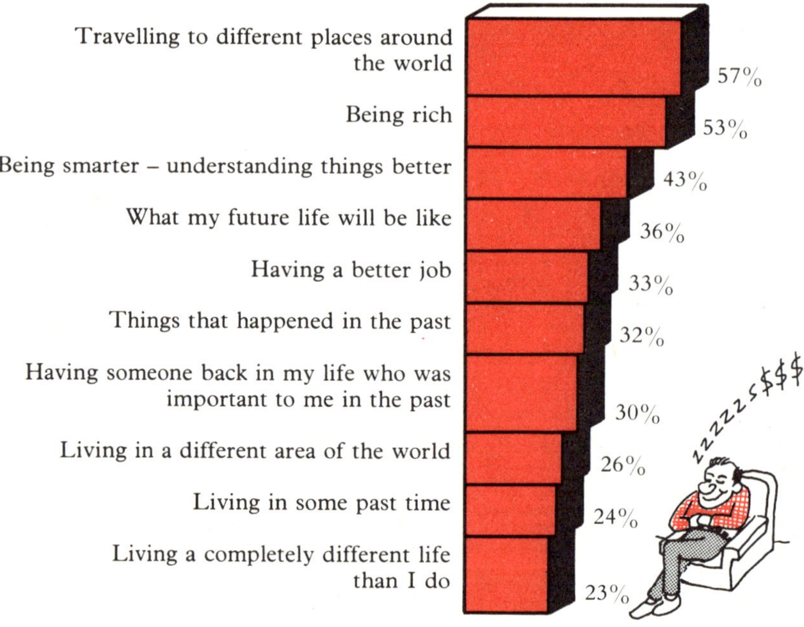

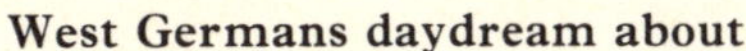

West Germans daydream about

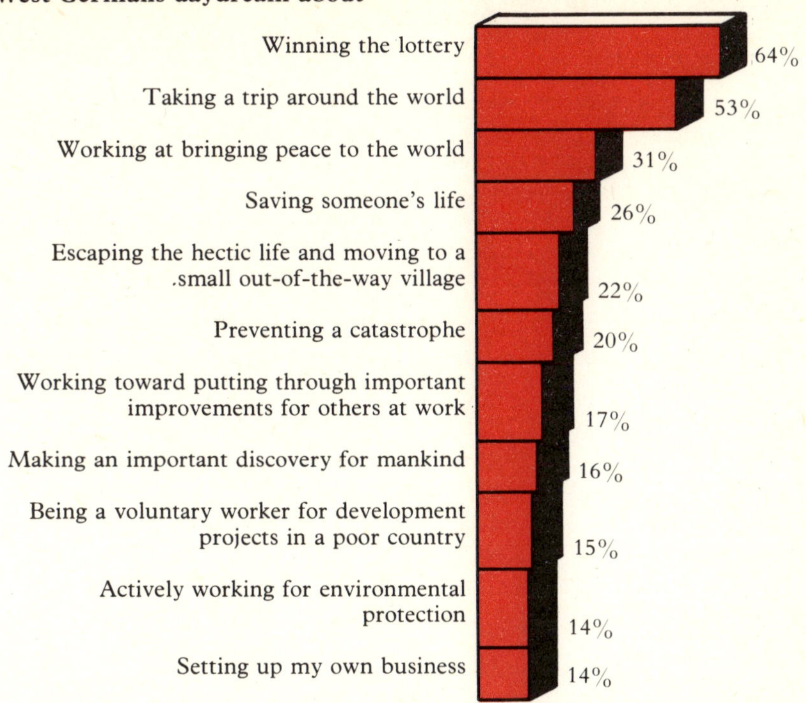

The survey in the United States showed that it is younger people who are more likely to dream about being rich – as many as 70 per cent of young Americans (aged 18–29) have this daydream, compared to 61 per cent of Americans aged 30–44 and 45 per cent of Americans aged 45–59. Only a quarter of Americans over 60 dream about being rich. Is that because they have made their fortunes or because they have come to believe that money isn't everything in life?

Americans who dream about being rich

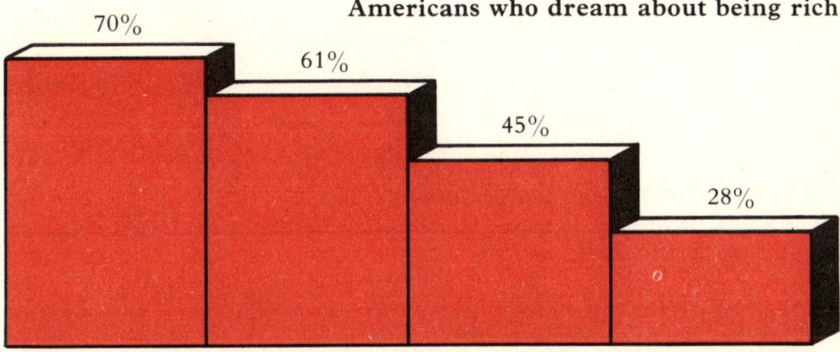

Nearly half of Americans over 60 still dream about travelling. So do 65 per cent of young Americans (aged 18–29).

Americans who dream about travelling to different places

Aged 18–29 years	Aged 30–44 years	Aged 45–59 years	Aged 60+ years
65%	59%	53%	47%

Older Americans, perhaps surprisingly, are only slightly more likely to dream about things that have happened (38 per cent do so) than younger Americans (aged 18–29), a third of whom dream about things in the past. More expected is the finding that over half of young Americans dream about their future (55 per cent) compared with only 16 per cent of older Americans.

Although the No. 9 American daydream – about living in some past time – did not feature in that West German table, such dreams are enjoyed by 15 per cent of West Germans. That was established in April 1983 when the Institut für Demoskopie Allensbach, using a sample of more than 2,000 adults, probed deeper into the subject of private yearnings.[3]

Perhaps this longing for life in an earlier century reflects a discontentment with modern hurly-burly, for it is strikingly stronger in the more heavily populated areas of Germany. Only 11 per cent of people living in villages wish they could slip away into the past. Thirteen per cent do so in small towns, 14 per cent in medium-sized towns and 18 per cent in major cities.

It certainly offers a rough guide to social standing, with the lower classes being more than twice as likely to prefer the past to the present as the upper classes. Twenty-one per cent of them do, compared with 10 per cent of the upper classes.

Five per cent of West Germans would sooner live after the year 2000 than at the present – with the lower classes again being the most eager to escape from the world of today.

Six per cent of West Germans would like to visit Hollywood but exactly twice as many would like to visit the Kremlin. Seven per cent would like to fly to the moon, but exactly twice as many would like to explore Jerusalem.

Nearly half of Americans (48 per cent) say they would like to travel in space, 57 per cent of men and 39 per cent of women.[4]

As an escape from reality, daydreams are less important, of course, for people who regard their lives as being very interesting. That means the Americans should need them far less than most nationalities. Their zestful enthusiasm for life was reflected in a ten-nation survey conducted between 1974 and 1976 by Gallup.[5]

The results showed that Americans are nearly twice as likely to consider their lives 'very interesting' as the West Germans – and six times as likely to do so as the Japanese.

International league of those who regard their lives as being very interesting

		Percentage			Percentage
1	AMERICA	36	6	SCANDINAVIA	26
2	AUSTRALIA	30	7	WEST GERMANY	19
2	BENELUX COUNTRIES	30	8	FRANCE	14
2	CANADA	30	8	ITALY	14
5	BRITAIN	28	10	JAPAN	6

The opportunity to experience other countries featured high in the Daydream Tables for America and West Germany, and a Japanese Government survey, published in 1984, explored the strength of that wish on a more universal basis – by questioning people aged 18 to 24 in America, Brazil, Britain, France, Japan, Korea, the Philippines, Sweden, Switzerland, West Germany and Yugoslavia.[6]

The survey asked: 'If you had the chance, would you like to live in a foreign country for a year or two?'

International league of those who would like to live abroad for a year or two

		Percentage			Percentage
1	SWEDEN	73	7	BRAZIL	48
2	BRITAIN	70	8	YUGOSLAVIA	42
3	THE PHILIPPINES	69	8	JAPAN	42
4	AMERICA	58	10	KOREA	29
5	FRANCE	57	11	WEST GERMANY	17
6	SWITZERLAND	54			

Youngsters in Sweden were the keenest. Nearly three quarters of them, 73 per cent, said so. Young Britons were second with 70 per cent, closely followed by those in the Philippines with 69 per cent.

Young Americans were in fourth place but, with 58 per cent, were far less enthusiastic than the leaders. The most stick-at-home youngsters of them all were the West Germans. Only 17 in every 100 fancied the idea of living abroad.

So much for wishes and daydreams. In the real world, what do people most enjoy – or most look forward to – in their day-to-day routine?

When the Roper Organization put that question to Americans in 1978, it emerged that one of the nation's favourite activities is checking to see what has come in the mail.[7] That is more than twice as popular as browsing through newspapers and three times as popular as having a drink after work.

According to this survey, Americans are also more likely to look forward pleasurably to having the telephone ring than to having their lunchtime. Similarly, they rate taking a shower more highly than meeting friends. And going to sleep at night is immensely more popular than getting up in the morning.

A list of 21 activities, times or situations was shown to respondents, who were then invited to pick those to which they most looked forward – with no limit set for the number they could choose. On the next page we show the order, with percentages, in which they were rated as agreeable to Americans, but maybe you would first care to see how your feelings match those of the average American – by deciding the order in which you would rate them.

Here they are, in scrambled order:

1 Having a break during work
2 Meeting friends after work
3 Watching television
4 Lunchtime
5 The morning newspaper
6 A drink or beer after work
7 Leaving the house in the morning
8 Cooking dinner
9 Having the telephone ring
10 Being by yourself
11 Taking a shower or bath
12 Having time to spend on a special interest or hobby
13 Checking to see what you have in the mail
14 Going to sleep at night
15 The trip to and from work
16 The afternoon newspaper
17 Listening to the radio
18 Getting in the house once your day is over
19 Having your doorbell ring
20 Getting up in the morning
21 Going out to shop for food

How Americans rated their favourite anticipations:

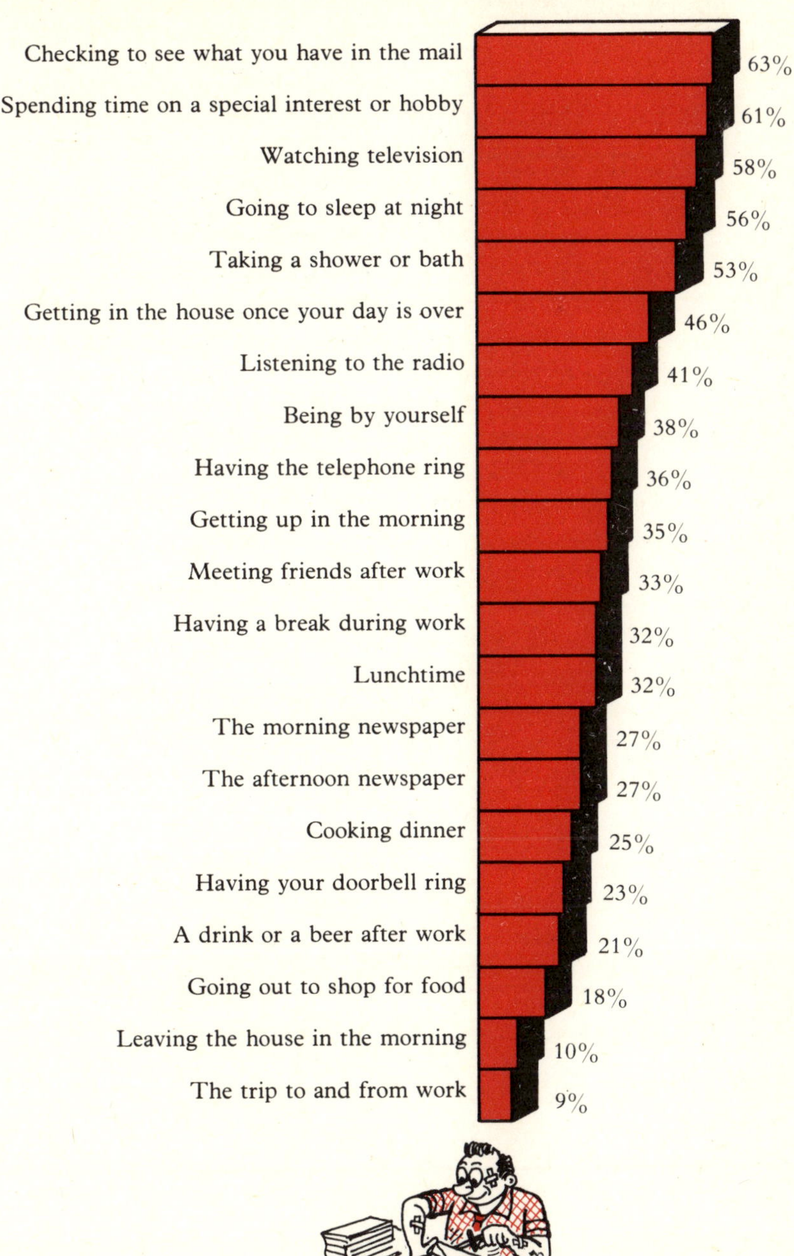

24 Who smiles most – or grumbles most – in Europe?

Dutch people are the most joyful in Europe – with 91 per cent rating themselves as 'very happy' or 'fairly happy' – and the most miserable are the Greeks (58 per cent) and the Italians (65).[1]

Despite their reputation for enjoying *l'amour* and fine food, only 13 French people in every 100 consider themselves 'very happy' – compared with 26 Belgians, 27 Britons and 36 Danes.

Among the gloomy Greeks, 41 in every 100 describe themselves as 'not too happy' – a description also chosen by 34 per cent of Italians. Other national percentages for that self-selected unsmiling label are France 23, West Germany 16, Denmark and Britain 14, Ireland 11, Belgium 10, Luxembourg 9 and Holland 8.

Worries over domestic bills may explain much of the despondency in Greece. Fifty-four people in every 100 there consider their families are 'poor' or 'badly off', compared with Denmark, at the other end of the scale, where that view is expressed by only 18 people in every 100.[2]

French people are also quick to plead family poverty, with 44 per cent of the population doing so – 5 per cent more than in Ireland. Britons have a percentage of 33 – three less than the average for all countries in the Common Market.

Germany is the European country with the most 'well-off' or 'rich' families – 33 in every 100, compared with Britain's 19 and Greece's 13.

How well do you understand attitudes and life in Europe? Find out by answering the following questions:

1 **Among the nations in the Common Market, the one in which people are most confident of their country's wealth is Germany.** TRUE OR FALSE?

2 **More shopkeepers are accused of having cheated customers in France than in any other country of Europe.** TRUE OR FALSE?

3 **No nation grumbles more about public services – such as trains and postal deliveries – than the British.** TRUE OR FALSE?

4 **The most patriotic people in Europe are the Greeks.** TRUE OR FALSE?

5 **The Dutch are keener on national defence than any other nation in Europe.** TRUE OR FALSE?

6 **The French are more suspicious of drinking water from the tap than any other nation in Europe.** TRUE OR FALSE?

Now see below for the answers.

QUESTION ONE **Among the nations in the Common Market, the one in which people are most confident of their country's wealth is Germany.** TRUE An analysis of answers gathered in ten nations provides this international league table of self-assessed wealth:

1	GERMANY	6	FRANCE
2	HOLLAND	7	BRITAIN
3	DENMARK	8	IRELAND
4	LUXEMBOURG	9	ITALY
5	BELGIUM	10	GREECE

QUESTION TWO **More shopkeepers are accused of having cheated customers in France than in any other country in Europe.** FALSE A far higher percentage of Italians report having been cheated by shopkeepers than people in other countries of Europe. Maybe that explains why so many of them are so unhappy![3]

Consumers in nine countries were asked if they could recall shops recently cheating themselves or their spouses.

Fifty-three Italians in every 100 did recall such cheating – particularly on purchases such as clothing and fresh food – compared with only 22 per cent of Belgians. This won shopkeepers in Belgium gold-plated haloes for straight dealing. Just behind them, qualifying for silver-plated haloes, were shopkeepers in Denmark, with complaints from only 25 per cent of their customers.

QUESTION THREE **No nation grumbles more about public services – such as trains and postal deliveries – than the British.** FALSE Italians get as much of a raw deal from their public services, in their opinion, as from their shopkeepers. Sixty per cent have reported themselves fuming about such services while the British, despite all their traditional moans about soaring gas bills and cancelled trains, clinch a mere second place with only 41 per cent.[4]

Despite being the happiest people in Europe, the Dutch rally to manage a 30 per cent score on this issue, pipped by Ireland (31) and West Germany and France (both 34).

However, the Dutch do live up to their happy-go-lucky reputation when it comes to actually *doing* something about their grievances. Sixty-seven per cent of them – 16 per cent more than their nearest 'forget it' rivals in West Germany – do absolutely nothing.

Europe's champion grumblers are the Luxembourgers. They have a triumphant complaints record of 84 per cent. Trailing in joint second place are the British and the French, who both have a score of 78 per cent.

QUESTION FOUR **The most patriotic people in Europe are the Greeks.** TRUE On their own reckoning, despite being the most miserable people in Europe, the Greeks are the most patriotic. Ninety per cent are 'very proud' or 'quite proud' of their nation.[5]

Jostling for second place as patriots among the ten nations surveyed are the British (88 per cent) and the Irish (84). However, a full analysis of all the answers cancelled Britain's slight lead and pushed the country into third place, behind Ireland.

Those with least pride in their country are the Germans and the Belgians, in both of which only 22 people in every 100 admit being 'very proud'. Twenty-eight per cent of Germans and 32 per cent of Belgians are either 'not very proud' or 'not at all proud'.

QUESTION FIVE **The Dutch are keener on national defence than any other nation in Europe.** FALSE In view of their fierce patriotism and prolonged experience of foreign occupation, it is hardly surprising that the Greeks should be more vigilant than other countries surveyed on the need for national defence – with 44 per cent voting it 'a great cause worth fighting for'. They consider it more important than religious faith – 41 per cent of them feel *that's* worth fighting for – and sexual equality (34 per cent).

National defence gets a 28 per cent rating as a Great Cause in Britain, France and Luxembourg, and there is impressive apathy in West Germany, where it gets only 17 per cent.

The Irish are even less impressed with national defence. Only 11 in every 100 people there agree it is a Great Cause. The country least interested is Holland, where it wins the vote of only 9 people in every 100.

QUESTION SIX **The French are more suspicious of drinking water from the tap than any other nation in Europe.** FALSE Among the ten nations surveyed, the Italians had the strongest reservations about the purity of their drinking water, with 27 per cent complaining either a 'great deal' or a 'fair amount'. The next most suspicious are the Germans (25 per cent). [6]

Only 9 per cent complain to that degree in Britain and the percentage in Ireland is 13. With a complaint percentage of 3, the most contented water-drinkers in Europe are the Danes.

How did your judgment rate? Take two marks for each correct answer. Scores of 0–4 show you are out-of-touch with modern Europe, 6–8 point to average awareness, 10–12 reflect an exceptional perception.

Acknowledgments and Sources

This book came about as a result of the enthusiasm of Leslie Watkins for the unusual and sometimes arcane results of MORI polls, but it would have been impossible without the helpful assistance of my colleagues in public opinion firms throughout the world. Thanks are due to colleagues and clients at MORI, among the latter *The Sunday Times*, *The Times*, *Daily Star*, *Daily Express*, *Scotsman*, *The Economist* and the BBC, among the former Theresa Moss and Kevin Soady, who checked and rechecked the sources; to Sally Clarke, my secretary; and to Dawn Blair for her research assistance. Especially heavily leaned upon in the compilation of the findings were the admirable volumes of public opinion data published annually under the title *Index to International Public Opinion*, by Philip and Elizabeth Hann Hastings (Greenwood Press, CT, USA); Elisabeth Noelle-Neumann's *The Germans, Public Opinion Polls 1967–1980*, a compilation of her firm, Institut für Demoskopie Allensbach's polls and her releases subsequently (Greenwood Press, CT, USA, 1981). Other key sources include America's Opinion Research Corporation, Harris and Gallup polls, Britain's Gallup poll, the Europe-wide *Euro-baromètre* led by Jean René Rabier and co-ordinated by Hélène Riffault, and many of our other colleagues of the World Association for Public Opinion Research (WAPOR).

It has, we confess, occurred to us that this one, if on the mark, could run and run. For that reason we would welcome contributions from readers of interesting and curious poll findings of the past that we have omitted – and especially in the future. We would also be grateful to anyone who discovers errors for them to be brought to our attention. We hope you've enjoyed reading *Private Opinions – Public Polls* as much as we have preparing it for your enjoyment.

Robert Worcester
32 Old Queen Street
London SW1H 9HP

December 1984

Chapter 1
Cupid under the microscope

1 Roper Organization, 1983, USA
2 Black Corporation, 1982, USA
3 MORI, 1983, conducted on behalf of Harlequin Books, GB
4 Audits & Surveys, for the Merit Report, 1983, USA
5 Black Corporation, 1982, USA
6 Ibid.
7 MORI, 1983, conducted on behalf of Harlequin Books, GB
8 Audits & Surveys, for the Merit Report, 1982, USA
9 Audits & Surveys, for the Merit Report, 1983, USA
10 MORI, 1983, conducted on behalf of Harlequin Books, GB
11 MORI, 1982, conducted on behalf of the *Daily Star*, GB
12 MORI, 1983, conducted on behalf of Harlequin Books, GB
13 Kirkpatrick & Caplow, 1945, USA

Chapter 2
Modern marriage – the uncensored facts

1 *Social Trends*, 1982, published by the Government Statistical Service, GB
2 MORI, 1982, conducted on behalf of the *Daily Star*, GB
3 MORI, 1984, conducted on behalf of *The Sunday Times*, GB
4 Geoffrey Gorer, *Sex and marriage in England today*, 1971, GB
5 Ibid.
6 MORI, 1984, conducted on behalf of *The Sunday Times*, GB
7 MORI, 1982, conducted on behalf of the *Daily Star*, GB
8 Brides survey, 1984, by *Wedding Day and First Home*, GB
9 Institute of Public Opinion, 1984, published in *Komsomolskaya Pravda*, USSR
10 MORI, 1982, conducted on behalf of the *Daily Star*, GB
11 National Opinion Polls, 1980, GB
12 Social Surveys (Gallup Poll) Limited, 1982, GB
13 MORI, 1982, conducted on behalf of the *Daily Star*, GB
14 MORI, 1982, conducted on behalf of the *Daily Express*, GB
15 Readers of *Better Homes and Gardens*, 1982, USA
16 MORI, 1982, conducted on behalf of the *Daily Star*, GB
17 Ibid.
18 National Opinion Research Center, General Social Surveys 1980–1983, 1970–1973, USA
19 ISOPUBLIC, 1977, conducted on behalf of *Weltwoche*, Switzerland
20 *Social Trends*, op. cit.
21 MORI, 1982, conducted on behalf of the *Daily Star*, GB
22 Readers of *Better Homes and Gardens*, 1982, USA
23 Elisabeth Noelle-Neumann (ed.), *The Germans, Public Opinion Polls 1967–1980*, CT, USA, 1981
24 Readers of *Better Homes and Gardens*, 1982, USA
25 Noelle-Neumann, op. cit.
26 Ibid.
27 Readers of *Better Homes and Gardens*, 1982, USA
28 MORI, 1982, conducted on behalf of the *Daily Star*, GB
29 Noelle-Neumann, op. cit.

Chapter 3
International sex – the amazing numbers game

1 Riksforundet für Sexual Applysning, Stockholm, 1967
2 MORI, 1984, conducted on behalf of *The Sunday Times*, GB
3 National Opinion Research Center, 1977, USA
4 Dr Pierre Charbon, *Rapport sur le comportement sexuel des Français*, Institute Français d'Opinion Publique, 1972
5 Gallup International Research Institutes, 1973, 1983
6 MORI, 1984, conducted on behalf of *The Sunday Times*, GB
7 Melvin Zelmich PhD and John D. Kanter PhD, *Sexual and contraceptive experience of young unmarried women in the USA 1971–1976*
8 MORI, 1984, conducted on behalf of *The Sunday Times*, GB
9 Riksforundet für Sexual Applysning, Stockholm, 1967
10 Dr M. Barrett and Dr M. Fitz-Earle, *Sexual experience, birth control usage and sources of sex education among unmarried university students*, Canada, 1974
11 Charbon, op. cit.
12 Schlackman Research Organization, 1976, conducted on behalf of *Honey*, GB
13 *L'Express*, 1977, France
14 Geoffrey Gorer, *Sex and marriage in England today*, 1971, GB
15 MORI, 1984, conducted on behalf of *The Sunday Times*, GB
16 Gorer, op. cit.
17 MORI, 1984, conducted on behalf of *The Sunday Times*, GB
18 Professor Robert E. Bell, *The sex survey of Australian women*, 1974
19 Morgan Research Center, 1974, conducted on behalf of *Cleo*, Australia
20 Bell, op. cit.
21 National Opinion Research Center, 1977, USA

22 Gorer, op. cit.
23 *Sexualiteit in Nederland*, 1968, conducted on behalf of *Magriet*, Holland
24 MORI, 1984, conducted on behalf of *The Sunday Times*, GB
25 Ibid.

Chapter 4
Homosexuality and morality

1 Gallup Organization Inc, 1977, USA
2 Social Surveys (Gallup Poll) Limited, 1981, GB
3 National Opinion Polls, 1975, conducted on behalf of *Gay News*, GB
4 Elisabeth Noelle-Neumann (ed.), *The Germans, Public Opinion Polls 1967–1980*, CT, USA, 1981
5 Ibid.
6 *Time* Magazine/Yankelovich, Skelly and White, 1977, USA
7 MORI, 1982, GB
8 *Time* Magazine/Yankelovich, Skelly and White, 1977, USA
9 Noelle-Neumann, op. cit.
10 Gallup Organization Inc, 1977, USA
11 *Weekend*, Toronto, 1977, Canada
12 *Sexualiteit in Nederland*, 1968, conducted on behalf of *Magriet*, Holland
13 Social Surveys (Gallup Poll) Limited, 1981, GB
14 Gallup Organization Inc, 1977, USA
15 Social Surveys (Gallup Poll) Limited, 1981, GB
16 Gallup Organization Inc, 1977, USA
17 Social Surveys (Gallup Poll) Limited, 1981, GB
18 National Opinion Polls, 1975, conducted on behalf of *Gay News*, GB
19 MORI, 1984, conducted on behalf of the Twenty/Twenty Vision television programme, GB
20 Finkelhor, 1979, Boston, USA

Chapter 5
Prospects of revolution

1 Gallup International Research Institutes, 1980
2 Warren E. Miller, Arthur H. Miller and Edward J. Schneider, *American Election Studies Data Source-book, 1952–78*, Cambridge, MA, USA, 1978; with 1980 figures from Center for Political Studies, University of Michigan
3 Opinion Research Corporation, 1959, 1969, 1981, USA
4 MORI, 1969, 1981, GB
5 Ibid.
6 The Harris Survey, 1966–1981, USA
7 Gallup International Research Institutes, 1980

Chapter 6
War and peace

1 Gallup International Research Institutes, 1982
2 Gallup International Research Institutes/International Research Associates, 1982
3 The Harris Survey, 1982, USA
4 Social Surveys (Gallup Poll) Limited, 1983, GB
5 Gallup International Research Institutes/International Research Associates, 1982
6 The Harris Survey, 1983, USA
7 Gallup International Research Institutes/Gallup Organization Inc, 1983
8 Canadian Institute of Public Opinion, 1983
9 Gallup International Research Institutes, 1982
10 The Harris Survey, 1983, conducted on behalf of the *Chicago Tribune*, USA
11 Social Surveys (Gallup Poll) Limited, 1983, GB
12 MORI, 1984, GB
13 Social Surveys (Gallup Poll) Limited, 1983, GB
14 The Harris Survey, 1982, 1983, USA

Chapter 7
Can foreigners be trusted?

1 Gallup International Research Institutes, 1980
2 European Economic Community, 1980
3 MORI, 1984, conducted on behalf of *The Sunday Times*, GB
4 The Gallup Poll, 1976–1977, USA
5 Elisabeth Noelle-Neumann (ed.), *The Germans, Public Opinion Polls 1967–1980*, CT, USA, 1981

Chapter 8
People at the top

1 MORI, 1984, conducted on behalf of *The Sunday Times*, GB
2 Institut Français d'Opinion Publique, 1984, conducted on behalf of *Nouvel Observateur*, France
3 Brule Ville Associes, 1984, France
4 Gallup Organization Inc, 1984, USA
5 MORI, 1984, conducted on behalf of the (London) *Standard*, GB
6 SOFRES, 1984, conducted on behalf of *Figaro*, France
7 Gallup Organization Inc, 1983, USA
8 MORI, 1983, GB
9 SOFRES, 1983, France
10 Gallup Organization Inc, 1948–1984, USA
11 The Harris Survey, 1983, conducted on behalf of the *Chicago Tribune*, USA
12 Gallup Organization Inc, 1981, conducted on behalf of NBC News/Associated Press, USA

13 CBS News/*New York Times*, 1981, USA
14 Roper Organization, 1981, USA
15 MORI, 1984, conducted on behalf of *The Sunday Times*, GB
16 Institut Français d'Opinion Publique, 1984, conducted on behalf of *Nouvel Observateur*, France
17 MORI, 1983, GB
18 Institut für Demoskopie Allensbach, 1982, conducted on behalf of *Der Spiegel*, West Germany
19 MORI, 1983, conducted on behalf of *The Sunday Times*, GB
20 Institut für Demoskopie Allensbach, 1982, conducted on behalf of *Der Spiegel*, West Germany
21 Institut Français d'Opinion Publique, 1984, conducted on behalf of *Nouvel Observateur*, France
22 MORI, 1984, GB
23 Chinese (Taiwan) Institute of Public Opinion, 1982
24 Gallup International Research Institutes/International Research Associates, 1981–1982
25 *Index to International Public Opinion, 1981–1982* (survey conducted in 1981, Thailand), CT, USA
26 Leisure Development Center, Tokyo, 1983, conducted on behalf of the International Conference on Human Values

Chapter 9
How did we get into this mess?

1 The Harris Survey, 1983, conducted on behalf of the Atlantic Institute for International Affairs
2 Trendex, 1980, 1982, conducted on behalf of General Electric Co, USA

Chapter 10
The rape of the environment

1 National Opinion Research Center, 1982, USA
2 Yomiuri Shimbun, 1982, Japan
3 Chinese (Taiwan) Institute of Public Opinion, 1982
4 *The Europeans and their Environment*, 1982, conducted on behalf of the Commission of the European Communities
5 MORI, 1983, conducted on behalf of the Conservation and Development Programme, GB
6 The Harris Survey, 1981, USA
7 *The Europeans and their Environment*, op. cit.
8 Opinion Research Corporation, 1981, conducted on behalf of the US Chamber of Commerce
9 Canadian Institute of Public Opinion, 1980
10 *The Europeans and their Environment*, op. cit.
11 NBC/Associated Press, 1981, USA
12 CBS News/*New York Times*, 1981, USA
13 *The Europeans and their Environment*, op. cit.
14 Canadian Institute of Public Opinion, 1983
15 *The Europeans and their Environment*, op. cit.
16 Trendex, 1979–1982, conducted on behalf of General Electric Co, USA
17 Canadian Institute of Public Opinion, 1980
18 Asahi Shimbun, 1979, 1981, Japan
19 *The Japanese Youth in Comparison with the Youth in the World*, 1984, conducted on behalf of the Youth Development Headquarters, Japan

Chapter 11
A boy's best friend

1 *The Japanese Youth in Comparison with the Youth in the World*, 1984, conducted on behalf of the Youth Development Headquarters, Japan
2 Black Corporation, 1984, conducted on behalf of *USA Today*
3 Ibid.
4 *The Japanese Youth*, op. cit.
5 *Images of Other Nations*, 1982, conducted by American Institute of Public Opinion, USA; Social Surveys (Gallup Poll) Limited, GB; Brule Ville Associes, France; Nippon Research Center, Japan; and EMNID Institut GmbH & Co, West Germany

Chapter 12
Verdicts on babies – and on parents

1 *Social Trends*, 1984, published by the Government Statistical Service, GB
2 *The Europeans and their Children*, 1979, conducted on behalf of the Commission for the European Communities
3 Ibid.
4 Gallup International Research Institutes, 1981
5 *The Europeans and their Children*, op. cit.
6 Morgan Gallup Poll, 1982, Australia
7 Social Surveys (Gallup Poll) Limited, 1982, GB
8 Canadian Institute of Public Opinion, 1982
9 *The Europeans and their Children*, op. cit.
10 *The Japanese Youth in Comparison with the Youth in the World*, 1984, conducted on behalf of the Youth Development Headquarters, Japan

Chapter 13
Britain's royal family

1 MORI, 1984, conducted on behalf of the *Daily Star*, GB

2 Public Opinion Surveys, 1984, conducted on behalf of the *Sunday People*, GB
3 MORI, 1982, conducted on behalf of the *Daily Star*, GB
4 Ibid.
5 Social Surveys (Gallup Poll) Limited, 1976–1982, GB

Chapter 14
Which countries are the healthiest?

1 Leisure Development Center, Tokyo, 1981, conducted on behalf of the International Conference on Human Values (1983)
2 Roper Organization, 1982, USA
3 *New York Times*, 1982, USA
4 Leisure Development Center, op. cit.
5 Gallup Organization Inc, 1984, USA
6 ABC News, 1983, USA
7 Roper Organization, 1982, USA
8 Gallup Organization Inc, 1984, USA
9 ABC News, 1983, USA
10 Elisabeth Noelle-Neumann (ed.), *The Germans, Public Opinion Polls 1967–1980*, CT, USA, 1981
11 Social Surveys (Gallup Poll) Limited, 1947, GB
12 The Gallup Poll, 1976–1977, USA
13 Gallup International Research Institutes, 1982
14 World Health Organization, 1974, 1975
15 Noelle-Neumann, op. cit.
16 Gallup International Research Institutes, 1982
17 Social Surveys (Gallup Poll) Limited, 1975, GB
18 Office of Population Censuses and Surveys, 1983, GB
19 The Gallup Poll, 1972–1977, USA
20 Canadian Institute of Public Opinion, 1981, 1982
21 World Health Organization, 1980
22 Euromonitor, 1977
23 World Health Organization, 1972–1974
24 United Nations, 1980
25 Peter Yapp (ed.), *The Travellers' Dictionary of Quotations*, London, 1983
26 Ibid.
27 Ibid.
28 National Family Opinion, 1983, USA
29 World Health Organization, 1974, 1975
30 World Health Organization, 1970

Chapter 15
Keeping fit

1 MORI, 1984, conducted on behalf of *Fitness*, GB
2 Research & Forecasts, 1982, conducted on behalf of the Miller Brewing Company, USA
3 Elisabeth Noelle-Neumann (ed.), *The Germans, Public Opinion Polls 1967–1980*, CT, USA, 1981
4 Gallup International Research Institutes, 1981
5 Chinese (Taiwan) Institute of Public Opinion, 1981
6 The Gallup Poll, 1976–1977, USA
7 Pan European Survey 3, 1984, conducted by Research Services Limited
8 Chinese (Taiwan) Institute of Public Opinion, 1981
9 MORI, 1984, conducted on behalf of *Fitness*, GB
10 Research & Forecasts, op. cit.
11 MORI, 1984, GB
12 MORI, 1983, conducted on behalf of the *Daily Express*, GB
13 MORI, 1982, conducted on behalf of the *Daily Star*, GB
14 Gallup International Research Institutes, 1982

Chapter 16
Alcohol – the pleasures and the perils

1 Leisure Development Center, Tokyo, 1981, conducted on behalf of the International Conference on Human Values (1983)
2 The Gallup Poll, 1976–1977, USA
3 Canadian Institute of Public Opinion, 1974–1983
4 The Gallup Poll, 1976–1977, USA
5 The Gallup Poll, 1972–1977, USA
6 MORI, 1981, conducted on behalf of the Brewers' Society, GB
7 Brewers' Society, 1975, GB
8 Pan European Survey 3, 1984, conducted by Research Services Limited
9 Ibid.
10 Central Statistical Office, 1980, GB
11 MORI, 1981, conducted on behalf of the Brewers' Society, GB
12 Euromonitor, 1977

Chapter 17
Gadgetry

1 Peter Yapp (ed.), *The Travellers' Dictionary of Quotations*, London, 1983
2 Government Statistical Service, 1984, GB
3 Elisabeth Noelle-Neumann (ed.), *The Germans, Public Opinion Polls 1967–1980*, CT, USA, 1981
4 Pan European Survey 3, 1984, conducted by Research Services Limited
5 Noelle-Neumann, op. cit.
6 Roper Organization, 1981, USA
7 Trendex, 1982, conducted on behalf of General Electric Co, USA
8 OECD, 1981, 1982
9 Roper Organization, 1983, USA
10 Reader survey of *Personal Computing*, 1984, USA
11 Yankelovich, Skelly and White, 1984, USA

Chapter 18
Cars – the great ownership race

1 Peter Yapp (ed.), *The Travellers' Dictionary of Quotations*, London, 1983
2 Ibid.
3 *Social Trends*, 1981, published by the Government Statistical Service, GB
4 Yapp, op. cit.
5 Pan European Survey 3, conducted by Research Services Limited, 1984
6 Elisabeth Noelle-Neumann (ed.), *The Germans, Public Opinion Polls 1967–1980*, CT, USA, 1981
7 Ibid.
8 MORI, 1983, conducted on behalf of *The Sunday Times*, GB
9 Social Surveys (Gallup Poll) Limited, 1982, GB
10 Noelle-Neumann, op. cit.
11 The Gallup Poll, 1976–1977, USA
12 Union Bank of Switzerland, 1976
13 MORI, 1983, conducted on behalf of *The Sunday Times*, GB
14 Noelle-Neumann, op. cit.
15 Roper Organization, 1984, USA

Chapter 19
The impact of television

1 Social Surveys (Gallup Poll) Limited, 1949, 1950, GB
2 Elisabeth Noelle-Neumann (ed.), *The Germans, Public Opinion Polls 1967–1980*, CT, USA, 1981
3 The Gallup Poll, 1976–1977, USA
4 Ibid.
5 Noelle-Neumann, op. cit.
6 Roper Organization, 1981, USA
7 Roper Organization, 1978, USA
8 Peter Yapp (ed.), *The Travellers' Dictionary of Quotations*, London, 1983
9 National Opinion Research Center, 1983, USA

Chapter 20
Crime and punishment

1 Atlantic Institute for International Affairs, 1983
2 Interpol, 1974
3 Gallup International Research Institutes, 1982
4 National Opinion Research Center, 1982, USA
5 Canadian Institute of Public Opinion, 1982
6 Institut Français d'Opinion Publique, 1983
7 Social Surveys (Gallup Poll) Limited, 1982, GB
8 Chinese (Taiwan) Institute of Public Opinion, 1969–1982
9 Canadian Institute of Public Opinion, 1982
10 National Opinion Research Center, 1982, USA
11 Canadian Institute of Public Opinion, 1982
12 Social Surveys (Gallup Poll) Limited, 1982, GB
13 The Harris Survey, 1973–1983, USA
14 Social Surveys (Gallup Poll) Limited, 1982, GB
15 ABC News, 1982, USA
16 National Opinion Research Center, 1984, USA
17 National Survey of Crime Severity, 1983, USA
18 National Opinion Research Center, 1982, USA
19 Gallup Organization Inc, 1981, conducted on behalf of the European Values Systems Study Group
20 Interpol, 1974
21 Government Statistical Service, 1982, GB
22 *The Japanese Youth in Comparison with the Youth in the World*, 1984, conducted on behalf of the Youth Development Headquarters, Japan

Chapter 21
Who cares about the Ten Commandments?

1 Gallup Organization Inc, 1981, conducted on behalf of the European Values Systems Study Group
2 *Europe at the Crossroads*, 1981, conducted on behalf of the European Values Systems Study Group
3 MORI, 1981, GB
4 Elisabeth Noelle-Neumann (ed.), *The Germans, Public Opinion Polls 1967–1980*, CT, USA, 1981
5 National Opinion Polls, 1981, GB
6 Canadian Institute of Public Opinion, 1982
7 Social Surveys (Gallup Poll) Limited, 1982, GB
8 Gallup Organization Inc, 1978, USA
9 *The Japanese Youth in Comparison with the Youth in the World*, 1984, conducted on behalf of the Youth Development Headquarters, Japan
10 Social Surveys (Gallup Poll) Limited, 1957, GB
11 Ibid.
12 Ibid.
13 Noelle-Neumann, op. cit.
14 National Opinion Polls, 1981, GB
15 Gallup Organization Inc, 1980, USA
16 Noelle-Neumann, op. cit.

Chapter 22
Being charitable

1 Roper Organization, 1981, conducted on behalf of Public Opinion Research for the American Enterprise Institute
2 Elisabeth Noelle-Neumann (ed.), *The Germans, Public Opinion Polls 1967–1980*, CT, USA, 1981
3 Ibid.

4 Ibid.
5 The Gallup Poll, 1976–1977, USA
6 Gallup Organization Inc, 1981, conducted on behalf of Independent Sector, USA
7 MORI, 1980–1984, GB
8 Social Surveys (Gallup Poll) Limited, 1983, GB
9 Gallup International Research Institutes, 1982

Chapter 23
Daydreams

1 Roper Organization, 1979, USA
2 Elisabeth Noelle-Neumann (ed.), *The Germans, Public Opinion Polls 1967–1980*, CT, USA, 1981
3 Ibid.
4 Roper Organization, 1979, USA
5 Gallup International Research Institutes, 1974–1976
6 *The Japanese Youth in Comparison with the Youth in the World*, 1984, conducted on behalf of the Youth Development Headquarters, Japan
7 Roper Organization, 1979, USA

Chapter 24
Who smiles most – or grumbles most – in Europe?

1 *Public Opinion in the European Communities*, published in *Euro-baromètre*, 1983, by the Commission of the European Communities
2 Ibid.
3 *European Consumers*, 1976, published by the Commission of the European Communities
4 Ibid.
5 *Euro-baromètre*, 1983, on behalf of the Commission of the European Communities
6 *The Europeans and their Environment*, 1983, published by the Commission of the European Communities

Index